NIGHTMARES

NIGHTMARES

The Science and Solution of Those Frightening Visions during Sleep

Patrick McNamara

Brain, Behavior, and Evolution

Westport, Connecticut
London

Library of Congress Cataloging-in-Publication Data

McNamara, Patrick, 1956–
   Nightmares : the science and solution of those frightening visions during sleep / Patrick McNamara.
     p. cm. — (Brain, behavior, and evolution, ISSN 1941-4099)
   Includes bibliographical references and index.
   ISBN 978-0-313-34512-8 (alk. paper)
   1. Nightmares. I. Title.
BF1099.N53M46 2008
154.6′32—dc22   2008009925

British Library Cataloguing in Publication Data is available.

Library of Congress Catalog Card Number: 2008009925
ISBN: 978-0-313-34512-8
ISSN: 1941-4099

First published in 2008

Praeger Publishers, 88 Post Road West, Westport, CT 06881
An imprint of Greenwood Publishing Group, Inc.
www.praeger.com

Printed in the United States of America

The paper used in this book complies with the
Permanent Paper Standard issued by the National
Information Standards Organization (Z39.48-1984).

10 9 8 7 6 5 4 3 2 1

For Reka and Ina Livia

Contents

Tables and Figures   xi

Preface   xiii

Acknowledgments   xix

Chapter 1. Approach to the Study of Nightmares   1

    Shortcomings of the Standard "Take" on Nightmares   1

    Nightmares Can Be Functional   2

    Definition and Diagnostic Criteria for Recurrent
    Nightmares   5

    Syndrome of Recurring Nightmares   7

    The Sharing of Nightmares with Others   8

Chapter 2. Why Do Nightmares Occur in Children?   13

    Sleep in Childhood   13

    Dreaming in Childhood   18

    Evolution of Childhood   20

    Cognitive and Psychological Growth of the Child   21

    Development of the Sense of Self in Children   22

    Impact of Developmental Milestones on Nightmare
    Propensity in Children   24

Chapter 3. Content of Nightmares   27

    Comparing Nightmare Content to Ordinary Dreams   27

    Nightmare Content Scoring   28

Word Count Analyses of Barb Sanders' Nightmares 39

Nightmares as Compelling: The Case of "Precognitive
Nightmares" 47

People Who Experience Extraordinary Dreams
Must Be Extraordinary People 51

Chapter 4. Nightmares in Premodern Societies 53

Nightmares as Evidence of Extraordinary Powers in
Ancestral Populations 53

Dreams in Premodern Societies 54

Cultural Context of Dreaming in Premodern Societies 55

Nightmare Sharing in Premodern Groups 60

Chapter 5. Biology of Nightmares 63

Normal Human Sleep Architecture 63

Sleep Rebound Effects and REM-NREM Imbalances in
Production of Nightmares 64

Special Link between Nightmares and REM Sleep 65

Summary of REM Properties and Nightmares 72

Key Role of the Amygdala 72

Selected Neuropharmacological Agents Can Induce
Nightmares 73

Neuroanatomy and Physiology of a Nightmare 73

**Chapter 6. Personality and Psychopathological Correlates of
Nightmares** 75

Nightmares Are Not Reliably Associated with Loss of
Function 75

Disorders Involving Nightmares 76

Nightmares and Psychopathology 82

Chapter 7. Phenomenology of the Nightmare 83

Basic Visual Features 83

Emotional Atmosphere 83

Automaticity 84

Cognitive Content Elicits the Emotional Content 84

Creativity 84

"Compellingness" 85

Narrative Form 85

Self-Identity 85

Lack of Metaphor 86

Self-Reflectiveness 86

Mind Reading 86

Summary of Formal Features of Nightmares 87

Chapter 8. Theoretical Accounts of the Nightmare 89

Facts That Must Serve as the Basis for Nightmare Theory 89

Proposed Functional Theory of Nightmares 92

Costly Signaling Theory (CST) 101

Freud's View of Nightmares 106

Fisher's View of Nightmares 106

Kramer's View of Nightmares 106

Hartmann's View of Nightmares 107

Nielsen and Levin's View of Nightmares 107

Theory and Treatment Strategies 108

Chapter 9. Nightmares and Popular Culture 111

Movies, Nightmares, and Spirit Possession 111

Nightmare-Related Spirit Possession Is a Universal Phenomenon 112

Alien Abduction 116

Books, Nightmares, and Spirit Possession 117

Chapter 10. Interpretation of the Possession Theme in Nightmares 119

Selection of Nightmares with Spirit Possession Themes 120

Caveats in the Interpretation of Nightmares and Standard Explanations of the Possession Theme 120

Recurring Patterns in the Spirit-Possession Theme 122

Chapter 11. Conflict Theory and the Nightmare 135

Mind Is Not a Unity 135

Paradox of Mind Reading in Dreams: The Role of the
"Stranger"   136

Male Strangers and Aggression in Dreams   138

REM-NREM Dissociations in the Dreaming Mind   138

Dreaming and Consciousness   140

Dream Agents/Characters Can Represent Genomes
within the Individual   141

Effects of Imprinted Genes on Physiologic Systems
Implicated in Growth   141

Effects of Imprinted Genes on Functional Brain Systems
Implicated in Sleep Processes   142

Genomic Imprinting and Sleep-State Biology   143

Genetic Conflict and Dream Phenomenology   146

Concluding Remarks   148

Appendix: Additional Resources   151

References   153

Index   171

Tables and Figures

Table 1.1. Diagnostic Criteria for Nightmares: Three Classification
Systems   6

Table 1.2. Prevalence, Themes, and Clinical Correlates of Recurrent
Nightmares   11

Table 3.1. Hall and Van de Castle Variables for Analyzing Dream
Content   29

Table 3.2. Means and Standard Deviations in LIWC Categories
for Barb Sanders' Nightmares and LIWC Norms:
Comparing Linguistic Markers of Nightmares with
Ordinary Narratives   41

Table 3.3. Comparison of Nightmare Content to Normal Dream
Content Using Hall and Van de Castle Norms   44

Table 7.1. Formal Features of Nightmares   88

Table 8.1. Facts That Must Serve as the Basis for Nightmare Theory   90

Table 9.1. Characteristics of Demonic Possession versus Holy
Spirit Possession in Nightmares   114

Table 11.1. Hall and Van de Castle Social Interaction Percentages in
Scored Dreams   139

Figure 11.1. Dreamer-Initiated Aggression/Befriending Percentages
Out of Total Number of Social Interactions in REM,
NREM, and Waking Reports   140

Preface

This nightmare was posted to an Internet site (www.nightmareproject. com) dedicated to the sharing of nightmares on March 12, 2000, by a 35-year-old woman. "This was a recurring nightmare. I had the first part repeatedly from the time I was sixteen until I was in my early twenties. That's when I had the second part."

Part One

I am a volunteer for an experiment dealing with people who have existed in a coma state for decades, without any life support or signs of decay. The duty of the volunteers is to form a psychic mind-link with their subjects and go through their memories to find a clue as to their current state.

My subject is a male from the Victorian era. As I go through his memories, I see a very spacious house decorated with Persian rugs, overstuffed furniture, and velvet curtains. But unlike most of the rooms of that time, it is very sparsely laid out. There is a woman who walks these rooms. She is his wife, Elizabeth. Her dark blond hair is up in a Grecian style, with ringlets on the back. She usually wears elegant dark green dresses. He treats her as if she is just another furnishing of the house. She is a very quiet woman, and seems very sad behind her statue-like expression.

Suddenly, I feel a consciousness discovering my intrusion. It has a very evil feel to it. I realize that it is the man I am linked to. I can feel his glee as he discovers another life force in his mind. He grabs me mentally and tries to take my life energy, stating that once he has taken my energy and killed me, he will be able to fully awaken his body and then feed upon the energy of others. I fight back and try to pull myself away from him. I state that I would never let him do it. He laughs at me and takes more of my energy. "What about Elizabeth?" I ask. He seems taken aback as I go on to say, "She deserves better."

"You don't know what you're talking about," he growls.

"You never paid any attention to her."

"Stop it!" he shouts.

"You can't even say her name," I say, watching him squirm. "Say her name!" I demand. "Say her name!"

It was usually at this part that I would wake up in a cold sweat and force myself to forget the dream. I'm not sure how many times I dreamed this part, because it was only when the dream was in progress that I remembered having it before."

Part Two

"I jerk back as I break contact with my subject. Shaken, I walk past the other tables, with their sides that suggest supermarket bins, and out into the hall. There I sit in a chair and try to explain what happened. One of the other volunteers is Sue, a lady who worked for the same company I once did. She is a very sweet and caring person. She and the others tell me there's nothing to worry about, and leave me to recover from my shock. I watch the clock on the wall as its hands slowly tick off the minutes.

I can't sit still any longer. I go outside to a field with children playing in the sun. I watch them until the sun begins to set. I shout to them to go home, before it gets dark. I go to the trench beside the field, where a line of trees is growing. As the sun sets, fireflies zip around me.

In remembrance of my childhood, I catch one in my hand. It is freezing cold. I release it and look back at the building in horror. I know my subject is now awake, and I run back. I am gasping for air as I approach the people in the hall. "Where is he?" I ask. "Where is he?"

They look at me in confusion and one tells me to calm down. I try to explain what is going on, but they think I am hysterical. Sue then comes out of the room of subjects, screaming. Her test subject has been strangled to death. I am certain that my person did it, but everyone tells me again to calm down. Before they can stop me, I run in and look. The table where he was, only a few yards away from the murdered subject, is empty. I begin to shake and swear that I will stop him.

The others take hold of me and set me back into the chair in the hall. They tell me to stay there and let them take care of it. I wait until they leave and then go looking for him, because I know that I am the only one who can find him.

I go through large, metal double doors and enter a world that looks like it has been wrapped in newspaper. I run down dark corridors and between buildings. I come across a large dark door. I can sense him behind it, but before I can open it, I find that two of my sisters and some of their friends are behind me. My heart stops for a moment. I can't let them be hurt. As I try to shoo them away, he comes through the door. He is living darkness in human form, his features indistinguishable. He sees the young women behind me and laughs.

We run. I shout out directions as we traverse the newspaper maze, only a few steps in front of this demon. We find another set of double doors. We enter a lit stairwell, with its steps going up in a square spiral. The walls and stairs are concrete and along the outer wall is a line of newspaper with ceramic greenware pots on top. We bar the door and start to run up the stairs. We are only one turn up before he crashes through the door and comes after us. I wish for some elders to get rid of this monster as I start throwing greenware at him. I yell to my sisters to get their friends farther up the stairs and away, but everyone is frozen in place as the demon comes for me. He tells me that he will get them too. They start passing down more greenware pots for me to throw.

I am out of greenware and he is only a few steps below me. He chuckles his glee as he reaches for me. "What about Elizabeth?" I shout. We have the same exchange as before, but this time as I tell him to say her name, I put my hands on his jaws and actually try to force him to say it, even as he is trying to subdue me. This is where I woke up, but I believe I won that battle.

This nightmare is extraordinary in several respects. The fact that the theme of the nightmare—confrontation with the mind of this tremendous evil, a demon and killer—was sustained over several years of the dreamer's life is remarkable. Part one recurred several times when she was a teenager and part two was a continuation of the recurring nightmare of her teenage years but now manifesting itself in her early adulthood. That nightmares can sustain a theme for so long belies the claim that they are just transient, meaningless, and spooky noise. The dreamer's confrontation with the evil demon was also noteworthy in that she used several techniques to "win the battle" against him, ranging from running away to throwing things at him to forcing him to recall a memory of a women he apparently loved and thus insinuating love into his consciousness. The demon apparently wanted to take control of the dreamer's will and consciousness—the dreamer's very mind—but she successfully thwarted the attacks.

This ability to win a battle against a demon in a nightmare is unusual. In premodern tribal cultures, it would have marked the dreamer off from the rest of the tribe as special. Someone who wrestled with a spirit-demon and won would have special powers, especially curative or healing powers. The dreamer would have been pressured or invited to become a specialist in the tribe's religious and ritual practices, particularly with respect to the healing arts. She would have been called upon to protect the tribe against other demons and to cure physical and mental illnesses—all on the basis of this recurring nightmare! One other exceptional feature of this nightmare is the dreamer's ability, at least fleetingly, to understand the mind of the demon. Typically, the dreamer's "mind-reading" abilities are suspended or unavailable to the dreamer during a nightmare. Most of us cannot fathom the mind of a supernatural being of immense evil. All we know is that the evil being in our nightmares intends to harm us. Beyond that, their thoughts, motives, and intentions are obscure to us in the dream/nightmare. Yet this dreamer's explicit aim, announced at the beginning of the nightmare, was to contact the mind of the demon and she succeeded—at least partially—and that contact allowed her to defeat the demon.

For most of us this strategy of contacting the mind of the demon in a nightmare would be disastrous, so I recommend against attempting to do so. Nightmares like this one contain hugely charged emotional material that cannot be integrated or assimilated in a healthy, constructive way by the dream ego without the help of a therapist or some other trusted source. The wisdom of the ages also recommends against attempts to contact the mind of the malignant beings that we meet during nightmares. You cannot control them. But you can defeat them with help. The kind of emotional material appearing in nightmares and sometimes represented by monsters or demons needs to be dealt with slowly, soberly, and during the daytime in the company of someone with the experience and expertise to help.

We will see in the chapters that follow that premodern tribal peoples believed that attempts to communicate with a demon-spirit in a nightmare could lead to possession by that spirit; that is, the dreamer's mind and personality would be destroyed and taken over by the demon. In the nightmare above the dreamer says "He (the demon) grabs me mentally and tries to take my life energy, stating that once he has taken my energy and killed me, he will be able to fully awaken his body and then feed upon the energy of others." That is what demonic possession is about—the destruction of one personality and the substitution of another, more destructive, personality. Nightmares, among other things, were considered portals or openings into the realm of the supernatural and thus were dangerous, terrifying, and powerful. Premodern peoples and our ancestors had a healthy fear and respect for the nightmare and the beings they encountered in nightmares. We will see in the chapters that follow that modern scientific approaches to the nightmare suggests that we should do likewise.

While this particular nightmare was remarkable for all of the reasons just adduced, it is unremarkable in the sense that it resembles all other nightmares in many other respects. That is, it contains many of the features that commonly occur in other nightmares. First, like all other nightmares it is emotionally compelling. It is a strangely compelling story that the dreamer had to share with others (over the Internet in this case) and that fascinates others. Nightmare images and stories also tend to linger—they haunt both the mind of the person who experienced it and the minds of persons who heard the story. Nightmares have a capacity to stay with people. They also have a capacity to jump from mind to mind like the contagious memes to which Richard Dawkins, the British biologist and evolutionary theorist who coined the term, has drawn attention. Perhaps nightmares can be treated as particularly virulent memes. We will see in the chapters that follow that recurring nightmares are more common in young women than in any other demographic group. We will see that like this nightmare, most nightmares involve the themes of being attacked by or chased by malignant strangers or monsters and that when the dreamer considers these malignant beings to be in some way "supernatural" or demons of some kind, the emotional distress associated with the nightmare increases dramatically and misfortunes for the dreamer within the dream/nightmare are much more likely to occur.

We will also see that recurrent nightmares can be one of two types: 1) the same nightmare, with similar thematic elements, which recurs again and again (as in our specimen dream here) or 2) dissimilar nightmares, which are experienced several times a week or a month (as in most cases of recurring nightmare "syndrome"). The first type occurs more often in the childhood and the teenage years than at any other time of life. The second nightmare type occurs to a select few individuals in the population at large. These recurrent nightmare sufferers are also likely to exhibit "fantasy proneness," "thin" emotional boundaries between themselves and others, increased levels of creativity, "openness to experience," and may have histories of significant emotional turmoil or even trauma. But we will also see that the experience of frequent nightmares does not necessarily imply psychopathology or that "something is wrong with you." In fact, a good case can be made for the theory that nightmares are functional, that they perform some service for the individual and the population.

In particular, nightmares help to solve the problems connected with mind, self, or identity. The ego is attacked, shaped, and often strengthened as a result of nightmares—though there is no guarantee that a strong sense of self will emerge from nightmare experiences. As we have seen in this specimen nightmare, it requires struggle on the part of the individual to resist what is considered and experienced as evil in the dream. At the very least, nightmares serve to mark off the individual who experiences them as in some way special. These individuals have, at a minimum, endured very frightening (nighttime) experiences and have lived to tell about them. Indeed, to our ancestors, the people who experienced frequent and terrifying visions during the night were considered to be in contact with supernatural beings and powers that could significantly influence the well-being of everyone in the tribe. Certainly the individuals who experienced the nightmares themselves would frequently speak of encounters with fantastic spiritual beings and with frighteningly evil beings. These reports, furthermore, were confirmed by all people who experienced nightmares. If only a single individual had reported interactions with demons during a nightmare people could pass off the report as the ravings of a lunatic. But many people reported such experiences and they still today consistently report such experiences.

Indeed, nightmares are universally attested across human cultures and varying historical epochs. People who report these experiences have always been considered special. They may speak of nighttime horrors and encounters with supernatural monsters but during the day-time they function normally. These are normal individuals who happen to experience extraordinary visions during the night. Once it had been demonstrated that the nightmare experiencers were not simply deranged, people were compelled to listen to them. They had tales to tell and visions to share. We will listen to them respectfully in this book.

Acknowledgments

I would like to thank my research assistants, Erica Harris and Deirdre McLaren, for their expert help on this book. Deirdre especially contributed to this book in myriad ways. She assisted with analyses reported in the chapter on nightmare content (Chapter 3) and is an expert in scoring dreams with the Hall and Van de Castle dream content scoring system, having scored literally hundreds of dreams with this system in the past. Several other research assistants including Emily Abrams, Catherine Beauharnais, and Alexandra Zaitsev assisted in tracking down references for me, formatting text, figures and tables, and troubleshooting the entire manuscript as it was completed in draft.

Some of the materials in Chapters 5, 8, and 11 were previously published in McNamara (2004a); McNamara (2004b); McNamara, McLaren, Smith, Brown, and Stickgold (2005); and McNamara and Szent-Imrey (2007).

Chapter 1

Approach to the Study of Nightmares

We have all experienced nightmares—dreams that can be intensely disturbing and frightening. We awaken from such a dream and thank God that it "was only a dream!" The images and emotions associated with the dream may haunt us throughout the day and sometimes for years. Nightmares prompt us to seek the company of others. Who prefers to be alone after a nightmare? The fear and sense of dread is so intense as to be palpable. We awaken drenched in sweat and with our hearts racing. The sense of vulnerability makes us quake with fear. For women and children the dream evokes fear of intruders or violent male strangers. For men and many women and children, the dream evokes fear of supernatural or unseen dangers.

SHORTCOMINGS OF THE STANDARD "TAKE" ON NIGHTMARES

Whence come such dreams? For most specialists in the study of nightmares these disturbing dreams represent a failure of normal dreaming processes. The surge of negative emotion in an otherwise typical rapid eye movement or REM dream (REM is one of the two major sleep states we experience, the one in which vivid dreaming occurs) rises to an unusually high level due perhaps to a failure in normal inhibitory processes that keep these surges of negative emotion in check. Nightmares have no positive function in themselves. They are unfortunate byproducts of an otherwise normal dream process that goes awry.

Yet, this explanation does not make much sense. Nightmares cannot be considered unfortunate and accidental byproducts of an otherwise normal sleep mentation system. If they were accidental breakdowns in the system that produces dreams, they would produce relatively random content and be relatively randomly distributed in people who experienced breakdowns in the sleep and sleep-mentation systems of the brain. Yet, nightmares do not occur randomly in the population. Their form and content are not random either. Instead, nightmares mostly occur in young children and in those adults who have a certain personality and cognitive makeup. We will see who those people are in later chapters. Because all of us to some extent share the personality and cognitive characteristics of frequent nightmare sufferers, we, too, occasionally experience nightmares.

NIGHTMARES CAN BE FUNCTIONAL

I will show in this book that nightmares must be considered as in some sense "intended" by Mother Nature. They are functional. They serve some purpose for the human organism. We currently do not know what that purpose is but the search has only recently begun. Hitherto most medical specialists considered nightmares an unmitigated negative. This of course is a reasonable position to take given the distress that nightmares cause. Nature does not always pause to ensure that her children feel good when she attempts to accomplish some purpose such as perpetuating the race or protecting her children from predation and the like. Life and health do not always feel good.

Evidence of purpose or function with respect to nightmares is rapidly accumulating in the scientific literature. As mentioned above, nightmares do not occur randomly or merely during stressful periods in a person's life. Distressing dreams and nightmares are common in childhood, become more prevalent in later childhood and adolescence (American Psychiatric Association 2000; Fisher, Pauley, and McGuire 1989; MacFarlane, Allen, and Honzik 1954; Mindell and Barrett 2002; Nielsen, Laberge Vela-Bueno et al. 1985) and then decline for most people throughout adulthood. In the elderly, reports of nightmares begin to increase again with 68 percent of older adults reporting nightmares at least "sometimes" (Partinen 1994). Females at all ages report nightmares more often than males (Hartmann 1984; Levin 1994; Nielsen and Levin 2007; Nielsen, Laberge, et al. 2000; Ohayon, Morselli, and Guilleminault 1997; Schredl and Pallmer 1998; Tanskanen et al. 2001). A longitudinal study by Nielsen and colleagues (2000) demonstrated a sex-by-age interaction effect for nightmare frequency with the prevalence in girls between the ages of thirteen and sixteen years almost doubling (2.7 percent to 4.9 percent) while the prevalence in boys dropped from 2.5 percent to 0.4 percent.

In short, what we have is a terrifying nighttime sleep-related emotional experience occurring mostly in woman and children, and in both men and women with a particular personality type to be defined later.

Do Nightmares Reflect Ancestral Dangers?

One immediate explanation of a functional role for nightmares suggests itself given these population data. Nightmares reflect the ancient vulnerabilities of these populations to those ancestral males who engaged in raids against neighboring tribes. These were murderous ancestral males. Women and children had good reasons to fear these marauding, pillaging, and raping ancestral males. Those women and children who had a lower threshold for experiencing a terrifying event may have been better suited or more ready to flee at the first signs of imminent threat from these bands of men. In other words, nightmares would have helped these individuals to recognize danger more quickly and presumably to escape more readily than people without nightmares.

This explanation seems plausible enough but there are major problems with it. First it cannot account for those males who experience frequent nightmares. It also does not account for the content of nightmares—even in women and children. The murderous ancestral male theory would predict that nightmare content would consist mostly of scenarios involving violent attacks on the individual female. This however is not the case. We will detail the data on nightmare content in a later chapter. The murderous ancestral male theory, furthermore, requires some sort of benefit in terms of survival success or reproductive success in those who suffer from nightmares. In other words, someone would need to show that nightmare sufferers or their immediate kin exhibited faster reaction times to threat or exhibited better survival skills in situations of war or ecologic stress. But unfortunately, I know of no such data. In summary, we will need to keep the murderous ancestral male theory in mind but my own feeling is that it cannot account for the facts concerning nightmare phenomenology or biology.

Nightmares Run in Families

Consistent with the idea that the nightmare is associated with some sort of reproductive benefit is the cumulating evidence of a genetic influence on frequency of nightmare production. (Hublin et al. 1999). Identification of a genetic influence on nightmare frequency of course does not require that nightmares be functional or confer reproductive benefits—only that the finding is consistent with such a claim. Clinicians have long noted that patients with recurrent nightmares also report that a parent, usually the mother, also suffered nightmares. Unfortunately, this finding of a link between genetic endowment and nightmare occurrence has not yet been followed up. This is an area ripe for breakthrough research.

Nightmares Do Not Necessarily Indicate Psychopathology

Nightmares can present in association with other neuropsychiatric disorders and their presence may warrant a neuropsychiatric work-up (Belicki 1992a; 1992b; Hartmann 1984, 1998; Hublin et al. 1999; Ohayon et al. 1997). For example, recurrent distressing dreams and nightmares may be associated with mood, anxiety, and/or personality disorders (Hartmann et al. 1987), post-traumatic stress disorder (Schreuder, Kleijn, and Rooijmans 2000) and although rarer, in the elderly, they may herald the onset of a neurodegenerative disorder (Boeve et al. 2007; Olson, Boeve, and Silber 2000).

On the other hand, nightmares can and do occur in the absence of any other significant psychopathology (Nielsen and Zadra 2005). For example, people with so-called "thin" personality boundaries and with high levels of creativity tend to experience nightmares more frequently than people with thick boundaries and low levels of creativity (Hartmann 1987). "Thin" or "thick" boundaries refer to how well-defined the lines are between you and others; and within yourself, between one cognitive system and others. Presumably the tendency to demarcate an area of "self" in distinction to an area or areas for other "selves" varies from high to low. People with marked or high tendencies to separate self from others would have thick boundaries while people with low tendencies to do so would have thin boundaries. Hartmann et al. (1987) studied twelve lifelong nightmare sufferers, twelve vivid dreamers who had no nightmares, and twelve persons who had neither nightmares nor vivid dreams. Relative to the other two groups the group with nightmares scored higher on a "boundary deficit" score of the Rorschach personality test, had more psychiatric symptoms, and had more first- and second-degree relatives with nightmares. In addition, lifelong nightmare sufferers had artistic and creative tendencies and interests not found in the other groups.

From an empirical perspective, nightmares should be studied without assuming that they are always pointing to some other significant psychopathology. Instead they can be and should be considered functional. When they become dysfunctional, when they interfere with daily functions, then interventions can be devised to reduce the distress associated with the nightmares. From a clinical perspective, treatment should be considered when distressing dreams and nightmares become frequent or recurrent, since the presence of nightmares can directly diminish the quality of sleep and indirectly increase daytime anxiety (Krakow 2006; Levin 1994; Ohayon et al. 1997).

In any case, because nightmares occur nonrandomly with nonrandom content themes and because they have profound effects on daytime functioning, they may in some sense be considered functional. In this book, we will keep an open mind about potential functions of nightmares. We caution, however, that the evidence for functionality is not yet convincing. We merely assert that it is time to at least consider this option when attempting to understand nightmares and their effects.

DEFINITION AND DIAGNOSTIC CRITERIA FOR RECURRENT NIGHTMARES

Nightmares are frightening dreams that most often occur during rapid eye movement or REM sleep (Hartmann 1984, 1998; Haynes and Mooney 1975; Krakow 2006). They "prefer" to appear during one of the late REM episodes that occur during the early morning period between 4 A.M. and 7 A.M. (Hartmann 1984; Nielsen and Zadra 2005; Spoormaker, Schredl, and van den Bout 2006). They may or may not be accompanied by signs of sympathetic surge (increased heart rate and blood pressure, as well as respiratory changes) and typically last between five and thirty minutes (Nielsen and Zadra 2005). For most persons with repeat nightmares, the dominant emotion is terror, overwhelming in its intensity. Frequent themes include the dreamer involved in aggressive encounters, being chased or attacked by unknown threatening men or animals or supernatural beings, enclosure in unpleasant surroundings, dread due to imminent violent assault by an unknown stranger, and so on (Hartmann 1984; Levin 1994). Pursuit nightmares are fairly common and occur in 92 percent of women and 85 percent of men who report nightmares (Nielsen and Zadra 2005). Attack dreams may carry a prevalence ranging between 67 percent to 90 percent (Harris 1948; Nielsen and Zadra 2005).

Violence by the dreamer against others is uncommon even when the dreamer is being physically attacked. Most interesting about nightmare content is the presence of unusual characters—characters that may be considered animalistic or supernatural or otherworldly, in short, nonhuman. It is the presence of these anomalous character types that crucially picks out nightmares from other unpleasant or intense dreams. Both of these latter types of dreams also very commonly contain pursuit or victimization themes. But these latter dream types *do not* typically contain nonhuman, supernatural characters. We will discuss nightmare content more thoroughly in a later chapter.

The Diagnostic and Statistical Manual of Mental Disorders, IV-TR, or DSM-IV-TR defines a nightmare as an "extremely frightening dream" that causes a person to awaken. Frequently, nightmares also result in difficulty falling back to sleep. Due to their intensity, nightmares produce a clear recall of the dream experience after awakening. Briefly, nightmares can be thought of as easy-to-remember frightening dreams that arise from REM sleep (American Academy of Sleep Medicine 2005; American Psychiatric Association 2000.) Table 1.1 compares three

Table 1.1
Diagnostic Criteria for Nightmares: Three Classification Systems

DSM-IV-TR Diagnostic Criteria for 307.47 Nightmare Disorder (American Psychiatric Association, 2000)	ICD-10, 2nd Ed. Diagnostic Criteria for 307.47 Nightmares (World Health Organization, 2004) The following clinical features are essential for a definitive diagnosis:	ICSD-R Diagnostic Criteria for 307.47 Nightmares (American Academy of Sleep Medicine, 2000)
A. Repeated awakenings from the major sleep period or naps with detailed recall of extended and extremely frightening dreams, usually involving threats to survival, security, or self-esteem. The awakenings generally occur during the second half of the sleep period.	A. Awakening from nocturnal sleep or naps with detailed and vivid recall of intensely frightening dreams, usually involving threats to survival, security, or self-esteem; the awakening may occur at any time during the sleep period, but typically during the second half ...	A. The patient has at least one episode of sudden awakening from sleep with intense fear, anxiety, and feeling of impeding harm.
B. On awakening from the frightening dreams the person rapidly becomes oriented and alert (in contrast to the confusion and disorientation seen in sleep terror disorder and some forms of epilepsy).	B. Upon awakening from the frightening dreams, the individual rapidly becomes oriented and alert ...	B. The patient has immediate recall of frightening dream context.
C. The dream experience, or the sleep disturbance that caused the awakening, causes clinically significant distress or impairment in social, occupational, or other important areas of functioning.	C. The dream experience itself, and the resulting disturbance of sleep causes marked distress to the individual.	C. Full alertness occurs immediately upon awakening, with little confusion or disorientation.
D. The nightmares do not occur exclusively during the course of another mental disorder (for example, post-traumatic stress disorder) and are not due to the direct physiological effects of a substance (e.g., a drug of abuse, a medication) or a general medical condition.		D. Associated features include at least one of the following: 1) Return to sleep after episode is delayed and not rapid; 2) The episode occurs during the latter half of an habitual sleep period.

prevailing sets of diagnostic criteria used to categorize nightmare disorders. These criteria can be found in the DSM-IV-TR of the American Psychiatric Association; the International Statistical Classification of Diseases and Related Health Problems, 10th Revision (ICD-10), of the World Health Organization, and the International Classification of Sleep Disorders Manual, Revised (ICSD-R) of the American Academy of Sleep Medicine.

No consensus definition of recurrent nightmares yet exists but a frequency equal to or greater than once per week should be considered recurrent. Nightmare distress is significantly related to nightmare frequency (Hartmann et al. 1987). Nightmare frequency, in turn, is correlated with neuroticism, anxiety, daytime physical and cognitive complaints, and stress-related symptoms (Spoormaker et al. 2006). The causal direction in these relationships remains unclear. Nevertheless, when nightmare frequency reaches a certain threshold, such that the individual experiences enough distress to complain of the nightmares, we say that he has recurrent nightmares.

As just summarized, the nightmare is generally considered to be a frightening dream that awakens the sleeper. In this book I will define a nightmare as any disturbing or terrifying dream, even in the absence of an awakening (Halliday 1987; Zadra and Donderi, 2000). I want to treat nightmares more broadly than the awakening criterion would allow. After all, many people report nightmares that did not cause an awakening. Indeed people with recurrent nightmares often do not awaken (till morning) from their disturbing dreams. Patients with psychosomatic disorders and nightmares do not always report awakenings, despite the severity of the nightmare (Levitan 1976; Van Bork 1982).

SYNDROME OF RECURRING NIGHTMARES

This syndrome is associated with recurring or frequent nightmares characterized by a recurrent theme. It is not uncommon that they are associated with increased frequency of dreaming. At least a subset of recurring nightmares has been linked to complex partial seizures (Penfield and Erickson 1941; Solms 1997). Some of these recurring nightmares have been considered to be manifestations of these seizures. On the other hand, recurring nightmares may be independent of any obvious epileptic activity. These latter recurrences tend to be less stereotyped and usually depict unpleasant conflicts and stresses that may vary over time (Cartwright 1979; Zadra 1996). Although some of these less well-stereotyped recurrences reflect significant trauma or psychopathology, many do not. It is not uncommon to encounter recurrent themes of being chased or threatened in some manner or being confronted with a natural disaster. Dreams with less recurrence and described as recurrent themes or recurrent content are not so clearly associated with psychopathology and may reflect adaptive functions (Domhoff 1993).

Up to 50 percent of children between three and six years of age, and 20 percent between six and twelve years experience "frequent" nightmares (American Psychiatric Association 2000; Fisher et al. 1989; Mac-Farlane et al. 1954; Mindell and Barrett 2002; Nielsen et al. 2000; Partinen 1994; Salzarulo and Chevalier 1983; Simonds and Parraga 1982; Vela-Bueno et al. 1985). Relying on parent reports about their children's sleep and dreams, Smedje, Broman and Hetta (2001a; 2001b) reported that children five- to seven-year-olds from the general population apparently experienced difficulty falling asleep (5.6 percent), frequent night wakings (15.5 percent), snoring (7.7 percent), nightmares (3.1 percent), and bedwetting (5.3 percent). Nightmares were associated with serious health problems or handicaps, sleep problems in conjunction with life events, and female gender.

Both the frequency of nightmares and the intensity of the distress they cause decline with age so that by the time an individual reaches maturity, nightmares are only rarely experienced. For some adult individuals, however, nightmares are not a rare occurrence. Epidemiological studies (Belicki and Belicki 1982; Bixler et al. 1979; Haynes and Mooney 1975; Levin 1994; Ohayon et al. 1997) indicate that 2 percent to 6 percent of the American population experience nightmares at least once a week. That translates into approximately eighteen million individuals in the United States alone who experience frequent nightmares.

Why is there this proportion of the population that experiences nightmares on a regular basis? Are they suffering from some medical condition that gives rise to the nightmare as psychological sequelae? Or are their nightmares functional in an as yet unknown way? There is no known psychopathology that alone could account for the frequency of nightmares in the vast majority of nightmare sufferers—never mind the millions of normal children ages three to six who regularly experience nightmares. Do we really want to pathologize these children for experiencing what is apparently a universal phenomenon for children their age?

THE SHARING OF NIGHTMARES WITH OTHERS

Early human groups are thought to have been composed of approximately two hundred individuals (Barrett, Dunbar, and Lycett 2002, 248). Three percent to six percent of two hundred individuals yields a mean of about eight individuals who likely experienced frequent nightmares. These eight individuals in a tribe of two hundred would have stood out from the crowd by sharing their frightening dreams with others in the tribe. If you share a frightening set of visions with some-one else in a small tribe then your reputation would certainly be affected, for better or worse, depending on how you shared the tale and how people reacted to it. Given what we know concerning the centrality of group dream sharing in premodern tribal groups (Gregor 1981a, 1981b, 2001; Schneider and Sharp 1969; Tedlock 1992a, 1992b), we can assume that dream sharing was a common practice in early human groups in the environment of evolutionary adaptation (EEA). If it was common, then people would very likely try to excel in the practice. People would attempt to share dream experiences in such a way as to be compelling and memorable so that their reputations would be enhanced and their prestige increased.

Even today young adults recall one to two dreams per week with 37 percent of these reporting that they recall a dream "every night" or "very frequently" (Belicki and Belicki 1986; Goodenough 1991; Strauch and Meir 1996). In representative samples of the general population, between 40 percent and 75 percent recall between one and five intense and "impactful" dreams per month (Borbély 1984; Kuiken and Sikora 1993; Stepansky et al. 1998). Once recalled, a dream is typically shared with another person (Stefanikis 1995; Vann and Alperstein 2000). For example, Vann and Alperstein reported that 98 percent of the 241 individuals they interviewed reported telling dreams to others, particularly friends and intimates. Once shared, they have the potential to go on influencing daytime mood and behavior of both self and others.

But what about nightmares? Why share nightmares? There are good reasons *not* to share nightmares. First of all nightmares contain a lot of scary and bizarre imagery. Second, given their intensity and fantastic imagery they are difficult to shape into a coherent meaningful narrative. Finally, and perhaps most importantly they contain a lot of negative emotion. Why would anyone else be interested in my negative emotion? Or better, why would I or any given person be interested in sharing my negative emotions with others?

Negative emotions can be powerful signals when used as leverage in social interactions (e.g., eliciting sympathy/empathy from conspecifics) (Hagen 2003; Sally 2003). When used thusly they enhance social ties/ alliances and powerfully influence the reputation of the individual reporting the emotion. The individual is marked either as a victim or as a powerful person who possesses resilience and therefore good genes. Scarifications, physical or emotional, testify to my ability to survive trauma.

In any case, at least 30–50 percent of the population exhibit and report a chronic experience of negative emotionality (Kessler et al. 2005; Riolo et al. 2005; Watson and Clark, 1984). Negative emotionality treated as a trait evidences moderate to high levels of heritability

(Bouchard 2004). Evidently people who exhibit high negative emotionality are considered attractive enough to at least a portion of the general population as they marry, mate, and produce offspring who inherit the disposition for negative emotionality.

REM sleep itself—never mind the dreams associated with REM—is certainly in a position to mark off a person as an individual who is resilient. REM can influence a person's waking mood state. REM involves regular, periodic, and intense activation of the limbic system and the amygdala—the two major emotional centers of the brain. As the night progresses, activation patterns become more intense and likely color the person's mood for the day upon awakening. If the sleeper awakes and remembers an emotional dream, waking-related mood states are that much more likely to be influenced by REM. Most but not all spontaneously recalled dreams are from late night/early morning REM period (Goodenough 1991; Schonbar 1961) or at least no different in content from late REM period dreams (Domhoff 2005).These are the dreams that get shared with others. Even specific dream content variables (such as number of characters appearing in early morning dreams) have been shown to have significant links with daytime mood (Kramer 1993).

Thus, nightmares gave a small number of individuals a chance to share exceedingly negative, even frightening, information with the group. Ethnographic evidence on dream sharing further suggests that early human groups very likely took the content of dreams, especially nightmares, very seriously. If nightmare sharing resulted in greater overall vigilance levels among tribal members, with many individuals on the lookout for potentially harmful events, then each individual in the tribe would have fared better than if they had not received the "warnings" in the form of nightmare images and content.

If the nightmares were taken as warnings or prophecies by early humans, then it is likely that the reputation of the nightmare sharers would rise or fall according to whether the prophecies were borne out in reality. In the long run, however, the reputations of frequent nightmare sufferers would likely suffer. Although unhappy events are frequent, nightmarish events were not that frequent even for early humans.

Another possibility is that nightmare reports would increase the reputation of nightmare sufferers since the experience would mark them out for some special religious, shamanistic, and leadership role in the tribe. Anyone who could experience such horrifying images would surely be considered special in some sense. Early human groups believed in the reality of a spirit world. Nightmare sufferers would have been marked as spiritual specialists. They were people who could wrestle with demons and survive. When nightmares occurred in children, these children would have been selected to be trained as a tribal shaman or to fulfill some

Table 1.2
Prevalence, Themes, and Clinical Correlates of Recurrent Nightmares

Population	U.S. Prevalence	Most Common Themes	Sleep State	Clinical Correlates
Children 3 to 6 years old	50%	Being attacked or chased by a monster or an animal	Late REM period	None definitively established
Children 6 to 12 years old	20%	Chased or attacked by strangers	Late REM period	Social anxiety
Adults	8%	Chased or attacked by male strangers or supernatural beings	Late REM period (Occasionally Stage II)	Neuroticism; thin boundaries; creativity; anxiety
Patients with post-traumatic stress disorder (PTSD)	Up to 70% of PTSD patients suffer recurrent nightmares (Wittmann et al. 2007)	Replay of trauma scenes	Any REM period and at sleep onset	History of trauma; anxiety
Patients with REM sleep behavior disorder (RBD)	Middle-aged and elderly men. No prevalence data available	Self or significant other under attack by male strangers	REM	"Acting out" dreams; violent movements while asleep; may herald onset of neurodegenerative disease

Source: Modified from Wittman, L., M. Schredl, and M. Kramer, 2007. *Dreaming in Posttraumatic Stress Disorder: A Clinical Review of Phenomenology, Psychophysiology, and Treatment.* Psychotherapy and Psychosomatics, 761: 25–39.

similar religious or healing role. We summarize prevalence, thematic, electroencephalograph (EEG), and clinical correlates of recurrent nightmares in Table 1.2.

Now that we have some basic facts regarding the prevalence, distribution, biology, and content of nightmares in hand we can explore each of these facets of the nightmare phenomenon in more depth in the chapters to come. We begin with the bald fact that nightmares occur in children. I want to suggest that this fact is odd and needs to be explained. Why would Mother Nature design a child who spontaneously produces nightmares?

Chapter 2

Why Do Nightmares Occur in Children?

We have seen that nightmares first appear in children ages three to six and then reach a peak frequency relative to other age groups in late childhood/early adolescence. Why is this the case? Why should nightmares appear and peak during childhood? How could nightmares possibly benefit a child? Perhaps they do not benefit children at all? In that case we would be left with the byproduct explanation for a major experience in the life of children. I have already discussed reasons to reject the byproduct explanation of nightmares in the previous chapter. I will now explore the nightmare experience in children from a functional point of view.

In order to get a handle on the problem of why nightmares occur at a relatively high frequency in childhood we will need to understand what is happening to the child biologically, emotionally, and cognitively. What is happening to the child during the period beginning around ages three to four and ending at onset of adolescence around ages twelve to thirteen? First, what is happening to sleep and dreams in childhood?

SLEEP IN CHILDHOOD

Carskadon and Dement's (2006) review of normal sleep variation as well as Anders, Sadeh, and Appareddy's (1995) review of the literature on sleep in children aged two to twelve showed that slow-wave sleep times (as a percentage of total sleep) are maximal at this age and that they decline steadily across the lifespan. Latencies in REM sleep are also longer in these children relative to other age groups. Beyond this meager bit of knowledge about sleep in children, little else is known. It is difficult to study sleep in children for a variety of reasons. Their neurophysiologic systems are still undergoing rapid development and these developmental changes make it difficult to identify stable EEG signals. Mothers too are reluctant to have their children sleep in a sleep lab or with electrodes attached to their scalps as children experience these manipulations as significantly stressful.

This is also the age at which nightmares and night terrors are more likely to occur as well. One can distinguish between a nightmare and other distressing dream disturbances like "night terrors" by identifying co-occurring symptoms of the nightmare event and by examining the EEG (electroencephalograph) record of the child. A nightmare typically occurs during late EEG stage REM while a night terror typically occurs during EEG stage non–rapid eye movement (NREM) sleep or during the transition from NREM into REM or waking consciousness. In stark contrast to a nightmare (where the child awakens frightened but oriented to self and environment), during night terrors the child may scream in terror with eyes wide open, yet seem otherwise asleep, hallucinating, and unaware of his surroundings.

In summary, we know very little about sleep in children and adolescents, except that slow-wave sleep (SWS) appears to be more potent (as measured by delta wave intensity and counts) in these children than at any other time in the lifespan. Because the changes in SWS intensity and duration are dramatic during childhood, children are more vulnerable to parasomnias associated with SWS, namely night terrors, sleepwalking, and presumably, nightmares. What is the function of slow-wave sleep? Let me digress here to say a few words about slow-wave sleep.

NREM Slow-Wave Sleep (SWS)

As in most other mammals, human sleep is composed of two phases/ types: 1) non–rapid eye movement (NREM) sleep, and 2) rapid eye movement (REM) sleep. NREM sleep is further divided into four substages with stages III and IV collectively known as SWS (Rechtschaffen and Kales 1968). The initiation of NREM sleep is gradual and characterized by slowing of EEG frequency. This initial phase is termed stage I. In stage II, we see a further decrease in EEG frequency and the appearance of intermittent high-frequency spikes called sleep spindles. Sleep spindles decrease in stage III as the amplitude of slow waves increases. This mixed pattern gives way to very high-amplitude delta waves in the deepest sleep, stage IV.

The delta waves characteristic of stage IV NREM constitute the intensity dimension of sleep. The greater the delta wave activity the more intense the sleep. It is very difficult to arouse someone who is in SWS. Something vitally important, apparently, is occurring in SWS.

The importance of the intensity dimension of sleep was first uncovered in experiments on effects of sleep deprivation. The most dramatic effect of sleep deprivation in every mammalian species studied thus far has been the phenomenon of "compensatory rebound," or the increase over baseline of sleep times and intensity, where intensity is measured by higher arousal thresholds, enhanced activity (particularly enhanced "delta power" when spectral EEG analysis is used), enhanced rapid eye movement frequencies per unit time and "deeper" and longer sleep cycles (Tobler 2005). After sleep deprivation, mammals contract a "sleep debt" and attempt to make up for lost sleep by enhancing the intensity and duration of subsequent sleep. During the wakefulness or deprivation period, neurochemicals are thought to accumulate in proportion to the length of the wake period. One such possible chemical is adenosine, which acts in a sleep center (possibly the basal forebrain) to inhibit arousal and increase sleepiness and then dissipates at a rate depending on sleep intensity until it returns to baseline during sleep. Birds too demonstrate a compensatory rebound after sleep deprivation, but the rebound involves increased overall sleep times and cycles rather than enhancements in slow-wave activity.

Borbély and Wirz-Justice (1982) first formalized the insight that mammalian sleep involved a balance between sleep amount and sleep intensity and that sleep was therefore under homeostatic control. In his "two-process" model of sleep regulation a sleep need process (Process S) increases during waking (or sleep deprivation) and decreases during sleep. This part of the model indexes restorative aspects of sleep and explicitly predicts that sleep is required for some restorative process of the brain, the body, or both. Process S is proposed to interact with input from the light-regulated circadian system (Process C) that is independent of sleep and wakefulness rhythms. Slow-wave activity (SWA) is taken as an indicator of the time course of Process S because SWS is known to correlate with arousal thresholds and to markedly increase during the previous waking period and during the rebound period after sleep deprivation in all mammals studied. Once a threshold value of Process S is reached (i.e., once the appropriate amount and intensity of SWS is reached), Process C will be activated. Simulations using the model's assumptions show that the homeostatic component of sleep falls in a sigmoidal manner during waking and rises in a saturating exponential manner during sleep.

The two-process model does not address homeostatic aspects of REM. Rapid eye movement, however, evidences rebound after sleep deprivation, but here the intensity component is likely to be some process associated with frequency (density) of rapid eye movements per unit time. In any case both REM and NREM are under homeostatic control and enhancements of sleep intensity over baseline address the homeostatic need for sleep. In short, these findings lead to the assumption that *sleep intensity indexes functional need*.

The potency, then, of SWS in children must be related to some physiologic functional need in these children. Presumably, SWS facilitates all of the things a growing child needs including brain sculpting and repair. During NREM sleep, for example, the hippocampus is thought to facilitate encoding of new declarative and episodic memories and to organize transfer of new memories to and retrieval of previously formed memories from neocortical sites. The amygdaloid complex (AC), which is developing rapidly in children, is thought to modulate these hippocampal activities during NREM sleep in such a way that the hippocampal-neocortical dialogue is enhanced especially for formation and consolidation of new emotional memories (Paré et al. 2003; Sterpenich et al. 2007). But memory consolidation and learning are only one of the things children need to do as they develop. Non–rapid eye movement SWS very likely also helps to orchestrate the hormonal cascade that regulates the timing for occurrence of developmental milestones.

NREM-REM Imbalances and Nightmare Propensity

But what is the relationship of SWS to nightmares? One possibility is that long durations of SWS (as occurs in childhood) disturb the balance that should obtain between NREM sleep and REM sleep states. If you get too much NREM, then REM will be inhibited and all of the brain and cognitive processes associated with REM will be threatened. This balance between NREM and REM is required for optimal mental functioning. REM and NREM sleep states are to some extent functionally connected and operate in an antagonistic manner. While, for example, NREM acts to enhance release of growth hormone (GH), REM is associated with enhanced release of somatostatin (SS), a growth hormone inhibitor (Van Cauter, Plat, and Copinschi 1998). Similarly, while corticotropin-releasing hormone (CRH) suppresses NREM, it enhances REM sleep indices, including rebound effects after REM sleep deprivation (Steiger 2003).

REM-NREM interactions may operate antagonistically with respect to other functions as well. While NREM enables an enhanced response to infectious challenge, REM seems to impair immunoregulatory functions (Krueger, Majde and Obal 2003). Fever and thermogenesis are difficult to mount during REM, and several proinflammatory cytokines such as interferon alpha, interleukin 1 (IL-1), and tumor necrosis factor (TNF) enhance NREM but suppress REM in rabbits (Inoue et al. 1999; Obal and Krueger 2003). While autonomic, cardiac, renal, and respiratory functions are stable in NREM, they are quite unstable in REM (Orem and Barnes 1980; Parmeggiani, 2000). While thermoregulatory capacities are intact (but down-regulated) in NREM, they are mostly absent in REM (Szymusiak et al 1998). While cerebral blood flow volumes are down-regulated in NREM, they are enhanced in REM (Maquet and Phillips 1999; Orem and Barnes 1980). Muscle tone is intact in NREM, but it is absent in REM (Lai and Siegel 1999). The EEG is synchronized in NREM, but is desynchronized in REM (Steriade and McCarley 1990). The list could go on but you get the point.

Given that nightmares are a phenomenon of REM, they are perhaps a response to something going on in both NREM and REM sleep. Perhaps there was too much NREM and you needed a big dose of REM to get out of the deep trance associated with NREM. Something along these lines has been suggested before by several of the pioneers of modern sleep medicine. The idea was that occasionally sleep would become too deep and you would need a special and very intense arousal process to emerge from SWS. Nightmares fit the bill. They are intensely arousing events if nothing else.

The problem with the above theory was that observations of arousal physiology during nightmares revealed a dampening down of the autonomic nervous system activity—not an increase. Fisher et al. (1970) found that nightmares were characterized by relatively low levels of autonomic nervous system (ANS) activation during REM sleep. In 60 percent (twelve of twenty) of the nightmares they studied with EEG and ANS recording equipment, ANS activity was absent altogether. Fisher and colleagues suggested that REM dreaming possesses "a mechanism for tempering and modulating anxiety, for desomatizing the physiological response to it … [for] abolishing or diminishing the physiological concomitants" (770). Nightmares result when the anxiety exceeds a certain threshold and the REM desomatization mechanism breaks down, allowing autonomic activation to occur. But this latter conclusion seems to contradict Fisher's own data as he showed that ANS activity did not occur at high levels during a nightmare.

Whatever the case may be with respect to ANS activity during REM-related nightmares, the available data suggest that REM-related ANS activity during a nightmare is not particularly high. This is surprising given that ANS storms are not uncommon during REM. Apparently one can have high ANS activity during REM without having a nightmare and vice versa; you can get low ANS activity and still have a nightmare. The fuel for nightmares then cannot be a response mechanism to reverse a particularly low level of arousal associated with SWS.

Nevertheless, the fact remains that children have particularly intense and long SWS episodes and this surely influences their vulnerability to nightmares. Unfortunately we just do not yet know why this is the case. There are clues, however, to the origins of nightmares in the content of children's dreams …

DREAMING IN CHILDHOOD

Nightmares in children occur as dreams so it behooves us to study dreams in children in hopes that these might tell us something unique about nightmares in children. In his landmark longitudinal studies of the development of dreaming in children, Foulkes (1978, 1982, 1999) showed children's dreams are characterized by relatively poor narrative structure and high levels of passive victimization. There may be a single scene of a monster threatening the dreamer for example. Interestingly there is also a high percentage of animals in children's dreams relative to adults' dreams.

In Foulkes' study, dream recall rates, not surprisingly, were predicted by age. Preschoolers reported dreams on approximately 15 percent of awakenings, and the narratives were not actively self-oriented. Adolescents, on the other hand, reported dreams on upwards of 80 percent of awakenings. Parents are invariably surprised when they hear the low dream recall rates reported by Foulkes. So, Resnick, Stickgold, Rittenhouse, and Hobson (1994) reinvestigated the issue. They had parents collect dream memories from their four- to ten-year-old children. Before falling asleep, children were encouraged to remember their dreams. Parents awakened their children fifteen minutes earlier than their usual wakeup time and asked for dream reports. Children as young as four and five years old were able to report their dreams in more than half of the awakenings. In addition, Resnick et al. (1994) reported that children's dreams were not lacking in narrative or particularly high in passive victimization.

There are obvious design limitations to this study such as its demand characteristic: Children want to please their parents so they may be inventing dreams. On the other hand, parents were convinced that their children were reporting real dreams and the narratives apparently exhibited typical dream characteristics. If we assume that the truth about children's dreams lies somewhere between the Foulkes studies and those of Resnick et al. then we can conclude that the dream life of young children begins as soon as they can report on them and that victimization themes, though present, are not ubiquitous and that animals appear as characters in nearly every dream. These content characteristics change as the child gets older with less victimization and the animal characters giving way to familiar characters.

Strauch's (2005) longitudinal data set on children's dream content changes confirms this general picture. Dream recall rates increase as the child gets older with boys lagging behind girls until middle childhood when they catch up with girls. Dreams in both girls and boys become more realistic and complex, with the dreamer taking a more active role in the dream scenario and interacting with other dream characters more frequently.

Oberst, Charles, and Chamarro (2005) collected dreams from four different age groups of children: seven- and eight-year-olds; eleven- and twelve-year-olds; thirteen- and fourteen-year olds; and seventeen- and eighteen-year-olds. They found that younger boys were victims more often than girls. Boys' victimization in dreams gradually decreased with age, however. In contrast, aggression in girls' dreams was lower in the youngest group, then increased, and eventually decreased with age. These data suggest that nightmares may not necessarily vary with victimization scenarios in children—after all, girls report more nightmares than boys—yet boys undergo a greater number of victimization dreams than do girls.

One unusual study of dreaming in children should be mentioned here as it dovetails nicely with what we will be discussing later in terms of development of theory of mind abilities in these children. Briefly, once children begin to understand that other people have minds like themselves, they begin to populate the world with all kinds of agents seen and unseen, including imaginary friends and beings we would call supernatural agents. In the study under discussion, Adams (2005) identified and analyzed dreams of children that reportedly contained spoken content or auditory messages. She reported that Christian, Muslim, and secular or religiously unaffiliated children had auditory message dreams with similar themes. Their dreams brought divine messages that gave them reassurance, predictions of future events, life directions, and guidance on mundane stresses, such as homework and peer conflicts.

Special Role of "Supernatural Agents" and Monsters in Children's Nightmares

Recall that the research on children's dreams shows that preschoolers start out with a fair amount of dreams of passive interaction and victimization but that these victimization scenarios decrease as children get older and social interactions, speaking, and taking active roles increase. Unlike older children and adults, preschoolers also evidence high percentages of animals in their dreams. Finally children also report hearing messages from adults and from counterintuitive supernatural agents in their dreams. It is this latter element—the presence and actions of "supernatural agents" in dreams—that I suggest is the added ingredient that, in a typically scary childhood dream, can tip the balance toward production of a nightmare experience. In short, children who experience frequent nightmares may also be particularly open to belief in imaginary beings including imaginary friends, supernatural agents, animals, and monsters.

Preschool and older children who report dreams also report fear of imaginary beings such as ghosts, monsters, and beings in the dark. It was originally believed that as children got older, nonhuman agents began to disappear from children's dreams. This supposition was based on the fact that fear of imaginary beings tends to decrease with age across the childhood years. Bauer (1976) studied the nighttime fears of four- to six-year-olds, six- to eight-year-olds, and ten- to twelve-year-olds (N = 54). Seventy-four percent of the four- to six-year-olds, 53 percent of the six- to eight-year-olds, but only 5 percent of the ten- to-twelve-year-olds reported fears of ghosts and monsters. These age-related differences were also reflected in the description of scary dreams reported by the younger and older children. The younger children reported that appearances of monsters caused their fear, while the older children imputed harmful actions to the monster. *In both age groups, however, supernatural agents and scary monsters were the objects of children's fears*—although fear of imaginary beings were less likely in the older groups than in the younger children.

It may be that one of the cognitive causes of nightmares is the presence of nonhuman, threatening agents in dreams. This idea has not yet been rigorously tested as far as I am aware, though the circumstantial evidence for it is fairly strong. We will pursue this theme in some of the chapters that follow. Whatever the proximate cognitive causes of nightmares in children we still have not answered the question as to why children are particularly vulnerable to nightmares. If nightmares are harmful then you would think that Mother Nature would have provided some sort of protection against them. Instead, nightmares are common in children.

It is worth considering these questions in the context of what has been learned about the evolutionary function of childhood itself.

EVOLUTION OF CHILDHOOD

Humans are unique relative to other animals in that we exhibit a developmental period of childhood inserted between the developmental periods of infancy and puberty. We have seen that one of the characteristics of this special developmental period is a relative high incidence of nightmares. How and why did childhood evolve?

Childhood is defined by specialists via several developmental characteristics, including a slowing and stabilization of the rate of growth relative to the period of infancy; dependence on older people for food; propensity for play; and immature motor control. Brain growth peaks at about seven years (Cabana, Jolicouer, and Michael 1993), with a small increase occurring later at puberty (Durston et al. 2001; Sowell et al. 2001). Myelination of neurons and some neuronal and synaptic proliferation continues into adulthood (Bjorklund and Pellegrinni 2002; Taupin and Gage 2002).

Childhood commences with the end of nursing and the beginning of a different kind of dependency on adults or older individuals. Specifically dependency on the mother lessens (but does not cease) and dependency on other adults increases. Anthropological data suggest that most children in premodern societies were/are weaned before their third birthday (Sellen and Smay 2001), with supplemental foods introduced early, usually within the first six months (e.g., Dupras, Schwarcz, and Fairgrieve 2001; Waterlow, Ashworth, and Griffiths 1980; Winikoff, Durongdej, and Cerf 1988). Thus, other adults besides the mother must step in to provision the child with food when the child is about three to four years of age.

The two most important other adults, from an evolutionary point of view, were the grandparent (usually grandmother) and the father. The switch in child-care responsibilities from the mother to other adults (and perhaps older siblings of the child) meant that the mother could now devote more of her resources to having another child. The evolutionary value of childhood, therefore, lay in the mother's freedom to initiate a new pregnancy because she could pass care of the current child to trusted others. Doing so enhanced the mother's reproductive fitness without increasing the costs to her infant or older children.

These trusted others who care for the child are highly skilled in providing specially prepared foods that are high in energy and nutrients until self-care becomes possible, and in various hunter-gatherer societies this is what was done (Blurton-Jones 1993; Estioko-Griffin 1986; Hewlett 1991). Summarizing the data from many human societies, J. B. Lancaster and C. S. Lancaster (1983) called this type of child-care and feeding "the hominid adaptation," for no other primate or mammal is so actively involved this way in provisioning the young. For humans, early weaning (by three years) reduces the birth interval and allows the mother to successfully produce two offspring in the time it takes chimpanzees and orangutans to successfully rear one. Thus, we see childhood as a suite of adaptations that enhances maternal reproductive fitness.

COGNITIVE AND PSYCHOLOGICAL GROWTH OF THE CHILD

In what has come to be known as the "five-to-seven-year shift" (Sameroff and Haith 1996), new learning and behavioral capabilities emerge, including development of so-called higher order "theory of mind" abilities where children can understand that person X thinks that person Y is thinking that Z and so forth. These abilities develop in concert with and partially dependent on children's amazing capacity for language learning. Children learn languages without tremendous effort or instruction. Surely the learning of language constitutes one of the great cognitive achievements of childhood.

DEVELOPMENT OF THE SENSE OF SELF IN CHILDREN

Another area where the child is doing an enormous amount of developmental work, and an area that is particularly relevant for nightmare phenomenology, is development of the "sense of self" or identity. One reason why children may experience a lot of nightmares is that their sense of self is still quite fragile. The self-concept, including the dream ego, is therefore correspondingly weak. One of the most common themes in nightmares is that the dreamer comes under intense attack by other characters, usually monsters or supernatural beings. Often the explicit aim of these beings is to take control of the dream ego—to invade the mind of the dreamer—or so the dreamer reports. Nightmares, then, must among other things be about the sense of self or identity. Children have a fragile sense of self—or at least a sense of a fluid and developing self. They are, not surprisingly, more vulnerable to nightmares. It behooves us then to look more carefully into how the self develops in children.

Loevinger, Wessler, and Redmore (1970) and Loevinger (1976) used a sentence completion procedure to gather data on the development of identity. She and her colleagues (Loevinger et al. 1970) utilized thirty-six sentence stems such as "The thing I like about myself is …," "What gets me into trouble is …," "I am …" etc. After testing hundreds of subjects, Loevinger et al. devised a coding system based on thousands of responses for each stem. The responses were classified into separate categories which seemed to reflect stable personality traits or modes of responding. Loevinger (1970; 1976) then noticed that these modes were characteristically associated with different age groups and so probably reflected distinct stages in the development of the sense of self or identity.

The general picture that emerges from Loevinger's (1970; 1976) analyses of identity development might best be illustrated with a description of typical response modes associated with the "I am …" stem. Impulsive personalities (classified as I-2) do not reflect on their responses but tend to provide short, simple, and uninformative responses such as "I am nice" or "I am tall." These young children tend to dichotomize all events into good and evil categories and do not consider the complexities of social life. They are concerned only with themselves rather than the world. At the next stage of ego development ("delta" transitional) the individual becomes more aware of the world around him but has no sense of the complexities of the world. There is an ego but it is small, weak, and fragile. It needs to be protected. So the child is suspicious, self-protective, and opportunistic. He eschews responsibility and is pre-occupied with staying out of trouble. His humor is often hostile and rejecting. The next (I-3) stage of development involves a broad socializ-ing trend. The child turns towards the world but often in a conformist way. He describes himself only in socially acceptable terms. He uses a kind of self-deprecating and ingratiating humor: e.g., "I am a big mouth." "I am such a ..." He uses broad, sweeping generalizations to describe others. He relies on formulistic and stereotyped responses in social interactions. His focus concerning self is concrete and oriented towards his physical appearance.

The next stage (I-3/4) involves a series of responses that are transi-tional between conformism and the I-4 stage: "conscientious." The I-3/4 transitional stage is characterized by self-criticism and self-consciousness. The child's view of the world and himself is now richer and more nuanced but negative reactions to self predominate. This is the stage where nightmares come in. The self is strong enough to reflect some complexity and to undergo some attacks but not strong enough to see the self-attacks as harsh and unjustified. No simple straightforward responses are given to the "I am ..." stem. Instead one gets responses like "I am ... not like anyone else." The next stage, I-4 is dubbed "con-scientious." There is a rich inner life and true conceptual complexity. The child has a strong sense of responsibility and has developed a moral sense and standards of excellence. There is a general awareness and orientation towards long-term goals and a restlessness and impa-tience to reach them. The I-4/5 transitional stage is characterized by complex responses. The child provides nuanced and contradictory descriptions of self. The teenager tries on all sorts of new identities and is happy with none of them. There is a tendency to try to justify all of one's responses. The I-5 "autonomy" stage is usually not reached till adulthood and is characterized by the ability to balance dimensions of personality that seem to be in conflict. The individual cultivates a rich array of preferences, inclinations, and behaviors but may not be able to integrate, and thus be enriched by, all these options. The last stage I-6 is characterized by "integration." Here the individual harmoniously bal-ances opposing tendencies within himself. He enjoys a rich internal life but is oriented to the world and sees service to others as his greatest concern.

Nightmares participate in the process of building a sense of self. In no other experiential arena is the self so threatened as in a nightmare. It is in nightmares that the individual really feels and believes that the self may truly be harmed or even annihilated—depending on the threat or monster the dreamer is facing during the nightmare. This emotional work must have an effect on the emotional and psychic balance of the individual. Nightmares are memorable and leave an indelible impression on the individual, and if they come at crucial transitional points in the development of the sense of self, they can surely shape the outcome.

In summary, early childhood is characterized for the child by a switch in dependency from the mother to the father and/or other adults and by an enormous investment of time and energy into learning very advanced cognitive skills including theory of mind skills, language skills, personal memory, and most importantly a development in the sense of self or identity. We have already seen that childhood is also characterized by an increase in slow-wave sleep intensity. Can any of these developmental milestones help us to understand why nightmares occur in early childhood?

IMPACT OF DEVELOPMENTAL MILESTONES ON NIGHTMARE PROPENSITY IN CHILDREN

The transition from the maternal to the paternal sphere, from breast-feeding to solid food provided by other adults besides the mother, must involve a huge psychological adjustment for the child. As has often been pointed out, the mother shares half her genes with her child while the father (given paternity uncertainty) may not. The father had to be made to believe that the child was his. The child could help to do this by developing cognitive and emotional specializations to relate to the psychology of the potential father. These specializations likely involved signaling genetic fitness and genetic likeness as well as emitting signals that elicited love and care from the father. Presumably both the acquisition of theory of mind abilities, of language skills, and of a "sense of self" facilitated father-child and adult-child interactions more broadly.

The acquisition of theory of mind skills must have created mental opportunities for the child that allowed for prediction and manipulation of the adults around him. But these skills must have also involved a dawning realization that all kinds of mental agents were "out there" and that these mental agents carry a variety of intentions towards the child. Among these intentional agents must have been imaginary, non-human agents that populated both the imagination and the child's dream life. It is these latter agents that will become the focus of discussion in later chapters.

Similarly, the development of language skills also facilitated interactions with adults besides the mother. The mother will feed the child whether or not he or she speaks to the mother. Speaking helps, of course, but the mother does not require extra coaxing to feed her offspring. She will do so instinctively. The father, on the other hand, does require extra coaxing and language must have helped the child in this respect. Language also gave the child access to other adults. With language the child can interact with anyone. Without language, his effective interactions are confined to the mother while all other interactions will be labored and difficult.

Finally, the sense of self greatly enhances the child's ability to interact socially with all kinds of others. The three great developmental achievements of childhood: "theory of mind," language, and "the sense of self" all have as their apparent aim the enhancement of the child's ability to interact socially with others, particularly adult others. The enhanced ability to interact with others was vital to the child's survival given his dependence on others for food.

How would nightmares fit in here? Well, nightmares might simply reflect the stresses of the childhood period, or they might facilitate development of one of the childhood skills. I suggest that they facilitate development of the sense of self. Nightmares assume theory of mind abilities and language abilities but they do not assume more than a fragile sense of self. They do assume a self as it is—the self that comes under attack in nightmares. But the attacks result either in a stronger sense of self in the child or a weakened one. For most children, the self is strengthened and nightmares disappear. For a small group of children, the sense of self is strengthened, but the nightmares do not disappear. Instead they recur when the children become adults, but these are, as we shall see in later chapters, special cases.

Chapter 3

Content of Nightmares

What are nightmares about? Surprisingly, there are few, if any, content analyses of large numbers of nightmares. Given the relative lack of study on the content of nightmares, I analyzed a small corpus of nightmares and compared them to ordinary dreams all of which I downloaded from the online DreamBank resource (www.DreamBank.net) created by Adam Schneider and Bill Domhoff (Domhoff 2003a).

COMPARING NIGHTMARE CONTENT TO ORDINARY DREAMS

Since we were interested in assessing nightmare content relative to typical dream content for children and adults I downloaded a recorded set of nightmares and then compared content indices of these nightmares to the publicly available norms for typical dreams. I selected a set of twenty-four nightmares from the series of dreams reported by a woman named pseudonymously as Barb Sanders. This woman had contributed thousands of dreams, which she had recorded over a period of years, to Professor G. William Domhoff, an expert on dream content analysis, so that he could analyze them and make them available, via a website, to other dream researchers. Here is what Professor Domhoff says about Barb Sanders at the website www.dreamresearch.net (downloaded on December 15, 2007).

Born in the 1940s and raised in a small town, "Barb Sanders" is the oldest of four children. She has a brother 2.7 years younger, a second brother 4.7 years younger, and a sister 6 years younger. Both of her parents earned college degrees at a small denominational college and worked all their lives in education and social work. Both parents had a strong interest in music and all the children sang and played musical instruments. Sanders was an average high school student who married after one year of college and had three daughters in the space of 4.5

years. Her husband was a very good student who earned an M.A. and then went to work in a technical profession for a natural resources corporation. She earned a B.A. degree in her mid-20s from a state college and left her husband at age 30, when her daughters were 7, 4.5, and 2.5. She left her daughters with her ex-husband and returned to her home state, where she earned an M.A. in a helping profession and worked in a community college setting for several years. She had several boyfriends after her divorce and never remarried. She became involved in local theater productions as an actress and director. She developed a strong interest in dreams and participated in dream groups.

She was not plagued by recurrent nightmares; we found only twenty-four in a series of more than a thousand of Sanders' dreams. These nightmares then are probably representative of the kinds of nightmares experienced by the general population. On the other hand "Barb Sanders" is unlike the rest of the population in that she is passionately interested in dreams and in fact studies them.

Once selected, the dreams and nightmares were then scored using the Hall and Van de Castle method. (See description below.) Both the Hall and Van de Castle adult dreams and the majority of Barb Sanders, dreams were already scored thanks to the hard work of the folks, presumably Bill Domhoff and Adam Schneider at the www.dreambank.net Web site. (Schneider and Domhoff 2007a). Deirdre McLaren, a research assistant in my lab scored the remaining Barb Sanders' nightmares for characters, for aggressive, friendly, and sexual/social interactions, and for successes, failures, misfortunes, good fortunes, and emotions.

NIGHTMARE CONTENT SCORING

Schneider and Domhoff (http://dreamresearch.net/DreamSAT/index. html) provide a spreadsheet program *DreamSat*, which allows for tabulation of dream content scores and automatic computation of derived scales and percents when using the Hall and Van de Castle scoring system (Schneider and Domhoff 2007a). This spreadsheet program greatly increases the reliability of results obtained with use of the system.

The Hall and Van de Castle system for scoring dream content (Domhoff 1996; Hall and Van de Castle 1966) is a standardized and reliable content scoring system which consists of up to sixteen empirical scales and a number of derived scales that are useful for an analysis of social interactions in dream content (see Table 3.1 for the Hall and Van de Castle variables). Three primary types of social interaction are scored: aggressive, friendly, and sexual; as well as subtypes (e.g., physical versus verbal aggression). The character that initiated the social interaction is identified as well as the target or recipient of the interaction. The "characters" scale allows for classification of characters known to the dreamer (e.g., family members, friends, etc.) as well as those

Table 3.1
Hall and Van de Castle Variables for Analyzing Dream Content

Variables	Meaning
Character Percentages	
Male/Female %	(Total male characters) / (Male characters + female characters)
Familiarity %	(N. of familiar characters) / (Total familiar characters + total unfamiliar characters)
Friends %	(Known characters / All human characters)
Family %	(Family + relatives) / (Familiar characters + unfamiliar characters)
Dead & Imaginary Characters %	(N. dead & imaginary) / (Familiar characters + unfamiliar characters)
Animal %	(Total animal) / (Total characters)
Social Interaction Percentages	
Aggression/ Friendliness %	(N. of aggressive interaction) / (Total n. of aggressive + friendly interaction)
Befriender %	(Dreamer as a befriender) / (Dreamer as befriender + dreamer as recipient)
Aggressor %	(Dreamer as aggressor) / (Dreamer as aggressor + dreamer as victim)
Physical Aggression %	(Physical aggression) / (Total aggression)
Social Interaction Ratios	
A/C index	(Total n. of aggressions / Total n. of characters)
F/C Index	(Total n. of friendliness interactions) / (Total n. of characters)
S/C Index	(Total n. of sex interactions / Total n. of characters)
Self-Concept %	
Self-Negativity %	(Dreamer as victim + d. involved in misfortune + d. involved in failure) / (Dreamer as victim + d. involved in misfortune + d. involved in failure + d. as befriender + d. involved in good fortune + d. involved in success)
Bodily Misfortunes %	(Bodily misfortune) / (All misfortunes)
Negative Emotions %	(Negative emotions) / (Negative emotions + positive emotions)
Dreamer-involved success %	(Dreamer-involved success) / (Dreamer-involved success + dreamer-involved failures)
Dreams with at Least One Occurrence:	
Aggression	(Dreams in which aggression occurs) / (N. of dreams)
Friendliness	(Dreams in which friendliness occurs) / (N. of dreams)

(Continued)

Table 3.1 (*Continued*)

Variables	Meaning
Sexuality	(Dreams in which sexuality occurs) / (N. of dreams)
Misfortune	(Dreams with misfortunes) / (N. of dreams)
Good Fortune	(N. of dreams with good fortune) / (N. of dreams)
Success	(N. of dreams with success) / (N. of dreams)
Failure	(N. of dreams with failure) / (N. of dreams)
Striving	(Dreamer-involved successes + dreamer-involved failures) / (N. of dreams)

unknown. Characters (known or unknown) can also be classified by age, gender, and relation to the dreamer. These scales allowed us to determine character frequencies and number and types of social interactions while adjusting for various baseline values in order to control for length effects.

We will see in later chapters that nightmares often concern threats to the dream-ego or the self-concept or identity of the dreamer. It is then particularly valuable that the Hall and Van de Castle system allows for scoring of self-related content experiences. Representation of self-related content is captured primarily by the self-concept scales. These are self-negativity, bodily misfortunes, negative emotions, and dreamer-involved success.

To calculate basic frequencies and the differences between content categories in Barb Sanders' nightmares versus norms, Deirdre McLaren, my research assistant who scored these dreams, used the *DreamSat* program to compute the scales, percent differences, and certain p values that we report. The program also produces Cohen's h statistic, which is an effect size value for samples involving nominal measurement scales.

To understand the content of nightmares, I reproduce here twenty-one of the Barb Sanders, nightmares I downloaded from DreamBank and that Deirdre McLaren scored. The number codes are consistent with the DreamBank.net codes for the same dreams. After each nightmare report I comment briefly on the content of that report.

Analysis of Barb Sanders' Dream Reports

Dream # 0021

I dreamed a lot last night, almost nightmares trying to get away from Howard.

Comment. Often we are amnesic about dreams and nightmares—we have only a vague awareness that we were struggling to free ourselves from some oppressive presence. In Sanders' case, if "Howard" is her ex-husband then he likely represents a mass of ambiguous feelings for the dreamer. After all it cannot be clear-cut when a mother leaves her children and takes up a new life elsewhere, but we cannot judge the situation from this vantage point. All we can say is that the character Howard is associated with a massive negative affect that gives rise to a nightmare report.

Dream # 0035

A nightmare about Howard. He is in bed with me and drooling at the mouth, etcetera.

Comment. This is another vaguely recalled dream about an individual who apparently was once important to Sanders' sense of self.

Dream # 0142

First dream of the night. Fear on bed, in the bedroom, rising up the curtain like in an elevator, but I am not. As I am going down, I get more fearful. There is a hole in the curtain and outside the hole is a cage, but my fear of it is like it is a Nazi concentration camp. I scream because I am going to be pushed out of the window into the cage. I push myself backwards. It was a weak push but I fall back hard. I fall across the room. I move furniture as I fall so I will not get hurt and land on the floor at foot of the bed. Two children are in the bedroom, a little boy and a little girl. A pouch with a banana is handed to me. I get sexually excited, aggressively, powerfully so. I grin and pull two legs out of the pouch and the banana turns into a penis. I want it badly. I kick the little girl out of the way. I place the penis in me and I can feel it, real. I hold the man tightly and the closer I get to orgasm, the fiercer I am. Then I see a "picture" of our faces. I am smiling, really into it. He is smiling because it gives him joy to see me feel so good (fierce, intense smiles). As I start to have an orgasm, a little boy is screaming, "Daddy! Daddy, do not!" Two policemen come in. I cannot talk. I try to but cannot. I want to finish. I can hear the screams. I wake up, feeling like it was a nightmare.

Comment. This nightmare obviously requires knowledge of the particular case of Barb Sanders in order to decipher it. Nightmares are unusual early in the night. There is a feeling of terror, of being pushed into a "cage." A child is kicked out of the way to satisfy sexual impulses but there is guilt and a police presence associated with satisfaction of sexual impulses. Once again we cannot pronounce on the individual herself, not having met her or talked with her. All we can say is that the dream apparently "pictures" the emotional and moral situation of the dreamer at the time of the dream. More importantly for the theory of nightmares is the fact that the dreamer's apparent identity is in flux: One identity is associated with a cage; a second with aggressive sexual gratification. These struggles around identity will become more manifest in future dreams of Barb Sanders.

Dream # 0225

A nightmare. Entities or souls or creatures from other planets are coming to meld with humans and take our spirits away. I am very frightened. The children are the first to go and then the adults. It is a terrible feeling of the fear of losing myself as through death or absorption into another. They come, three of them. The one coming for me is a big man in a chicken hawk suit with red and blue fluffy feathers. He talks like an English pirate (irate)? We meld and a transparent form of my body is tucked under his wing and off we fly. What a ride. I can feel my stomach lurch as we go zipping up to the cosmos and down again. It is like a jet plane. We get to their planet. Then a man gets shot and falls. I am surprised because I thought, "1) No one dies here, and 2) Ugly, mean people do not exist here." They take the body of a two-year-old baby and this shot man's soul goes into the baby. His face is only softened and rounded like a baby. I am appalled because they had told me we were just being borrowed. Now I know we were being lied to. I feel awful. I tell Nate to run. "I am sorry I got you into this mess."

Comment. The struggles around identity become intense. An alien force is attempting to devour the dreamer's identity. Her developing sense of self in her waking life may later be influenced by these night-time struggles.

Dream # 0334

I am in my house, only it is M City or someplace isolated. It is late at night and I am alone. I lock all the doors. I put the cats out. I have a feeling of deep fore-boding. I feel afraid. I get to my bedroom and step outside to look. There is an airport across the way, a county airport. I see a plane coming in for a landing. It crashes into something or explodes. I feel sick because I am witnessing an awful thing. I see it explode and I see the flames. I say, "Oh no!" It crashes into places and buildings and people on the airport ground. I run into my bedroom. Now I am asleep in my bed feeling the fear of what I had witnessed. I am trying to wake up. I have to wake up because the awfulness of the crash has affected the girls/women at the airport. They are coming to my house. I try to turn on the light on my bed. It will not go on. I feel this is sinister. I grope for a flashlight. It rolls and nearly falls off the headboard. I catch it just as it almost falls. I am so afraid it is a terror, a nightmare. I turn it on. A weak light shines. I try to get up and I fall out of bed. I know something is very wrong. I get back in bed. I get out of bed. I look out the window. I must call the police. I get the phone. It is a wall phone. It is dead. I look and the women are swarming all around me, like zombies or crazies. They moan and cry out, "Do not let the police catch you." A policeman comes to the door. He picks me up to take me over to the airport. I am paralyzed with fear. I do not know who to trust. Then I hit out at the policeman. I knock his head off. It does not matter. He is carrying me away. Then I am trying to wake up and write the dream down. I see myself writing the dream down. It was hard to wake up. It is an awful feeling.

Comment. In this, as in many nightmares, there is a background awareness that something has gone terribly wrong—a major catastrophe has occurred. There is no one she, the dreamer, can trust. The authorities she thought were trustworthy really are not trustworthy. She attempts to wake up but it is difficult. The phony policeman is carrying her away to an uncertain fate.

Dream # 0478

A frightening dream. I went to a party. Everyone is drinking, laughing, and frenetic. I hesitate to join them. They swirl around me, encouraging me to join them. Darryl sits across from me. He teases me and says something about a girl he used to know. I feel the same old distance from him (placed by him). I call him Howard and feel embarrassed. A lot of people disappear. The party seems to have moved on down the street, maybe to Aunt Elaine's house. I belatedly want to join them now. I drink some wine. I feel slightly high. Instead, I end up in my living room. An uncle and a cousin are there. I greet them. I laugh at my cousin because he carries a rifle on his shoulder everywhere he goes. I say, "How silly, you are getting carried away." A man then appears at the door. He is smiling gently and wants me to join the party. I feel a desire and a fear to go. There is some danger to me if I go. I clutch my cousin and say, "Look at my hand. See the bullet wounds?" He looks. He says, "There is poison here, you have been poisoned." The man beckons me to come to the party. I realize then that they have gotten their poison into me, but not quite enough. I still can resist. I say, "I do not want to be a part of your project." It is hard for me to say because the drug makes me want to go. I say it several times and he just stands there waiting for me, because he knows the drug is powerful. I will be sucked into another being like in the *Invasion of the Body Snatchers.* I run to my "dad" and plead with him, telling him I do not want to, and to please help! I am trying to but I am growing weaker. "Please help me!" He does not respond to me other than to weakly smile at me to acknowledge that he has heard me. I grab my cousin, who before I had seen as weak and silly, and cling to him, hugging him hard, hanging on like he was my anchor to that room. Then a fat lady, mostly naked, is dancing at a party. Her husband picks her up off the floor and makes love to her. He is detached, fully clothed, and his back is to me. She is fully exposed. I see her vagina. I see her face clearly. A prim blonde woman sits rigidly beside them. I am shocked. This is on television. After he is done, the man sticks a fat piece of paper in the blonde woman's mouth. She is disgusted. It is a symbol of a large penis. Her red lipstick forms an "o" around it. Then I am upstairs in my bedroom. I wake up from a nightmare. I run downstairs, crying, "The little men are inside my stomach!" I am crying. My uncle or grandfather soothes me. He says, "No, it is not possible. I have been barricading the stairs for you all night." I am not comforted. I go back upstairs. I sit on the bed and hug my nanny. She is an old square robot and not very sophisticated. I ask it, "Why are there not any nice men for me?" It says, "Look, there are," and shows me two of them (on a screen on its chest). I say, "But if I take them, what will be left for my brother!" Nanny laughs and shows me many women for Dwight. I am still worried. Then I am at a dance, watching the musicians. One cannot find his banjo. Then he finds it and sees that something has eroded the outside. I realize that what ever "they" touch, corrodes like that and that "they" are there. I turn and the man is standing there, smiling. He says, "It is so close. We almost had you." I try to resist.

Comment. The dreamer has been putting up a fight against the forces that would destroy her self and enslave her. I will have more to say about these dreams in a later chapter. Suffice it to say here that the dream ego successfully resists the poison given her by these demonic characters who are interested only in her enslavement.

Dream # 1010

The Drapes Nightmare. Ellie kept bothering me. She came into my house and was not thinking, just kept being in the way or annoying me. I tried to get her to leave me alone. I wanted to go to bed. I got into a small, thin brass bed but the covers and pillows would not stay put. It was uncomfortable. I was very angry. I pushed and shoved to throw her out and she would keep popping back in. I looked out the window and Arvonne was dressing up to go out. She was putting on a blond wig. It was a brassy, bright beehive blonde hairdo. I was glad she was getting out of my way too. Now I am in my room and sort of on a boat in a closed up space. A horrible dog/boy creature is attacking me and it bites savagely. A man behind me says, "I will help. Let me do that." I say nothing but continue to take the attack. It is very painful; constant and scary. Ellie is also attacking. I throw it away and it lunges back at me. I scream in agony and frustration. The man cannot take it anymore. He grabs the horrible attacking thing and throws it into a garbage disposal. I scream, "No!" and hear the grinding up of its body and cannot bear the thought of its pain or death. I do not want to cause anyone else pain. Then I look again in renewed horror because the thing is now four times larger, an ugly large boy, and he is crawling out of the garbage disposal to get me even worse. I run to escape. I go into a room, like a living room or a captain's bedroom of a boat. I go to the tall windows and try to climb up, pulling myself hand over hand up the drapes. Each drape I try to climb up falls and is replaced by another drape. This happens over and over and over. I know now I am trapped. I panic, sobbing. I pick up objects off the dresser to heave it at the window to break it open and it just bounces off like it was Mylar plastic windows. Nothing I do helps. I am condemned to this hell for eternity.

Comment. The dream-ego is attacked by vicious, small animals and humanoid monsters that cannot be killed off. Sanders struggles to free herself from danger by climbing up drapery but this is a losing proposition and she knows it. She gives into despair and anguish in the dream and feels herself condemned. She is losing the battle against the alien forces in the nightmare that seek to harm and enslave the dream ego. They will haunt her mercilessly.

Dream # 1854

Nightmare. I wake up frightened. I was being chased.

Dream # 2652

I walk into a room with two bathtubs and a shower. A man is taking a bath in one tub and I decide to take a bath. I then decide to shower. I get in and am wiggling around to get all the spray because it feels so good and warm, and I know the man can see my movements through the glass shower door. Then suddenly the shower door slides open and two naked men come in to rape me. I bite and kick and scream, "Stop it, stop it." I then see myself from behind and see the purple welts I have (from the arthritis) and bunches of single strands of course black stubby hairs growing out of my butt. Not very pretty. I wake with my voice screaming, "Stop it," in my head, very loud and realistic. Nightmare quality.

Comment. The dream-ego is being badly beaten and bruised and weakened in this nightmare. The alien "evil" forces are winning.

Dream # 2730

Nightmare. Stabbing, hurting someone and them hurting me. Anger and pain.

Dream # 2808

Nightmare. I have red, white, and blue poker chips and these black men are trying to take them from me. I run away and dive in the river. I swim just to the left of the other woman captive, only I am just under the surface of the water. I know it is a good, safe spot for me. They are looking for me. They will rape and hurt me if they find me, and take away my poker chips.

Comment. The dreamer's resistance to relentless attacks on her sense of self is beginning to pay off. The dream ego has finally found a safe zone (under water). This safe zone will give her cover and some protection against attacks. She can now gather her strength to formulate a concerted response to these attacks. But it will take great effort with many ups and downs in the battle.

Dream # 2878

I am in some mad nightmare where tremendous forces of hate and violence are coming at me and I must fight it off by sending back blasts of intense love. People come at me, wanting to kill me and I send back intense love, trying not to succumb to the hate and violence. It is pretty overwhelming.

Comment. The dream ego's response to assaults on its integrity is to return love for attack. This is a significant dream and a significant breakthrough in the developing sense of self.

Dream # 2957

Charla is lying on a bed, she is perhaps been overstimulated, maybe by me, or maybe by Ellie. She (Charla) suddenly goes into a grand mal seizure. She vomits and starts to choke on it. I feel horror. I am waiting passively for Ellie to do CPR. I want Ellie to do it and am aware that I should do it, but it would be messy and stinky, so I do not. Then Charla dies. I am grief-stricken and sob and feel terrible guilt for not taking action quickly, which could have saved her life. It is a terrible nightmare.

Comment. On the surface what we have here is a straightforward anxiety and guilt dream. The adults, including the dreamer, have overstimulated a child who reacts violently and dies through the neglect of the adults. Many nightmares are straightforward anxiety/worry and guilt dreams.

Dream # 2973

I am a woman who is being terrorized by a man who takes a medicine and is invisible. He grabs the steering wheel of the car I am driving and tries to crash us and so on. I flee. Now I am a man and the same invisible man is after me. It is a life and death situation. I suspect my psychiatrist. I go into his office to see if I can find evidence. He comes in and I hide in his closet. A roomy coat closet. He comes in and I hide behind coats. He says to me, "I can smell you. I know you are here." He tries to feel me but barely misses me. He leaves. Now I have driven up to my own cabin or house. I sing opera and a rock group wants me to sing with their band, blending the two forms of music. The invisible man comes. There are lots of people in the room and I fire my pistol into the invisible man many times. Everyone thinks I have gone crazy and I ask them to leave. The supposedly dead, invisible man lays under my pool table. I feel for a pulse; he is still alive and I shoot many more bullets into him. Finally he is dead. Then a second invisible man is after me. I fight him too. It is terrorizing a nightmare.

Comment. Again there are struggles around identity themes. The dreamer is at one point a man and at another point a woman. An invisible man, a demon of sorts, is after her and she cannot kill him. Sanders does not have access to the "sending love" strategy announced in an earlier nightmare she had reported. Nor does she have access to the safe zone under water that she had discovered in yet another nightmare. Instead she tries to deal with the threat violently with a gun but no amount of shooting can eliminate a threat to the self.

Dream # 3963

"Aliens kill nightmare." I/a woman is entering an airplane. The dream ego is watching from behind her. I see her feet stepping into the raised carpeted stairs in the aisle as she steps down each step like in a raked seating situation. She walks to the front. She turns to the right and pulls out a black pistol and fires into the chest of a passenger, male. A man stands up and also pulls out a gun and begins to kill passengers. Between the two they kill every passenger. Then they throw the bodies out the windows on one side. They are aliens. Another I (the dream ego) is in another airplane, in the cockpit. The captain tensely says to his crew to lock the door. I see people falling out of the other airplane. The crew member nearest the door is afraid and fumbles as he tries to lock the door. The lock turns and holds. They know it is aliens and they are next. I wake up afraid.

Comment. The threat to identity continues. Aliens once again are attempting to kill and enslave humans and the dreamer. Yet in this dream the dream-ego is partially fused with one of the aliens. She has partially allied herself with the entity that is trying to destroy the dream ego as the dream ego now sees matters from the perspective of the alien. In this nightmare the long fight to preserve an identity against a debased and enslaved dissolution of the ego continues, but the dreamer is losing the war.

Dream # 3971

A nightmare. Woke me up.

Comment. The struggle continues but we are given no new details.

Dream # 4026

A young teen woman and me (a young teen woman) are on the run from a policeman who is after us. He is ruthless and out to get us. I try and protect my friend but the policeman (plain clothes man) grabs her and drags her with him. He is interrogating her, threatening her, yelling at her. She yells out "Officer Dunn," a kind of officer at a lower level. He hears her and races up to where she is to help protect her. He races right up to the bad cop, in his face, yelling, "Let her go." The bad cop shoves him aside. He had forced her and me to give samples of our blood. We each have our sample in vials in our hands. He demands hers. She tries to fight him off. She manages to throw her vial so he cannot get it. She runs toward Officer Dunn. The bad cop comes after me, livid with hate and rage. I run into a small lab room and out again. I yell, "I threw it away." He sneers and goes into the lab room and picks up a vial. He says, "If you say you threw it away, then you did not and this is it." He tips up his head and drinks it down fast. I scream "No, No!" It was some kind of acid poison. He convulses out of the chair onto the floor screaming in his horror and the pain. "Oh, God!" he screams. He is seated now cross-legged in an upright fetal ball position. He says in pain I must not be so loud. I scream "Oh God! Oh God!" as loud as I can. He dies quickly. I wake up hearing both our screams echoing loudly in my mind. Horror. Nightmare. I felt shocked.

Comment. The theme of an assault on the dream-ego continues but this time the dreamer manages to find some sympathy for the devil— for the bad cop who attempts to drink her blood. This dream may be a turning point in her struggles with the forces that are impairing the dream-ego and that attempting to enslave and degrade the self.

Dream # 4052

I am excited about sharing my results from my dream program. I have lots of numbers. I call a man over to where I am working. I tell him I want to show him my results. He is an official. Then I get the attention of a woman, well known in dreams, who becomes curious about all my numbers. I am trying to explain my dream program to her. There is a man near. I know we like each other but I do not know why. A mysterious feeling of knowing him. Then I see a group of men in brown security guard uniforms, all wearing masks of famous people. They sit like they were on a plane or train. I begin to feel fear. Something awful is happening and I am afraid. I keep forgetting things. The woman runs. I say to the man, "Are we moving? Are we moving?" It feels like we are on some vehicle. Then the woman runs out screaming hysterically "Why would they want to kill me?" over and over. I wake up, feeling fear. Night terror or nightmare?

Comment. Even though all feels well at first, signs begin to appear (people wearing masks in a vehicle that is moving) that something horrible is happening. The dream ego is threatened again. "Why would they want to kill me?"

Dream # 4053

I must remember to write down what is happening. I call that official man out of his office to look over the weird things that happened over my dream program. He looks like he is in a trance. The man I am attracted to is still there. We do not remember why we met or how, just that we love each other. A pretty woman is there. Everyone else is gone. I look with fear down a flight of stairs. "They" are down there. We have to protect ourselves from the aliens. The mayor and several other people stand around in a trance. I and the man's mother move into a room. She lost lots of weight and her clothes are huge, nearly falling off her. We gasp. Proof. Time has passed, but not normally. I notice with irony even under these circumstances I do not lose weight. Now these few other people are coming back in with rags on. That is all that is left. Decaying, rotting rags. The pretty woman still looks pretty even though her clothes are mismatched. I think that is ironic as well. We must remember to gather and store water. To survive. A man points to a circular patterned woven basket mat in a front window of a house. "Bees" he says in fear. They are like bees. We begin to run to find a place to hide. Little bees appear near us and try to sting us. We swat at them. We run into a room with a bathroom and try to lock the doors. They will not lock no matter how hard I try. I say get some pots. I turn on the faucet for water and plug the sink. The pretty woman brings small paper cups "because they are prettier." She said. Even she realizes this is illogical and non–survival-like. I try and fill the sink but the water escapes down the drain. I am afraid and continue to try and lock the doors. Holes appear. They are coming. I wake up. Fear like monsters are under the bed. Nightmare.

Comment. The dreamer and someone close to her are under threat. Once again aliens are trying to enslave and or kill them. Efforts at protection from the alien assault are ineffectual.

Dream # 4155

I am in a square bus. Men keep coming in. Gaston sits across from me. He acts silly. I keep trying to keep these men out but they keep coming back in. I feel scared of them. They mean me harm. I ask the bus driver to help me, but he is one of them. I realize they are aliens in human form. I am very afraid. I try to escape them. They follow me out of the bus. They are surrounding me. I feel terror. I wake up, afraid. Nightmare.

Comment. The dream ego is under sustained attack from aliens and no help is to be found from any quarter, unless help or a response can be found, the dream ego is likely to fail and a full scale personality disorder to emerge.

Dream # 4190

I am standing on a lawn in front of a white house shaped like the Mac House, but it is not. A horrible plant is growing out of a small buried mess of body parts in the lawn. It is angry. Its leaves are like tentacles reaching out to try and grab me, to kill me. I had been lazy and irresponsible when I buried the stuff there. I run madly and it grows very fast to try and get me. I run down a street near a parked car. The tentacles could only reach that far and it is screaming (sounds like Godzilla) with fury and frustration that I am just out of its reach. I stand there listening to its screams and watch as it dies. I walk around the block to stay safely out of its way. Someone insists I go back and look at it now that it is dead. I am fearful to do so, but I do it. I am afraid it will spring to life and kill me. I wake up, afraid. Nightmare.

Comment. The dreamer manages to find a safety zone, out of reach of the threatening alien monster. The inability of the monster to "feed off" of the dreamer leads to its death.

WORD COUNT ANALYSES OF BARB SANDERS' NIGHTMARES

Aside from the apparent themes surrounding preservation of the dream ego in Barb Sanders' nightmares, I want to present a solid picture of the basic characteristics of these nightmares. By comparing them to norms for everyday dreams, we can identify distinctive markers of nightmares. I will analyze both linguistic indices and content indices for these nightmares. I will begin with the language-related markers for the dreams.

To identify any potentially distinguishing content differences of these nightmares as compared to ordinary narratives about everyday events, we compared key word counts in these nightmares and in a body of discourse samples analyzed by an independent research group. This "control" group of everyday narratives was taken from the Web site describing the Linguistic Inquiry and Word Count (LIWC) Program at www.liwc.net. (Pennebaker, Francis, and Booth 2001). This word count program automatically tabulates numbers of words in several categories such as self-related pronouns, emotions, and social interactions. The LIWC program is able to tabulate such words, thus providing an independent check on, say, self-related content in nightmares versus everyday discourse. The output from this program consists of a spreadsheet with total number of words in each sample, as well as percentages of words in each of several target categories. LIWC 2001 is a well-validated instrument (Pennebaker, Francis, and Booth, 2001, and see www.liwc.net). For the purposes of the current study, we had the program tabulate all instances of "I", "we" self-related words, social processes, and emotion. The Emotion category contains 615 words drawn from two subcategories: positive emotions and negative emotions. Positive emotions is further divided into two subcategories: 1) positive feelings (e.g., happy, joy, love) and 2) optimism and energy (e.g., win, excitement). Examples of negative emotion words include hate, worthless, and enemy. The negative emotion subcategory also includes three further subcategories of anxiety/fear (e.g., nervous), anger (e.g., hate, pissed), and sadness/depression (e.g., cry). The target category, Social Processes, is made up of social pronouns (first-person plural, second- and third-person pronouns), communication verbs (talk, share), and references to family, friends, and other individuals. In addition to the overall social processes category, we analyzed the references-to-other-people category as it potentially contains instances of nonhuman agents such as animals or monsters.

As a check on the procedures' reliability, we compared the word counts we obtained to the LIWC program's published norms (available at www.liwc.net). The mean word count for our sample of nightmares was 210—about 100 words less than published norms. (Results for only twenty-one of the twenty-four nightmares that we analyzed appear in this text for space reasons.) Inspection of Table 3.2 shows that the means for each of the categories that we analyzed approximate the published norms, thus increasing our confidence in the reliability of the LIWC analyses. We hypothesized that, relative to the norms, nightmares would evidence higher mean numbers of negative emotions, other-related pronouns and words, and social process words. These predictions were largely confirmed; but we also found that words indicating anomalous cognitive processing of temporal reference, spatial terms, and references to the physical body were altered in the nightmares relative to norms.

The word count analyses reveal some predictable differences and yet some surprising differences with more typical daytime discourse samples. Nightmare narratives are slightly shorter than daytime narratives; they contain fewer questions, fewer positive emotion words, and fewer references to time (particularly past tense) than do daytime narrative samples. Conversely, nightmare narratives contain more negative emotion words, more references to physical states, and more references to sleep and dreams compared to daytime narratives. The only surprising finding in these nightmare analyses was an increased number of references to spatial location than typically found in daytime narratives.

Table 3.2
Means and Standard Deviations in LIWC Categories for Barb Sanders'
Nightmares and LIWC Norms: Comparing Linguistic Markers of
Nightmares with Ordinary Narratives

Category	Barb Sanders (SD)	LIWC Norms (SD)
Word count	210.25 (174.99)	353 (278)
Words per sentence	10.14 (3.878)	18.2 (29.9)
Sentences ending with ?	.07 (.33)	5.4 (13.1)
Unique words (type/token ratio)	59.93 (14.54)	50.8 (9.8)
% words captured, dictionary words	79.47 (4.98)	79.9 (7.8)
% words longer than six letters	13.1 (7.27)	13.1 (5.1)
Total pronouns	17.11 (4.61)	15.2 (5.2)
First person singular (I, me)	9.95 (4.18)	8.5 (4.7)
First person plural (we, us)	.55 (1.04)	1.1 (1.6)
Total first person	10.5 (3.9)	9.5 (4.7)
Total 2nd person (you)	.15 (.3)	1 (1.9)
Total 3rd person (other)	4.24 (3.79)	2.0 (2.8)
Negations (no, never)	.9 (.83)	
Assents (yes, ok, mmhmm)	.009 (0.043)	.4 (1.7)
Articles (a, the)	7.25 (4.09)	2.8 (5.8)
Prepositions	13.72 (4.10)	12.9 (3.5)
Numbers	3.14 (4.39)	1.1 (1.2)
Affective or emotional processes (happy, ugly, bitter)	5.67 (6.61)	4 (2.4)
Positive emotions (happy, pretty, good)	.90 (1.08)	2.4 (1.6)
Positive feelings (happy, joy, love)	.34 (.79)	.7 (.8)
Optimism and energy (certainty, pride, win)	.08 (.16)	.5 (.6)
Negative emotions (hate, worthless, enemy)	4.82 (6.63)	1.6 (1.7)
Anxiety or fear	1.28 (2.09)	.4 (.6)
Anger	1.37 (2.28)	.5 (0.8)
Sadness or depression	1.02 (3.36)	.4 (.7)
Cognitive processes (cause, know, ought)	4.85 (3.09)	6.4 (3.2)
Causation (because, effect, hence)	0.47 (.067)	.9 (.9)
Insight (think, know, consider)	1.60 (1.68)	2 (1.5)
Discrepancy (should, would, could)	1.21 (1.23)	2 (1.5)
Inhibition (block, constrain)	0.29 (0.50)	.3 (.4)
Tentative (maybe, perhaps, guess)	1.59 (1.85)	2.1 (1.5)
Certainty (always, never)	.45 (.58)	1.1 (0.9)
Sensory and perceptual processes (see, touch, listen):	2.84 (2.05)	2.4 (1.6)
Seeing	.80 (.87)	.7 (.8)

(Continued)

Table 3.2 (*Continued*)

Category	Barb Sanders (SD)	LIWC Norms (SD)
Hearing	.85 (.88)	1.1 (1.1)
Feeling	1.15 (1.69)	.5 (.7)
Social processes (talk, us, friend)	8.46 (6.31)	8.8 (4.9)
Communication (talk, share, converse)	1.14 (1.15)	1.7 (1.4)
Other references to people (we, you, personal pronouns)	5.37 (4.87)	5 (3.6)
Friends	.014 (.067)	.4 (.7)
Family	.15 (.36)	.7 (1.3)
Humans	1.48 (1.43)	.6 (.8)
Time (hour, day, o'clock)	2.18 (2.64)	5 (2.8)
Past tense verb	2.14 (3.75)	6.2 (4.4)
Present tense verb	12.37 (5.04)	10.1 (5.1)
Future tense verb	.31 (.39)	1.2 (1.6)
Space (around, over, up)	4.87 (3.6)	2.8 (1.7)
Up	1.48 (1.22)	1.8 (1.6)
Down	.57 (.61)	.3 (.5)
Inclusive (with, and, include)	6.91 (4.39)	6.2 (2.4)
Exclusive (but, except, without)	1.92 (1.63)	3.5 (1.7)
Motion	1.48 (1.22)	1.8 (1.6)
Occupation (work, class, boss)	1.32 (1.43)	
School	.09 (.19)	1.5 (1.9)
Work or job	.17 (.39)	.6 (1)
Achievement	1.09 (1.38)	.8 (.8)
Leisure activity (house, TV, music)	1.36 (1.69)	1.5 (1.9)
Home	1.06 (1.61)	.9 (1.3)
Sports	.08 (.26)	.4 (1)
TV and movies	.07 (.16)	.1 (.4)
Music	.17 (.4)	.2 (.4)
Money and financial issues	.018 (.09)	.3 (.6)
Metaphysical issues (God, heaven, coffin)	.63 (.89)	.3 (.7)
Religion	.15 (.36)	.2 (.5)
Death and dying	.48 (.82)	.1 (.5)
Physical states and functions (ache, breast, sleep)	6.42 (7.7)	1.6 (1.8)
Body states, symptoms (ache, heart, cough)	1.49 (2.08)	.7 (1.1)
Sex and sexuality	.44 (.88)	.2 (.5)
Eating, drinking, dieting	.06 (.17)	.5 (1)
Sleeping, dreaming	4.83 (7.75)	.3 (.6)
Grooming	.26 (1.14)	.2 (.7)
Swear words	.09 (.24)	.1 (.4)

Table 3.2 (*Continued*)

Category	Barb Sanders (SD)	LIWC Norms (SD)
Nonfluencies (uhh, rr*)	0 (0)	.1 (.4)
Fillers (you know, I mean)	0 (0)	.04 (.3)

Note: "rr" is a place-marker in the LIWC program that flags filler words, such as "like" that have no meaning when used out of context.
Sources: Schneider, A. and G. W. Domhoff, 2005. DreamBank. Accessed on December 20, 2007 from http://www.dreambank.net.
Pennebaker, J. W., M. E. Francis, and R. J. Booth, 2001. *Linguistic Inquiry and word count: LIWC.* Mahwah, NJ: Erlbaum Publishers.

Perhaps this is not surprising either as most people need to explain the setting in which a dream or nightmare occurs in order for the vision to make sense to the listener.

While the word count analyses confirmed distinctive linguistic characteristics of nightmares, what about content analyses themselves? In order to identify potentially distinctive content indicators of nightmares, we compared nightmare content to content derived from ordinary dreams that comprised the Hall and Van de Castle "norms" (Hall and Van de Castle 1966; Domhoff 1996). These norms describe what is typically found in ordinary dreams of ordinary people taken as averages from hundreds of dream reports and hundreds of individuals. Comparing the Barb Sanders' nightmare series to the Hall and Van de Castle norms we find some interesting content differences, as seen in Table 3.3.

The male to female character percentage was higher in the Sanders' nightmare series than in the Hall and Van de Castle norms (Hall and Van de Castle 1966; Domhoff 1996). Seventy percent of the characters in Barb Sanders' nightmares were male while only 48 percent were male in the female norms. This is statistically significant in comparison to the female norms (p < .001), and the effect size (reflecting the reliability of the result) is moderate (h = +.45).

Also, with regard to "familiarity" percentage differences, only 24 percent of the characters in Barb Sanders' nightmares were familiar to the dreamer. Compare this result with the Hall and Van de Castle female norms: More than 50 percent of the characters in the dreams of females are familiar to the dreamer. The differences between the familiarity percentage in the nightmare sample and the norms for females is highly significant (p < .00001) and the effect size was high as well (h = −75).

Only 7 percent of the human characters in Barb Sanders' nightmares were her real-life friends. This is significantly lower than the female norms (37 percent of human characters were "known characters" in the female norms; (p < .001) with high effect sizes (h = −.65; −.77). The percentage of animal characters in dreams tends to be very low, and of the

Table 3.3
Comparison of Nightmare Content to Normal Dream Content Using Hall and Van de Castle Norms

	Barb Sanders' Nightmares	Female Norms	h Statistic Barb Sanders to Female Norms	p Value Barb Sanders to Female Norms	N Barb Sanders' Nightmares	N Female Norms
Characters						
Male/female percentage	70%	48%	+.45	.000**	77	1054
Familiarity percentage	24%	58%	-.72	.000**	100	1363
Friends percentage	07%	37%	-.77	.000**	100	1363
Family percentage	15%	19%	-.11	.270	100	1363
Dead & imaginary percentage	01%	01%	-.00	.961	115	1423
Animal percentage	02%	04%	-.15	.124	115	1423
Social Interaction Percentages						
Aggression/friendliness percentage	69%	51%	+.37	.001**	98	530
Befriender percentage	50%	47%	+.06	.780	26	225
Aggressor percentage	15%	33%	-.43	.004**	54	231
Physical aggression percentage	56%	34%	+.45	.000**	86	337
Social Interaction Ratios						
A/C index	.75	.24	+1.20		115	1423
F/C index	.27	.22	+.13		115	1423
S/C index	.04	.01	+.07		115	1423
Indoor setting percentage	68%	61%	+.14	.457	28	1423
Familiar setting percentage	50%	79%	-.61	.012*	18	591

44

Self-Concept percentages

Self-negativity percentage	75%	66%	+.20	.052	101	306
Bodily misfortunes percentage	29%	35%	−.12	.565	24	865
Negative emotions percentage	89%	80%	+.23	.091	62	206
Dreamer-involved success percentage	33%	42%	−.19	.406	27	420 / 78
Torso/anatomy percentage	43%	20%	+.52	.007**	30	314

Dreams with at Least One Occurrence:

Aggression	79%	44%	+.74	.000**	24	500
Friendliness	50%	42%	+.16	.453	24	500
Sexuality	17%	04%	+.46	.028*	24	500
Misfortune	54%	33%	+.42	.044*	24	500
Good fortune	08%	06%	+.11	.606	24	500
Success	46%	08%	+.93	.000**	24	500
Failure	54%	10%	+1.02	.000**	24	500
Striving	67%	15%	+1.12	.000**	24	500

Note: * p < 0.05; ** p < 0.01

Sources: Hall, C., and R. Van de Castle, 1966. *The Content Analysis of Dreams*. New York: Appleton-Century Crafts.

Domhoff, G. W., 1996. *Finding Meaning in Dreams: A Quantitative Approach*. New York: Plenum Publishing Co.

Schneider, A. and G. W. Domhoff, 2007a. DreamSAT: Automated Dream Data Entry System and Statistical Analysis Tool. Accessed December 20, 2007 from http://www.dreamresearch.net/dreamSAT/index.html.

characters in the Sanders nightmares only 2 percent were animals; slightly lower than the norms.

The aggression/friendliness percentage was higher in the Sanders' nightmares than in the female norms. When looking at the dreamer-involved social interactions, 69 percent were aggressive. The difference is statistically significant in comparison to the female norms, where only 51 percent of social interactions were aggressive; (p = .001; h = +.37).

Of aggressive social interactions in the nightmares, 56 percent involved physical aggression (as opposed to verbal aggression or unexpressed feelings of aggression). This is statistically significant compared to the female norms (34 percent; p < .001) with a high effect size (h = +.45).

The A/C index shows that the ratio of aggressive social interactions to characters (86/115 = .75) was more than three times higher in the nightmares than in the norms, with high effect sizes (A/C = .24; h = +1.20 for female norms).

The self-negativity percentage was not significantly higher than the female norms (66 percent; p = .052).

The torso/anatomy percentages were more than twice as high as the female norms (20 percent; p = .007).

When we examine how many nightmares registered at least one of the major content indicators, we find that aggression indicator was significantly higher in the nightmares. Seventy-nine percent (79 percent) of Barb Sanders' nightmares had at least one aggressive interaction, compared to 44 percent of the female norms (p < .001), with high effect sizes (+.74 for female norms).

Notably, the nightmares were very high in "striving." Sixty-seven percent (67 percent) of Barb Sanders' nightmares contained some goal-driven action that resulted either in success or failure. That's more than four times higher than the female norms (15 percent; p < .001), and had very high effect sizes (h = +1.02). Concerning the results of striving, 46 percent of Barb Sanders' nightmares contained a success. This is significantly higher than the norms, more than five times higher than the female norms (8 percent; p < .001) with high effect sizes (h = +.93 compared to female norms).

More than half, or 54 percent, of Barb Sanders' nightmares contained a failure; which is five times more often than in the female norms (10 percent; p < .001), with very high effect sizes (h = +1.02 compared to female norms).

In summary, interesting differences emerge between nightmares and more typical everyday dreams. The most consistent content difference between nightmares and garden variety dreams is that nightmares contain the "unfamiliar." Characters are less familiar than in normal dreams; friends and family show up less often than in normal dreams; the settings in which the dream action occurs is unfamiliar, and aggressive interactions are very common. In most of those aggressive interactions, the dreamer is *not* the aggressor. More often the dreamer is the target of an aggression. Finally, the sense of striving is extremely high in nightmares relative to common dreams. Presumably the striving is linked to a motivation to escape the aggression or the striving was interrupted by an aggression.

In any case, a most striking content index that distinguishes nightmares from ordinary dreams is the number of unfamiliar characters that occur in nightmares. Deirdre McLaren discovered that of the 115 characters in Barb Sanders' nightmares, 13 were creatures (neither human nor animal). These included a recurring group of aggressive aliens, a dog/boy creature, and a killer plant. Eight of the 24 (30 percent) Barb Sanders' nightmares that we analyzed (remember only 21 of the Sanders' nightmares were reproduced above) contained these creatures. The corresponding percentage for the norms is near zero percent. McLaren also found that the presence of creatures in a nightmare predicts misfortune in the dream. Compared to the nightmares without creatures, misfortunes occur more than twice as often in nightmares with creatures. Eighty-nine percent (89 percent) of nightmares with creatures contained misfortunes compared to 36 percent of nightmares without creatures ($p = .006$) with a very high effect size ($h = -1.18$). These misfortunes differed in nature depending whether or not creatures appeared in the dream. Only 12 percent of misfortunes in nightmares with creatures tended to be bodily misfortunes (a character is killed or physically killed or injured). The other 88 percent were other kinds of misfortunes such as accidents, obstacles, environmental threats, falling, etc. On the other hand, 71 percent of misfortunes in nightmares *without* creatures were bodily misfortunes, leaving only 29 percent of other kinds of misfortunes ($p = .003$; $h = +1.31$).

This link between creatures and major misfortunes in nightmares may be clinically significant as the presence of misfortune in dreams is very likely a causative factor in the emotional distress associated with the nightmare. It is the distress associated with some nightmares that best predicts daytime clinical disturbances.

We have seen that nightmare content differs from typical dreams along several content dimensions, most especially the dimension of familiarity. There are anomalous agents—nonhuman supernatural agents who act aggressively toward the dreamer and this causes significant "misfortune" in the dream and distress upon awakening.

NIGHTMARES AS COMPELLING: THE CASE OF "PRECOGNITIVE NIGHTMARES"

One of the most important and most unremarked distinguishing features of nightmares is that nightmares are taken more seriously by the dreamer than are typical dreams. Nightmares carry a huge significance for the dreamer. *The single most defining emotional characteristic of the nightmare is that it is terrifying and therefore compelling.* People feel changed emotionally by the nightmare. They feel driven to extract some meaning from the experience. This search for meaning can last anywhere from a few minutes after the experience to days or even weeks after the experience.

Nowhere is the link between the need for meaning and the nightmare experience more clearly seen than in the case of "precognitive" and "prophetic" nightmares. "Precognitive dreams appear to anticipate events in a dreamer's life." "Prophetic" dreams and nightmares contain references to cosmic, apocalyptic, and historical catastrophies and events.

In the latter part of the nineteenth century, the International Society for Psychical Research sent out questionnaires to 5,360 persons asking each one if he had had in the last twelve years a vivid dream of the death involving someone known to him. Approximately one of every twenty-six persons questioned replied in the affirmative (Gurney, Myers, and Podmore 1886, Vol. I, 299–300).

The second largest category of telepathic dreams uncovered by Gurney, Myers, and Podmore contained those in which a target person (known to the dreamer) was in distress or danger. Here is a classic example of a death or distress dream cited by Ullman and Krippner (1973). The percipient (dreamer), was a Mrs. Morris Griffith, who wrote her account in 1884.

On the night of Saturday, the 11th of March, 1871, I awoke in much alarm, having seen my eldest son, then at St. Paul de Loanda on the southwest coast of Africa, looking dreadfully ill and emaciated, and I heard his voice distinctly calling to me. I was so disturbed I could not sleep again, but every time I closed my eyes the appearance recurred, and his voice sounded distinctly, calling me "Mamma." I felt greatly depressed all through the next day, which was Sunday, but I did not mention it to my husband, as he was an invalid, and I feared to disturb him. We were in the habit of receiving weekly letters every Sunday from our youngest son, then in Ireland, and as none came that day, I attributed my great depression to that reason, glad to have some cause to assign to Mr. Griffith rather than the real one. Strange to say, he also suffered from intense low spirits all day, and we were both unable to take dinner, he rising from the table saying, "I don't care what it costs, I must have the boy back," alluding to his eldest son. I mentioned my dream and the bad night I had had to two or three friends, but begged that they would say nothing of it to Mr. Griffith. The next day a letter arrived containing some photos of my son, saying he had had fever, but was better, and hoped immediately to leave for a much more healthy station, and written in good spirits. We heard no more till the 9th of May, when a letter arrived with the news of our son's death from a fresh attack of fever, on the night of the 11th of March, and adding that just before his death he kept calling repeatedly for me. I did not at first connect the date of my son's death with that of my dream until reminded of it by the friends, and also an old servant, to whom I had told it at the time....

Here is another precognitive nightmare cited by Ullman and Krippner (1973). It was originally reported by a Dr. Walter Bruce of Micanopy, Florida.

February 17th, 1884: "On Thursday, the 27th of December last, I returned from Gainesville (12 miles from here) to my orange grove, near Micanopy. I have only a small plank house of three rooms at my grove where I spend most of my time when the grove is being cultivated. There was no one in the house but myself at the time, and being somewhat fatigued with my ride, I retired to my bed very early, probably 6 o'clock; and, as I am frequently in the habit of doing, I lit my lamp on a stand by the bed for the purpose of reading. After reading a short time, I began to feel a little drowsy, put out the light, and soon fell asleep. Quite early in the night I was awakened. I could not have been asleep for very long, I am sure. I felt as if I had been aroused intentionally, and at first thought someone was breaking into the house. I looked from where I lay into the other two rooms (the doors of both being open) and at once recognized where I was, and that there was no ground for the burglar theory; there being nothing in the house to make it worth a burglar's time to come after.

I then turned on my side to go to sleep again, and immediately felt a consciousness of a presence in the room, and singular to state, it was not the consciousness of a live person, but of a spiritual presence. This may have been part of the dream, for I felt as if I were dozing off again to sleep; but it was unlike any dream I ever had. I felt also at the same time a strong feeling of superstitious dread, as if something strange and fearful were about to happen. I was soon asleep again or unconscious, at any rate, to my surroundings. Then I saw two men engaged in a slight scuffle; one fell fatally wounded, the other immediately disappeared. I did not see the gash in the wounded man's throat, but knew that his throat was cut. I did not recognize him, either, as my brother-in-law. I saw him lying with his hands under him, his head turned slightly to the left, his feet close together. I could not, from the position in which I stood, see but a small portion of his face; his coat, collar. Hair or something partly obscured it. I looked at him the second time a little closer to see if I could make out who it was. I was aware it was someone I knew, but still could not recognize him. I turned and then saw my wife sitting not far from him. She told me she could not leave until he was attended to. (I had got a letter a few days previously from my wife, telling me she would leave in a day or two, and was expecting every day a letter or telegram, telling me when to meet her at the depot.)

My attention was struck by the surroundings of the dead man. He appeared to be lying on an elevated platform of some kind, surrounded by chairs, benches, and desks, reminding me of somewhat of a schoolroom. Outside of the room in which he was lying was a crowd of people. Mostly females some of whom I thought I knew. Here my dream terminated. I awoke again about midnight; got up and went to the door to see if there were any prospects of rain; returned to my bed again, and lay there until nearly daylight before falling asleep again. I thought of my dream and was strongly impressed by it. All the strange, superstitious feelings had passed off.

It was not until a week or 10 days after this that I got a letter from my wife, giving me an account of her brother's death. Her letter, which was written the day after his death, was missent. The account she gave me of this death tallies most remarkably with my dream. Her brother was with a wedding party at the depot at Markham station, Fauquier County, Va. He went into a store nearby to see a young man who kept a barroom near the depot, with whom he had some words. He turned and left the man, and walked out of the store. The barroom keeper followed him out, and without further words deliberately cut his throat. It was a most brutal and unprovoked murder. My brother-in-law had on his overcoat, with the collar turned up. The knife went through the collar and clear to the bone. He was carried into the store and laid on the counter, near a desk and showcase. He swooned from loss of blood soon after being cut. The cutting occurred early Thursday night, December 27th. He did not die, however, until almost daylight, Saturday morning....

Dr. Bruce's account continues with reference to another dream about that time, reported by his sister-in-law, Mrs. Stubbing, who was visiting her cousin in Kentucky. Here is Mrs. Stubbing's account of her dream.

... I saw two persons—one with his throat cut. I could not tell who it was, though I knew it was somebody that I knew, and as soon as I heard of my brother's death, I said at once that I knew it was the person that I had seen murdered in my dream; and though I did not hear how my brother died, I told my cousin, whom I was staying with, that I knew he had been murdered. This dream took place on Thursday or Friday night, I do not remember which. I was in the exact spot where he was murdered, and just as it happened.

Here is another precognitive nightmare recounted in Robert Van de Castle's (1994, 406–7) book on dreams.

Walter Franklin Prince, a psychologist and Episcopal minister, experienced a very striking and precognitive dream, which, unlike most such dreams, involved a stranger. His dream occurred on the night of November 27, 1917, and he told it to his wife and his secretary the next morning, before the tragic events foreseen in it unfolded.

Prince dreamed that he had in his hand a small paper, with an order printed in red ink for the execution of the bearer, a slender woman with blond hair about thirty-five years old. The woman appeared to have brought the execution order to Dr. Prince voluntarily and indicated her willingness to die, if only he would hold her hand. After he examined the execution order, the lights went out and it was dark. Prince could not determine how the woman was put to death, but her soon felt her hand grip his and knew that the deed was being carried out. Then he felt one of his hands on the hair of her head, which was loose and severed from her body, and he felt the moisture of her blood. The fingers of his other hand were caught in the woman's mouth, which opened and shut several times. Prince was horrified at the thought of the severed but living head. Then the dream faded.

Two days later, the local newspaper, *The Evening Telegram*, carried an article how a Mrs. Sara Hand, at approximately 11:15 on the night of November 28, had deliberately placed her head in front of the wheels of a train that had stopped in a Long Island Rail Road Station, so that the wheels would pass over her neck and decapitate her when it started. Near the body was a new butcher knife and cleaver, which Hand had apparently intended to use for her self-decreed "execution" before deciding to lay across the railroad tracks. In her handbag nearby, a letter was found with this message:

"Please stop all trains immediately. My head is on the track and will be run over by those steam engines and will prevent me from providing my condition ... My head is alive and can see and talk, and I must get it to prove my case to the law. No one believed me when I said I would never die and when my head was chopped off I would still be alive. Everyone laughed and said I was crazy, so now I have proved this terrible life to all.

Please have all the trains stopped to save my head from being cut in fragments. I need it to talk to prove my condition and have the doctor arrested for this terrible life he put me in."

Hand, who fit the physical description in Dr. Prince's dream, had been mentally disturbed since the death of her young daughter a few months earlier. Dr. Prince's dream can be considered precognitive, since Hand carried out her own execution the next night. The dream could also be considered telepathic, since she seemed to be planning her death when she purchased the butcher knife and cleaver on November 27. The dream dealt with a highly unlikely event: an unfamiliar woman decapitating herself in the darkness to prove that her head could continue to live, and talk, after being severed from her body. Prince's dream also contained many prominent references to hands.

PEOPLE WHO EXPERIENCE EXTRAORDINARY DREAMS MUST BE EXTRAORDINARY PEOPLE

What are we to make of such "precognitive" dreams or nightmares? As to their precognitive status the scientific community is skeptical. Many dream researchers who work day in and day out studying dreams appear to be open-minded about dreams' abilities to pick up faint signals and make sense of them. At present, however, there is no scientific way to account for these extraordinary nightmares. I recommend keeping an open mind about them so as not to foreclose thorough investigation of these nightmares. We have to operate on the assumption that dreams or nightmares cannot foresee the future. On the other hand, it is possible that cognitive processing routines during dreams and nightmares are sophisticated inference machines. We may be underestimating the power of the inferential capacities of dreams and nightmares. It is also possible that people who report these kinds of extraordinary precognitive nightmares have gathered clues that escape the notice of others and can use these clues about impending disasters to compute probabilities and inferences that are beyond the powers of the rest of us.

In any event, precognitive nightmares demonstrate how compelling the content of a nightmare can be. It is so horrifying or anomalous that the dreamer feels compelled to share its content with others. Our ancestors would have felt the same. *Nightmares therefore are mental experiences that have a high probability of being passed from one mind to another*. This fact gives us a clue about functionality. Nightmares force an individual to interact socially with others. Why? To warn a kinship group about impending danger? To pass on a mental virus? To pass on some other pathogen that uses its victim as a jumping off post to get to other mind/brains? We simply do not know. Certainly the sharing of terrifying scenarios with others would heighten vigilance levels in the group and this could only have enhanced survival prospects in marginal circumstances. But all of these conjectures are hard to test. Much more probable is that the persons who shared such frightening dreams really impressed their listeners. Their listeners would have remembered the narrative and the person sharing it. They would have held that person in some awe—even if they did not like the person. Persons sharing nightmares would have a chance to increase their status and prestige in the group if they shared the vision in a way that awed their listeners and avoided terrifying their listeners such that they ostracized the dreamer or worse, killed him outright as a sorcerer of some kind. We will see that if nightmare sharing became linked with enhanced social status and prestige, the capacity for nightmare experiences and the sharing of such experiences would have come under positive selection and thus could be considered an adaptation.

Chapter 4

Nightmares in Premodern Societies

We have seen that nightmares are very often shared with others. They are so scary that one feels compelled to share the story with another. I have been arguing that this need to share the terrifying dream gives us a clue as to the function of nightmares for our ancestors. If nightmares were meant to be shared with others then it follows that nightmares carried some sort of important information, either about the individual dreamer or about the group or both. At first this claim seems absurd. Most nightmares have no rational content at all. How could they convey anything of substance or value to anyone?

NIGHTMARES AS EVIDENCE OF EXTRAORDINARY POWERS IN ANCESTRAL POPULATIONS

If nightmare content carried information about the psychic state of the dreamer, then nightmares could serve as signals to indicate the dreamer's fitness or willingness to cooperate with others. Furthermore, if the sharing of a nightmare with the group caused the group to increase its vigilance levels against attack by neighboring tribes or marauding bands of raiders or even of animals or diseases … then individuals who report nightmares would have been held in high regard and their reproductive fitness would have correspondingly increased.

Regardless of these conjectures however, the sharing of a nightmare, in a culture that believed in the power of a spirit world and spirit beings, could indicate that the dreamer had had interactions with spirits and other supernatural beings and thus had valuable information. This individual would therefore increase his prestige if he let it be known that he had had interactions with spirits or dead ancestors in a dream or nightmare.

Is there any evidence that our ancestors held such individuals in high regard? Were persons who reported interactions with the spirit world in frequent nightmares treated with respect or honor? Were they given special treatment? Or were they considered deranged and pitiable? One way to answer these questions is to look at the available ethnographic evidence that anthropologists and trained observers have collected from modern societies that resemble early ancestral societies in crucial respects. To appreciate how nightmares were understood by premodern societies we first need to investigate how dreams were understood in premodern societies. Premodern societies are generally understood to be small-scale, traditional tribal societies.

DREAMS IN PREMODERN SOCIETIES

Lohmann (2007) has provided a recent survey of the literature on dreams in premodern cultures. In general, ancient peoples distinguished among several types of dreams. Some dreams were considered products of the imagination and therefore useful for entertainment in the form of storytelling. Most premodern peoples, however, regarded dreams as arenas for interaction with the spirit world. Michael Harner (1972) reports that the South American Jivaro considered dreams to reveal a more true spiritual reality behind the illusory images people perceived in waking life. The Zuni and Quiché Maya traditions that Barbara Tedlock (1987) studied, for example, saw dream images as communications from ancestors, spirits, or divinities. The Tikopia (Firth, 2001) in Polynesia saw dreams as opportunities for visitation of spirits to the dreamer. Perhaps most commonly among premodern peoples, dream images are explained as the experiences and perceptions of the dreamer's soul, as it wanders outside the body (e.g., Gregor 1981a, 1981b on Amazonia; Lohmann 2003a, 2003b on Oceania; and Tonkinson 1974, on aboriginal Australia).

In short, premodern peoples respected dreams but knew when a dream story or image was just good storytelling. Premodern peoples certainly reported nightmares as well. Achte and Schakir (1985) studied the dream content of 282 bushmen (aged eighteen to seventy years) from Southwest Africa. Through interviews conducted in 1970, 1971, and 1973, subjects described a dream they recalled. Nightmare themes included falling, violence, death, and threatening animals; themes of other dreams included food, foreboding, and hunting. This report of nightmares, however, in bushmen does not mention nonhuman supernatural agents as part of nightmare content, but we can suppose such content was ubiquitous in nightmares of premodern peoples. It should not be surprising that their dreams were concerned primarily with the spirit world. Their very cultures were suffused with supernatural entities and spirits.

CULTURAL CONTEXT OF DREAMING
IN PREMODERN SOCIETIES

What kinds of cultures did our ancestors live in? Premodern cultures respected the dream and gave it a central place in their lives. What kinds of cultures allowed for a central role for dreams and nightmares? Many ethnographers, evolutionary psychologists, and anthropologists point out that many of these premodern cultures were influenced by what is now called shamanic religious imagery, which placed dreams at the center of society's rituals. (Dunbar and Barrett 2007, 521–25; Hitchcock and Jones 1976; Jacobs 1990; Winkelman 2000.)

Shamanic Cultures

It is worth discussing these shamanic studies as shamanic culture was central to the cultures of aboriginal and premodern peoples. The shaman specializes in use of dreams, psychological dissociation, trance, and other altered states of consciousness to accomplish various tasks such as healing ill people, providing social information about others, foretelling the future and compiling information about myths and religious rituals of the tribe. The shaman engages in imaginary travels (usually in a dream state) to spiritual realms, meets spirit beings, retrieves lost souls, speaks with the gods and returns with new information as to how to perform ceremonies or rituals, and so forth (Lewis 1971). Alternatively the shaman may be possessed by such entities who speak through him when in trance.

The shaman often acquires his status after an illness involving apparent possession by spirits or via a series of dreams, nightmares, and visions concerning the fate of the tribe itself. For example, many people know the story of Black Elk as vividly described in the book *Black Elk Speaks* (Black Elk and Neihardt, 1932). While a boy, Black Elk had a series of dreams and nightmares predicting an invasion of white men against his tribe. Some of these nightmares also contained prescriptions for how to prepare for the coming invasion. These preparations entailed a series of dances and costumes and festivals involving his entire tribe. When he shared his dream-nightmare with tribal members, the entire society ceased its regular ongoing life and spent weeks creating the costumes, dances, and events Black Elk had seen in his "visions." They then spent several more weeks enacting the contents of these visions. In short some nightmares, if shared with others in a way that convinces the others of the meaningfulness of the visions, can confer shamanic status on the dreamer.

A shaman may attain high status in a tribe. He certainly undergoes extensive training in order to become a healer and a leader in the tribe.

In particular he is trained to use his dreams to contact the relevant spirits who hold the key to a cure for his patients. One of the finest accounts of the world view of a shamanic society prior to any major impact of the modern world comes from the research among the Tukano Indians of the northwest Amazon by Gerardo Reichel-Dolmatoff (1997).

The dream visions of shamans are interpreted as a return to a time of origin when all things were created by the gods. The ancestors may appear, special spirit beings may also appear who hold a special relationship with the shaman. The shaman may receive a gift from the beings or take it by force and this gift will confer power on the shaman henceforth. Dreams are central to this imaginal work. The images seen in dreams become the topics of discussions the shamans lead. The experiences are not private but freely shared and interpreted in a group led by a shaman.

Research on Asian shamanism is extensive (Hitchcock and Jones 1976; Samuel 2003). In his pioneering work, Eliade (original pub. 1913; republished 1964) considered this to be the fundamental shamanic type. A major variation is the Tibetan lhapa however, who becomes possessed by gods, spirits, or other spiritual agents while in trance. Here the "gods" come to the shaman rather than vice versa. These shamanic types have been particularly studied in Ladakh, North India, where they perform psychological functions as they heal those possessed by witches or spirits of place, etc. (Brauen 1980; Crook 1997, 1998; Day 1989; Kuhn 1988; Phylactou 1989; Rösing 2003). These shamans may interact with an amazing number of spirit entities. These include ancestor spirits, spirits of the dead, spirit beings seen in dreams, the god of local shrines, and high gods of mountains. In a healing ceremony the lhapa's task is to find, via dreaming or trance, the spirit causing the illness, retrieve the ill person's soul from that spirit or demon, and expel the demon from the person's body.

Winkelman's (1992) seminal cross-cultural study of shamanism sought to identify distinctive characteristics of shamans as opposed to other magico-religious practitioners across forty-seven cultures for which data were available. Winkelman's (1992) statistical analysis yielded four practitioner groups: 1) the shaman complex (shamans, shaman–healers, and healers), 2) priests and priestesses, 3) diviners, seers, and mediums, and 4) malevolent practitioners (witches and sorcerers). Independent evidence has shown that all of these spiritual specialists use dreams and nightmares to interact with the spirit world and to carry out their work of healing or divining. Unlike the other specialists, the shamans were almost always controlled the interaction with spirits or demons rather than being controlling by them. Shamans enter their profession by displaying behavioral evidence that they are called to shamanize (Heinze 1991). Reports of persistent dreams, visions, and nightmares with the right content constituted evidence that the individual was being called to be a shaman. That content will usually involve interactions and transactions with spirit beings or one particular spirit being who imparts to the dreamer special knowledge about treatment of illness, contacting and working with benevolent spirit entities, fighting malevolent demons or spirits, performing religious rituals, interpreting dreams, and predicting future events. To accomplish these feats, shamans typically either incorporate the target spirit being into their own consciousness or dream states and do battle or negotiate with them "there" or they engage in out-of-body experiences to send (once again via trance or dreaming) their spirit to where the target spirit being is and interact with them "there." Peters and Price-Williams (1980) compared shamanic practices in forty-two societies from four different cultural areas. They reported that shamans specialized in spirit incorporation in half of the forty-two societies they surveyed, while in about a quarter of the cultures shamans were engaged in out-of-body journeying, and the final quarter of shamans engaged in both spirit incorporation and out-of-body journeying.

Shamans are typically men and women of exceptional cognitive talent with prodigious memories and a dedication to service to other members of the tribe. Basilov's (1997) case studies of Turkic shamans in Siberia showed that they were capable of expertly memorizing an extensive body of knowledge concerning healing procedures, religious rituals, medicines, and the pantheon of spirits in the spirit world. Sandner (1979) described the remarkable abilities of the Navajo hatalii. To attain their status, they must memorize at least ten ceremonial chants, each of which contains hundreds of individual songs.

In short, shamans were high-status individuals in their cultures and their facility in dreaming and in reporting dreams and nightmares in a compelling way was a route to high-status occupations in these cultures. Winkelman (1992), in fact, found that shamans hold high status in hunter-gatherer and forager societies and lower status in agricultural states. With the rise of agriculture some fifteen thousand years ago, shamanism began to decline while other spiritual specialists replaced them. In any case, it seems reasonable to conclude that among our ancestors, spiritual specialists, exemplified by the shaman, were held in high regard and were quite prestigious. To become a spiritual specialist in one of these cultures required evidence that one was called to the profession and a major source for that evidence was dreams, visions, and nightmares.

How did shamanism evolve? McClenon (1997a, 1997b) hypothesized that shamanic practitioners capitalized on human's innate abilities to go into dream states or trances. The shaman specializes in these trance states and uses them to heal the sick. In short shamanic spiritual practices arose and developed because they were linked with effective healing techniques. Another possibility is that shamanism and kindred spiritual practices arose because they were prestigious. Anyone who could wield the power or stand up to the power of a spirit being was a man or woman to be reckoned with.

Sources of Social Prestige of Spiritual Specialists

What evidence is there that interactions with spirit beings in dreams and nightmares were prestigious? Among adults in premodern tribal societies, nightmare sharing was associated with attempts to enhance social prestige or change the dreamer's social status (Jedrej and Shaw 1992; Lohmann 2003a). For example, the waxing and waning social power of Temne diviners depended upon active accomplishment in the realm of dreaming (Shaw 1992). Temne diviners derived their abilities from an initial dream or nightmare in which they meet some supernatural agent that then serves as a source of power and prestige for the dreamer. The diviner argues that his spirit has particular powers to heal or to provide favors for the dreamer's clients and so forth. The diviner attempts to gain power from subsequent encounters in his dreams with his patron spirit and other spirits in the "dream town" or *ro-mere*. The diviner then asserts authority as a spiritual specialist to interpret the dreams of others and to predict fortune or misfortune for these others.

Similarly, Ray (1992) studied the role of dreams in the formation of ritual kingship among the Igbo culture as it persisted into the early decades of the twentieth century. After the death of the sacred king, the *eze Nri*, the new king, must be chosen by the spirit of his predecessor, or by the deity whose power the ritual office mediates. In the case of the *eze Nri* a group of assessors deliberated on the choice of the rivals, but their decisions were based at least as much upon a reading of extra-human signs that were communicated to them by their own and others' dreams. If the dream teller had a series of nightmare visions about the *eze Nri*, his testimony and advice on the kingship would carry more weight as the sharing of his visions would be compelling, prophetic, and awe-inspiring.

The Yansi from the Democratic Republic of Congo begin each day with a discussion of the dreams of the night. Those who share especially compelling dreams are accorded more attention and consideration. The sharing of a nightmare has material consequences for the individual and others extending widely through the society. Dreaming in Yansi society, for example, appears to be integral to the Yansi witchcraft-sorcery-medicine complex with certain nightmares marking out individuals for special treatment depending on its interpretation by the specialist. In his studies of the Toraja, wet rice farmers who live in hamlets throughout the central highlands of South Sulawesi, Indonesia, Hollan (2003) reported that the Toraja, despite being Christianized, still encounter ancestor spirits (nene') and other spiritual beings (deata) in their dreams and nightmares. When Hollan asked Nene'na Limbong, a Toraja man in his seventies whether he had had any really bad dreams, Nene'na answered:

One time I dreamed that my throat had been cut! There was a man who cut my throat. I fell down dead! And I was very frightened. I woke up frightened think- ing, "I'm dead." A man cut me with a machete and I fell down dead and my eyes went dark. Then my body was cut up and distributed to A and B and C (he whispers in a low terrified tone of voice). "Oh this is my body being cut up!" But I could see it happen! I was cut up and distributed (voice continues low, quiet, horrified). I was very frightened. (Hollan 2003, 174–75)

Nene'na then told Hollan the meaning of the dream. "The dream really meant that I would eventually slaughter many buffalo and become an im- portant man" (Hollan 2003, 175).

When Hollan directly asked Nene'na if he had ever had a nightmare (tuan) Nene'na replied:

I went to sleep about 10 P.M. but my eyes were still open! But my body was al- ready asleep. But my eyes were still open and I could see. I thought, "Oh what is this?" Then it came. It came and trampled on my stomach! Then it trampled on my hands and legs. I wanted to say something, but I couldn't speak! I wanted to yell, but nothing would come out. I was frightened! And my heart inside was pounding. [He speaks louder to convey his sense of fear and anxi- ety.] So my heart was pounding, beating hard! People die from experiences like that. They can die? Yes, die, because of the restricted breathing. [And the spirit that jumped on you, was he/she a man or woman?] A woman. [And what did she look like?] Like a human but her hair wasn't tied up. Her hair was very long. [Women unbind their uncut hair only in very private contexts such as bathing and lovemaking, and when they are possessed by spirits during the course of special rituals.] I was very frightened to see her. But I saw her with my own eyes! I have seen many people die because of an experience like that, because they can't fight back and they can't survive. (Hollan 2003, 174)

Many cultures have reported these sorts of "spirit attack" night- mares. A spirit attack nightmare marks the person out for special treat- ment in the tribe and the individual has to interpret the dream in such a way to show that he foiled the attack and thus enhance his social prestige. The Tiwi describe attacks by *mabidituwi* during nightmares. The Parintintin attribute nightmares to the proximity of a demon (anang) that chokes the dreamer and so on. How an individual handles interactions with the spirit world, particularly with the challenging case of malicious spirits, contributes to his reputation and his social standing (Hollan 2003).

Robbins (2003) studied the ways in which dream-sharing allowed Melanesians to channel charismatic leadership into roles that benefited rather than threatened tribal political stability. He notes that "Throughout Melanesia, people are regularly thought to have contact with supernatural beings, and in the eyes of those around them these contacts endow them, at least momentarily, with exceptional powers to foretell the future, heal others and so on" (23). Robbins then notes that "… it is in dreams that Melanesians most regularly come into contact with supernaturals and with supernaturally given knowledge that may afford them extraordinary powers" (23).

These brief snippets of the role of dreams and nightmares in the social interactions in a small number of premodernized tribal societies are meant only to illustrate the larger claim that nightmare sharing among our ancestors very likely enhanced the *prestige* of the individual who did so—especially those individuals who could do so convincingly, eloquently, and compellingly. Prestige did not necessarily mean that the individual in question was liked or adulated. Instead it meant that the individual was regarded with respect, sometimes with adulation, and sometimes with fear and awe, but always with respect.

NIGHTMARE SHARING IN PREMODERN GROUPS

Given what we know concerning the centrality of group dream sharing in premodern tribal groups (Gregor 1981a, 1981b, 2001; Jedrej and Shaw 1992; Schneider and Sharp 1969; Tedlock 1992a), we can assume that dream and nightmare sharing was a common practice in early human groups in the environment of evolutionary adaptation (EEA). Given that nightmares are more memorable than ordinary dreams, it seems likely that most nightmares are shared with others. In representative samples of the general population, between 40 percent and 75 percent of individuals surveyed recall between one to five intense and impactful dreams per month (Borbély 1984; Kuiken and Sikora 1993; Stepansky et al. 1998).

Mannix (2006) examined relationships between dream recall frequency and a host of daytime mental health variables. She reported that many individuals report dreams that they claimed caused them to experience a negative emotion (anxious, scared, distressed, sad) or negative physical sensation (tense, drained, heart racing, tears) upon waking. Once recalled a dream is typically shared with another person (Stefanikis 1995; Vann and Alperstein 2000). Once shared it has the potential to influence social appraisals of the dreamer.

Nightmares have the added advantage of being considered as utterly involuntary cognitive and emotional experiences and thus, are unfakeable. They provide honest information about the dreamer and the dream contents to others. Sharing a nightmare with another gives the "other" a direct window onto recent brain/mind REM activity of the dreamer when under duress and thus a direct window into the quality of the individual sharing the dream. In short, the sharing of a nightmare with others impresses these others because nightmares are compelling, memorable, fantastic, vivid, scary, and convey important information about the dreamer.

Therefore, I suggest that the adaptive function of nightmares is to provide an opportunity for the dreamer to enhance his or her prestige by sharing the nightmare in a compelling way. You cannot share them in a compelling way unless you really experience them and you cannot really experience and gain practice at sharing them unless you experience them on some sort of a regular basis—thus the phenomenon of recurrent nightmare sufferers. Note, however, that enhancing the prestige of the dreamer requires more than just getting people to pay attention to the dreamer ... the nightmare sufferer is not just seeking attention. We are not talking here about any strategy of secondary gain or the like. The nightmare sufferer is not out to fool people. Instead he shares an experience that cannot be faked, a very costly experience, a vision that our ancestors believed carried vital information about both the dreamer and the welfare of the group.

Chapter 5

 Biology of Nightmares

This chapter will focus on the biology of rapid eye movement or REM sleep since this is the sleep state where most nightmares occur.

NORMAL HUMAN SLEEP ARCHITECTURE

As mentioned earlier, when measured electrophysiologically, the human sleep state consists of five major stages. The first four stages constitute non–rapid eye movement (NREM) sleep, and are best described by polysomnographic and electroencephalographic (EEG) criteria. The fifth stage is not part of NREM sleep and is characterized by periodic or phasic bursts of rapid eye movements (REM) under the closed eyelids. REM sleep is indicated by EEG data, electroculographic (EOG) activity, and a reduction in electromyographic (EMG) activity. Electromyographic electrodes are usually placed under the chin and indicate when the muscle paralysis characteristic of REM sleep occurs (Rechtschaffen and Kales 1968).

REM and NREM sleep states alternate throughout the night in a period of about ninety minutes. Stages III and IV constitute slow-wave sleep (SWS), which is particularly potent during the childhood phase of human development. If, as some sleep scientists believe, SWS operates in a kind of mutual inhibitory balance with REM sleep, then SWS may be particularly important for production of nightmares that occur in REM. In stage II, the amplitude of slow waves increases and gives way to very high-amplitude delta waves in the deepest sleep, stage IV or SWS. NREM stages dominate the first third of the night, while REM dominates the last third (Carskadon and Rechtschaffen 2000).

A sleep cycle is defined as a period of NREM sleep followed by a period of REM sleep. During a single night, a person will progress through three or four NREM-REM sleep cycles, each lasting between 90 and 110 minutes and becoming progressively longer through the night.

Usually, the NREM period will last about eighty minutes or longer, followed by a REM period that can be as short as one minute in the early cycles. Towards the morning REM periods can last as long as forty-five minutes.

When studying nightmares, sleep scientists measure several important sleep parameters including REM sleep duration and NREM sleep duration, both of which are usually expressed as a percentage of total sleep time. The time from sleep onset to the onset of the first REM period is known as REM latency. The number of eye movements per minute of REM is called REM density. It is usually expressed as a total for the night, and reflects the intensity of REM sleep.

SLEEP REBOUND EFFECTS AND REM-NREM IMBALANCES IN PRODUCTION OF NIGHTMARES

The longer you go without sleep the more vivid your dreams are once you fall asleep. Sometimes these vivid rebound dreams turn into nightmares. Rebound sleep contains a large amount of slow-wave sleep or SWS. Sleep deprivation studies have provided much insight into our need for SWS. When people or animals are deprived of SWS they must make it up the next time they sleep. The amount of SWS made up depends on the amount of time the person went without SWS (Dijk, Hayes, and Czeisler 1993; Webb and Agnew 1971). The effects of sleep deprivation on SWS suggest the existence of a compensatory mechanism that attempts to recover from SWS loss. The magnitude of this compensation or rebound depends on the length of sleep loss. In short, like many other body chemicals, signals and processes, SWS is homeostatically regulated. We need a certain amount of it to function well. Too much or too little will have detrimental effects on the individual. Too much SWS may be associated with greater nightmare production.

Sleep deprivation studies have indicated that there is a possible interaction between REM and NREM sleep. Sleep deprivation invariably involves deprivation of both NREM and REM sleep. Thus sleep rebound also involves high amounts of both NREM and REM. After sleep deprivation, SWS shows an immediate rebound effect while REM sleep is made up only after SWS is recovered. Only when REM sleep is selectively deprived is there a significant REM sleep rebound (Beersma 1990). Even when a specific REM deficit is created, REM rebound will occur only during times that SWS is normally decreased, such as in the later parts of the night. But it is here that we get nightmares. High amounts of REM late in the night yield nightmares. Conversely high amounts of SWS early in the night may yield nightmares as well. In short, too much REM or too much SWS can yield nightmares. You need a balance between REM and NREM to prevent nightmares.

Sleep rebound effects suggests that NREM sleep is controlled by mechanisms that take precedence over REM sleep. Since NREM sleep does seem to take precedence over REM sleep, there is support for NREM sleep as a restorative or revitalizing sleep process. At the least, the mechanisms that control each stage of sleep are in a balance that tends to favor one over the other depending on the circumstances.

Non–rapid eye movement and REM also interact in their control of hormonal states in the organism. Circulating levels of a number of growth-related factors appear to be influenced by REM-NREM interactions. Nighttime levels of these hormones typically exceed their daytime levels. Nocturnal growth hormone (GH) levels, for example, are at least four times the daytime level of GH in young men (Mueller, Locatelli, and Cocchi 1999). Slow wave sleep of NREM is associated with a major surge in GH release (Mueller, Locatelli, and Cocchi 1999; Van Cauter, Plat, and Copinschi 1998). The surge in GH release in humans is particularly marked in males. Growth hormone-releasing hormone (GH-RH) promotes NREM sleep, while somatostatin (SS) inhibits both GH and GH-RH release. Somatostatin release appears to be partially dependent on REM activation, as SS levels rise with onset of REM. Stimulation of GH secretion and promotion of NREM sleep are dependent on activity of GH-RH-ergic neurons of the anterior pituitary and the medial pre-optic region. In addition to the regulatory control of SS, GH and insulin-like growth factor I feedback on GH-RH to inhibit GH release and regulate GH levels.

Fisher et al. (1970) found that nightmares occurring in REM sleep were characterized by reduced autonomic nervous system (ANS) activity relative to nightmares occurring in other stages of sleep and thus, REM nightmares could dampen down intense affect and were "desomaticized" when compared to other forms of nightmares.

When considering the associations between sleep and nightmares, it is important to keep in mind the possible interactions between NREM and REM sleep. It may be that nightmares occur when the NREM-REM inhibitory balance is upset or put off kilter in such a way as to yield too much REM or too much SWS. When you have too much of either of the sleep states it becomes more difficult to transition from one sleep state to another and thus the individual becomes more vulnerable to the so-called parasomnias and other sleep-related disorders such as night terrors.

SPECIAL LINK BETWEEN NIGHTMARES AND REM SLEEP

Nightmares typically occur during REM sleep periods for both children and adults. When trauma is present in the history of the individual, nightmares will be due to a derangement of the balance between

SWS and REM. When nightmares occur in otherwise healthy adults or in children then we are likely dealing with the extreme end of a continuum of REM sleep that extends from small to large amounts of REM. *Frequent nightmare sufferers experience too much REM sleep.* Too much REM in turn exerts a moderate inhibition on SWS. This nature-induced "imbalance" favoring REM yields nightmares in these otherwise healthy individuals. We therefore need to look more closely at REM properties that make it the main culprit in frequent nightmare sufferers who have no history of trauma.

REM Properties

Rapid eye movement (REM) sleep accounts for about 22 percent of total sleep time in humans. Although the cortex is activated in REM, arousal thresholds are higher in REM than in the waking state (or in SWS for that matter). The phasic aspects of REM sleep, such as intermittent muscle twitching, ANS discharges, and rapid eye movements, occur in some mammals in association with bursts of pontine-geniculo-occipital (PGO) waves. Mammals (with the possible exception of humans) also exhibit a theta rhythm in the hippocampal formation during REM. Rapid eye movement is also associated with ANS instabilities that become more extreme as duration of REM episodes increases throughout the night. It is unclear if ANS activity during nightmares is elevated relative to nightmare states arising out of other sleep states. Like NREM, REM deprivation results in a rebound phenomenon indicating that a certain amount of REM is required and must be made up if lost. Interestingly, as mentioned above, after total sleep deprivation, NREM sleep is made up first before REM.

Thus, REM's tonic characteristics are a desynchronized electroencephalogram (EEG), penile erections, and atonia of the antigravity muscles. Its phasic characteristics include bursts of rapid eye movements under the closed eyelids; myoclonic twitches of the facial and limb muscle groups; increased variability in heart rate, respiration, and blood pressure; and ANS discharges. Other correlates of REM include effects on release of selected hormones, especially growth factors. Virtually all mammals (with some crucial exceptions such as certain sea mammals) exhibit both SWS and REM sleep.

REM-On and REM-Off Cellular Networks

Rapid eye movement sleep onset is triggered by cholinergic neurons originating within the peribrachial regions of the brain, known as the laterodorsal tegmental (LDT) and pedunculopontine tegmental (PPT) nuclei (LDT/PPT). Noradrenergic and serotonergic neurons in the locus coeruleus and dorsal raphe nucleus (LC/DRN), respectively, may inhibit REM sleep. Activation of cholinergic REM (including phasic REM) is related to removal of inhibition exerted by these aminergic efferents on cholinergic cells in the LDT/PPT. When the aminergic neurons decrease their firing, cells of the LDT/PPT are released from inhibition and increase their firing.

The release of acetylcholine from terminals of LDT/PPT cells triggers the onset of REM by activating brain regions that control various components of REM, including brain stem sites, the hypothalamus, limbic system, amygdala, and the basal forebrain. Cholinergic collaterals to the LC/DRN exert an indirect excitatory effect on aminergic cell groups in these nuclei. As REM proceeds, this excitatory effect on these aminergic cell groups eventually reaches a threshold at which point their activation results in a feedback inhibition on REM—on cells of the LDT/PPT—thus ending the REM period. The initiation of NREM sleep may be a GABA-ergic–mediated process characterized by loss of wake-related alpha waves and slowing of EEG frequency.

Selective Cerebral Activation in REM

Recently a number of positron emission tomography (PET) and functional magnetic resonance imaging (fMRI) studies of the sleeping brain have revealed that REM demonstrates high activation levels in pontine, midbrain tegmentum, anterior cingulate, limbic, and amygdaloid sites, and deactivation of prefrontal areas, parietal cortex, and posterior cingulate (Braun et al. 1997; Hobson, Stickgold, and Pace-Schott 1998; Maquet and Franck 1997; Maquet et al. 1996; Nofzinger et al. 1997). Crucially, these imaging studies have consistently revealed exceptionally high activation levels in the amygdala during REM.

Brain activation patterns are significantly different and even opposing for REM and NREM, demonstrating high activation levels in limbic/amygdaloid sites and deactivation of dorsolateral prefrontal cortex sites (Braun et al. 1997; Hobson, Stickgold, and Pace-Schott, 1998; Maquet and Franck 1997; Maquet et al. 1996; Nofzinger et al. 1997), while regional cerebral blood flow studies for NREM/SWS indicate deactivation of thalamic functions and activation in secondary association areas in the temporal and parietal lobes, including the language-related planum temporale and the inferior parietal lobule areas (Hofle et al. 1997).

REM Dream Content

When subjects are awakened from REM, they generally report a narrative involving the dreamer, with vivid visual detail, unpleasant emotions, and occasional bizarre and improbable events (Domhoff 2003b;

Hobson and Pace-Schott 2002; Nielsen et al. 2001; Strauch and Meier 1996).

PGO Waves

Pontine-geniculo-occipital (PGO) waves are associated with several of the phasic (or variable) events of REM, including rapid eye movements and ANS instabilities. These waves are generated in the pons and are propagated up through the lateral geniculate body (LGB) of the thalamus and then up to occipital and other cortical brain sites. Because the LGB and the occipital cortex are visual centers, it was originally thought that PGO waves could account for visual phenomena of dreams. It now appears that PGO waves are not confined to visual centers but may instead be quite prominent in the amygdala and in limbic and disparate cortical sites. PGO waves occur in bursts or spikes and thus are correlated with many phasic phenomena of REM. At the level of the pons, Datta (1999) has shown that PGO state-on cells in the caudolateral peribrachial (C-PBL) region of the cat and the subcoreleus\ edq5\ region of the rat contain the triggering elements of PGO wave generation. During waking and NREM sleep, these cells are silent due to presynaptic inhibitory inputs from aminergic (5HT and noradrenergic) cells in the DRN, LC, and local C-PBL state-off cells. The local inhibitory cells may be GABA-ergic. When aminergic and local inhibitory inputs are removed from the state-on neurons of the C-PBL, they start discharging. PGO state-on cells activate LDT/PPT cells rostral to the peribrachial region and these, in turn, interact with triggering elements to generate PGO waves.

Morrison and colleagues (Morrison 1979; Morrison, Sanford, and Ross 1999) have suggested that PGO waves are comparable to the well-known orienting reflex (OR) that occurs after startle, interest, or fear during waking. If PGO waves are associated with orienting, startle, and fear reactions, then organisms experiencing PGO waves during REM are likely undergoing regular and repeated startle reactions, orienting reflexes, and stress-inducing mobilizations to defend against hallucinatory threats each time they go into REM.

Activation of the Amygdala in REM

As mentioned above, a number of PET and fMRI studies of the sleeping brain have revealed that REM demonstrates high activation levels in pontine, midbrain tegmentum, anterior cingulate, limbic, and amygdaloid sites, as well as deactivation of prefrontal areas, parietal cortex, and posterior cingulate (Braun et al. 1997; Hobson, Stickgold, and Pace-Schott 1998; Maquet and Franck 1997; Maquet et al. 1996; Nofzinger et al. 1997). These imaging studies have consistently revealed exceptionally high activation levels in the amygdala during REM, suggesting that the amygdala is *key* to REM physiology.

Maquet and Phillips (1999) point out that REM-related amygdaloid activation may contribute to the profile of forebrain sites that are activated and deactivated during REM. Specifically, activated cortical areas receive amygdaloid projections, while deactivated sites do not. Maquet and Philips also report significant positive interactions between amygdaloid blood flow and occurrence of REM in the temporal cortex.

The high activation levels of amygdaloid circuits during REM may be an especially important process in the production of nightmares. The central nucleus of the amygdala is known to be a regulatory center for neural circuits involved in fear, aggression, defense, the fight-or-flight response, and autonomic reactivity (Ledoux 2000; Sah et al. 2003). The central nucleus is particularly important for mediation of fear responses. Fear-related responses are characterized by freezing, startle, release of stress hormones, rises in blood pressure and heart rate, respiratory distress, piloerection, and stereotypical threat displays. In humans, these autonomic responses are accompanied by a sense of anguish, anxiety, dread, despair, and intense distress. Activation of the central nucleus induces autonomic instabilities associated with these negative emotions. The medial portion of the central nucleus has substantial projections to the hypothalamus, bed nucleus of the stria terminalis, and several nuclei in the midbrain, pons, and medulla, associated with regulation of the ANS. Projections to the brain stem are to three main areas: 1) the periaqueductal gray matter, which mediates startle, analgesia, vocalizations in response to threat, and cardiovascular changes; 2) the parabrachial nucleus, which is involved in pain transmission; and 3) the nucleus of the solitary tract, which contributes to regulation of the vagal system. The neuroanatomy of the amygdala thus allows it to regulate fight-or-flight responses, cardiac and respiratory functions, and other fundamental ANS responses. REM-induced phasic discharges occurring in the central nucleus may help to explain REM-related cardiac, respiratory, and autonomic instabilities.

Animal studies have, in fact, linked amygdaloid activation to phasic signs of REM. Electrical stimulation of the central nucleus of the amygdala increases PGO wave frequency (Calvo et al. 1987) and other signs of phasic REM. Carbachol injection within the same nucleus increases REM sleep duration and other REM indices (Calvo, Simon-Arceo, and Fernandez-Mas 1996). Activation of the amygdala during REM may be considered a phasic process of REM that is superimposed on a more tonic activation of the limbic forebrain in general during REM. Interestingly, measures of both REM and amygdaloid activation are enhanced in depression (Whalen et al. 2002).

REM Sleep and Autonomic Nervous System Storms

Relative to the waking state, sympathetic activity rises during phasic portions of REM. As the duration of phasic REMs increases over the course of the night, so do the durations of sympathetic discharges giving rise to periodic REM-related sympathetic discharges or "storms." These sympathetic discharges, in turn, may be linked to a host of negative cardiopulmonary changes that occur during phasic REM.

REM Sleep and the Cardiovascular System

Cardiac output declines over the course of the night, reaching its lowest levels during the last REM period. During all REM periods, an acceleration of heart rate occurs at least ten beats before EEG signs of phasic arousal, and then fluctuates dramatically during phasic REM. Systemic arterial blood pressure (BP), pulmonary BP, and intracranial arterial BP all exhibit increased variability relative to NREM and waking levels. There is marked vasodilation in all of the major vascular beds, including selected cerebral vascular systems. Because of the hemodynamic, ANS, and sympathetic alterations of REM, plaque rupture and coronary arterial spasm become more likely.

There is a well-documented increased risk for cardiac arrest during the late morning hours coincident with the final REM period (Asplund and Aberg 1998; Peters, Zoble, and Brooks 2002). As mentioned, cardiac output is lowest during this REM period. Individuals with cardiopulmonary disease are more likely to die during this REM period than at any other time of the day. Sei and Morita (1999) report that REM-related phasic increases in arterial BP are associated with hippocampal theta activity in rats. Similarly, Rowe et al. (1999) report that REM-related heart rate surges were associated with increased frequency of hippocampal theta and increased PGO waves in cats. Heart rate surges were dramatically reduced by administration of atenolol, indicating that the phenomenon is sympathetically mediated by beta-adrenergic synapses.

REM-Related Respiratory Changes

Both REM and NREM show reductions in ventilation (alveolar hypoventilation), but the REM-related reduction is severe (Douglas 2000). During this REM period, oxygen desaturation levels are maximal and Cheyne-Stokes-like breathing patterns predominate. As a result of the fall in alveolar ventilation, there are changes in blood gas levels, with rises in CO_2 and decreases in oxygen saturation. During phasic REM, respiration becomes irregular, with a waxing and waning of tidal volume that resembles Cheyne-Stokes breathing. The natural response to lowered O_2 levels is to increase inspiratory breathing, but this response (the hypoxic ventilatory response) is decreased by more than 50 percent of normal capacity during REM. The REM-related hypoxemia and abnormal breathing patterns may cause life-threatening complications in vulnerable persons, including infants with immature lung capacity and in adults with various respiratory ailments and disorders.

REM-Related Lapse in Thermoregulation

Rapid eye movement sleep appears to involve a reversion to a poikilothermic state (Bach, Telliez, and Libert 2002; Parmeggiani 2000; Szymusiak, et al. 1998). Although brain temperature rises during REM, thermoregulatory responses such as sweating and panting do not occur in REM, although they are present in NREM. Sleep onset in humans is associated with a reduction in body temperature of about one to two degrees centigrade. The reduction appears to depend on NREM SWS, as it does not occur if the organism is selectively deprived of SWS. If body temperature increases during waking hours, SWS increases during sleep. Thus, NREM SWS appears to serve a thermoregulatory function. Given that body temperature influences metabolic rates, NREM SWS may also be implicated in energy conservation functions. REM sleep, however, does not appear to serve clear thermoregulatory or energy conservation functions because it cannot mount an effective defense against thermal loads.

REM-Related Motor Paralysis

One of the most paradoxical features of REM is that phasic eye movements and muscle twitches occur against a background of paralysis in the antigravity musculature, including the jaw, neck, and limbs. Two major pathways seem to be involved in REM-associated muscle atonia. The first includes the pontine cholinergic neurons that activate glutaminergic neurons in the medullary reticular formation. These in turn activate glycinergic neurons that inhibit motor neurons. In the second pathway, GABA-ergic neurons inhibit serotonin and noradrenergic neurons that "normally" maintain excitatory drive on motor neurons.

Penile Erections

Every REM period is associated with penile tumescence. These REM-related erections apparently occur even in infants. They persist throughout the lifespan but are not reliably associated with erotic desire. There is some evidence that REM-related sexual activation may also occur in women as uterine contractions and pelvic thrusting, appearing with

REM onset, but too few studies have been done on this topic to draw any firm conclusions.

Muscle Twitching

During phasic REM, a number of muscle groups begin to twitch, including the middle ear muscles, legs, arms, and selected facial muscles. Occasionally the twitching in the legs becomes so prominent as to cause restless legs syndrome, whereby the patient experiences an uncontrollable urge to move the legs, and this keeps the patient awake all night.

SUMMARY OF REM PROPERTIES AND NIGHTMARES

This review of major physiologic properties of REM, including REM-related PGO waves, activations of the amygdala, ANS storms, cardiovascular instabilities, respiratory impairment, thermoregulatory lapses, dynamic changes in GH release, and so on, suggests that these phasic properties of REM are a good substrate for production of nightmares. Even the tonic properties of REM (limbic forebrain activation with prefrontal deactivation, muscle twitching and muscle atonia, penile erections, etc.), however, may increase vulnerability to nightmares. In short, REM's properties appear to be the sort of properties we associate with nightmares. Yet not all REM dreams are nightmares (though virtually all nightmares occur in REM).

Perhaps nightmares emerge from REM activation when REM activation levels are particularly high or intense thereby yielding a concomitant inhibition of SWS. While there is some evidence for this point of view, you can have very intense REM dreams that are not called "nightmares" by the subject who reports these dreams, so intensity alone cannot account for nightmares. We will need to delve more carefully into the bio-psychology of nightmares before we can sort out their potential functions.

KEY ROLE OF THE AMYGDALA

The high activation levels of amygdaloid circuits during REM may contribute significantly to the occurrence of nightmares. Individuals with higher baseline levels of amygdalar activation would theoretically be at greater risk for nightmares, although this idea has not yet been adequately tested. Nevertheless, the available data are consistent with this idea. Nightmares, for example, appear to be a stable trait from childhood to middle age (Hublin et al. 1999). If you had them frequently in childhood you are more likely to suffer them as an adult. Further, a nationwide twin-cohort study in Finland (Hublin et al. 1999) has revealed strong genetic effects on nightmare frequency. The heritability estimate was approximately 0.45 for childhood nightmares and 0.37 for adult nightmares.

Presumably these genetic effects shape and regulate structure and activity of REM-related activation of amygdaloid circuits. As mentioned above, the amygdala is known to be a regulatory center for neural circuits involved in fear, aggression, defense, the fight-or-flight response, and autonomic reactivity (Ledoux 2000; Sah et al. 2003). A role for the amygdala in production of nightmares is supported by neuroimaging and pharmacologic investigations into the pathophysiology of post-traumatic stress disorder (Nutt and Malizia 2004; Rauch, Shin, and Phelps 2006).

SELECTED NEUROPHARMACOLOGICAL AGENTS CAN INDUCE NIGHTMARES

Many neuropharmacological agents such as antidepressants, narcotics, and barbiturates can cause nightmares. Intense, frightening dreams may occur during the withdrawal of drugs that cause REM sleep rebound, such as ethanol, barbiturates, and benzodiazepines. Agents affecting the neurotransmitters acetylcholine, GABA, and histamine, as well as some anesthetics, antipsychotics, and antiepileptic agents are particularly effective at inducing nightmares (Pagel and Helfter 2003).

NEUROANATOMY AND PHYSIOLOGY OF A NIGHTMARE

Pulling all this neurophysiologic data together, presumably what occurs in production of a nightmare is the following: An individual via genetic endowment or via a stressor event has an over-reactive amygdala. When for some reason (e.g., sleep deprivation, stress, trauma) NREM SWS is reduced, REM gets released from inhibition and the amygdala becomes very sensitive to stimulation. REM-related activations of the amygdala can now easily push it over the edge into an over-activated state and Fisher's desomaticization process fails.

Regardless of the sequence of neurophysiologic events that lead to a REM nightmare, it is clear that REM–related activation of the amygdala plays a key role. Pharmacologic agents that inhibit stimulatory or noradrenergic receptors on the amygdala could reduce the likelihood that a nightmare would arise during REM periods. Other nonpharmacologic interventions to reduce the occurrence of nightmares are also possible but will require more study of nightmare content in order to target the images that reliably produce stress.

We turn next to a survey of the clinical correlates of nightmares. This survey will tell us when nightmares appear as part of other clinical syndromes. We will see that REM sleep and the amygdala are implicated in each case.

Chapter 6

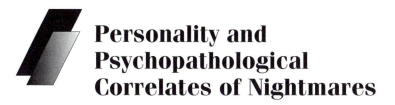

Personality and Psychopathological Correlates of Nightmares

One way to investigate potential functions of nightmares is to examine how nightmares are related to other clinical phenomena. If nightmares always co-occur with some loss of function, such as an increase in daytime anxiety, then we can be more confident that nightmares are not adaptive or functional. If on the other hand we find that nightmares frequently or always co-occur with a functional effect on some other behavior or state then the case for functionality is improved though not of course proved. A third possibility is that nightmares will co-occur with both functional and dysfunctional states. In that case, nightmares themselves will only be markers for functionality and the genes coding for nightmares might be passed along with other genes that code for a behavior or capacity that confers reproductive benefit on its bearers. Given their marker status, nightmares will either die out or be selected as a signal or indirect indicator of fitness. Like a costly set of useless feathers or antlers, nightmares will encumber their bearers only to signal "Look at the extreme visions I can bear. My genes must be extraordinary!" So let us now quickly sift the evidence for the clinical associations of nightmares.

NIGHTMARES ARE NOT RELIABLY ASSOCIATED WITH LOSS OF FUNCTION

The first thing we notice when we examine whether nightmares are associated with any other clinical states is that nightmares are not always associated with loss of function. Instead nightmares can be associated with extraordinary cognitive skills and creativity. This is true even when nightmares are in fact co-occurring with mental dysfunction.

For example, although recurrent nightmares in adults are associated with high levels of anxiety and neuroticism and other distinctive personality characteristics, Hartmann (1984, 1998) reported that chronic nightmare sufferers evidence "thin" boundaries in both the interpersonal sphere and in the cognitive sphere. Thin boundaries may sound bad but they are just a description of a cognitive style, one that happens to be ubiquitous among creative people. Nightmare sufferers with thin boundaries are no different. These people evidence long histories of unusual artistic and creative interests and accomplishments. Now if recurrent nightmares really were nothing but pathological states it is hard to account for the fact that they can co-exist with consistently high accomplishment in the creative arts. Yet that may be, in fact, the case.

This line of inquiry needs more follow up; unfortunately, I know of no other rigorous studies that have examined the cognitive talents of recurrent nightmare patients. This unfortunate state of affairs is undoubtedly due to the fact that most investigators and most sufferers/patients view nightmares as things to be eliminated—as unmitigated evils. The distress caused by nightmares *is* an evil or at least a serious clinical problem. But, to diminish the distress associated with nightmares we need to know more about the immediate sources of the distress. It is not helpful to say that the nightmare causes the distress. What elements within the nightmare are most responsible for the distress? I will return to that question in the chapter on treatment options for nightmare sufferers.

DISORDERS INVOLVING NIGHTMARES

With respect to nightmare's association with loss of function there is an abundance of evidence suggesting that that is the case. Nightmares most frequently are associated with mood and sleep disturbances. Among individuals (n = 718) who sought medical help for a sleep disturbance of any kind, 26 percent report experiencing nightmares (Krakow 2006). Moreover, among the patients who reported having nightmares, nightmares ranked among their major sleep problems, with 66 percent claiming that their bad dreams contributed to their disrupted sleep. In addition, this subset of patients evidenced greater insomnia, sleep-fragmentation, sleep-related daytime impairment, psychiatric history, and various medical conditions compared to the sleep patients who did not report having nightmares.

REM Behavior Disorder (RBD)

When recurrent nightmares occur in middle-aged or elderly individuals there may be indications that the patient is suffering REM sleep behavior disorder or RBD. This is because RBD, although rare, often heralds onset of a neurodegenerative disorder like Parkinson's disease or some form of dementia (Boeve et al. 2007; Olson et al. 2000). If a neurodegenerative disorder can be identified early in the course of the disease, treatment can be initiated in a timely fashion either to delay onset or at least to increase the patient's quality of life. Thus, recurrent nightmares in older individuals need to be taken seriously.

Patients with RBD often present with a history of bad dreams or nightmares. Nightmares of RBD are vivid, action-filled, violent dreams that the dreamer acts out, sometimes resulting in injury to the dreamer or the sleeping partner (Schenck and Mahowald 1996). The acting out of dreams is due to failure of normal REM-associated inhibition of antigravity muscles. No REM-related paralysis occurs so when the patient enters a REM episode, he is free to act out his dreams, which are all too often nightmares where the dreamer or his wife (most of these patients are men) is being attacked by strangers—including supernatural strangers like aliens or demons.

Patients with idiopathic RBD typically complain of a history of vivid unpleasant dreams or nightmares and excessive movements in sleep. They typically do not evidence a degenerative dementia until very late stages of the disease. There appears to be enactment of violent dream content and a concomitant failure of REM-related muscle atonia. Like Jouvet and colleagues' (1964 and Jouvet 1999) study of pontine-lesioned cats, who were thought to exhibit oneric behaviors that were normally under output inhibition, these patients are thought to suffer from a similar disinhibition of selective brain stem motor pattern generators. The disinhibition, in turn, is thought to be due to a pathologic process that affects pontine and some basal ganglia sites and other midline structures.

RBD has been found to occur in about 47 percent of Parkinson's patients (Olson et al. 2000), both in treated and untreated patients, with some patients reporting symptoms before the onset of Parkinson's. A great deal of dopaminergic cell loss occurs before the first signs of motor dysfunction. Perhaps early dopaminergic cell loss promotes vulnerability to both nightmares and RBD. Albin et al. (2000) determined the density of striatal dopaminergic terminals with [11C] dihydrotetrabenazine PET in six elderly subjects with chronic idiopathic RBD and nineteen age-appropriate controls. In subjects with RBD, there were significant reductions in striatal [11C] dihydrotetrabenazine binding particularly in the posterior putamen implying significant dopamine deficit.

Patients with RBD-related nightmares exhibit a cognitive profile consistent with frontal lobe impairment. Ferman et al. (1999) compared cognitive performance of nondemented idiopathic RBD patients to a group of patients with Alzheimer's disease (AD) and found that patients with RBD evidenced greater deficits on attention/concentration, perceptual organization, visual memory, and verbal fluency tests than did the AD patients. Shirakawa et al. (2002) used magnetic resonance imaging (MRI) and single-photon emission computed tomography (CT) of the brain to study the neurologic basis of RBD. Blood flow in the upper portion of both sides of the frontal lobe and pons was significantly lower in patients with RBD than in a normal elderly control group.

Olson et al. (2000) reported that 25.8 percent of their patients had histories of psychiatric illness or neurotic profiles, a figure somewhat lower than the 35 percent reported by Schenck and Mahowald (1990).

As in typical nightmares, the content of RBD nightmares involves the patient under some sort of threat, directed either against himself or his wife or significant others. Most patients report that they repeatedly experienced this RBD-related "nightmare" of being attacked by animals, monsters, demons, or unfamiliar people. The dreamer attempts to fight back in self-defense. Fear rather than anger is the usual accompanying emotion reported.

Despite these self-reported emotions in RBD dreams, content analyses of the dreams of RBD patients reveal a very high degree of aggression (Fantini and Ferini-Strambi 2007). Compared to controls, patients with RBD report a very high frequency of aggression, expressed by various indicators, namely a higher percentage of "dreams with at least one aggression" (66 percent versus 15 percent), an increased aggression/friendliness interactions ratio (86 percent versus 44 percent), an increased aggressions/characters (A/C) ratio (0.81 versus 0.12). A similar profile of high aggression indicators was associated with the nightmares we analyzed in an earlier chapter.

Polysomnographic studies show loss of muscle atonia with RBD and thus the patients are in danger of acting out their nightmares and causing injury to themselves or their bed partners. According to Mahowald and Schenck (2000) the overall sleep architecture is typically intact but most patients show increased SWS for their age. Schenck and Mahowald (1990) found that twenty-eight of sixty-five patients they evaluated evidenced increased REM (>25 percent) as a percentage of total sleep time. In the Olson study of ninety-three consecutive patients with RBD (Olson, Boeve, and Silber 2000), ninety showed increased phasic activity in REM.

In summary, the nightmares exhibited by people with REM Behavior Disorder or RBD are similar to nightmares other people without neurologic disease experience. They are under attack by anomalous agents such as dangerous strangers or animals and they strive to defend themselves.

Depression

One frequently reported clinical correlate of recurrent nightmares is depression. Reduced REM sleep latency was identified as an objective indicator of depressive disorder and an inverse correlate of its severity

30 years ago (Kupfer and Foster 1972). In subsequent years, reduced REM latency has proved to be one of the most robust and specific, if not exclusive, features of sleep in depressed patients (Benca 2000). Other reported abnormalities in REM sleep linked with depression include a prolonged duration of the first REM period, an increased density of the eye movements, and an increased REM percentage of total sleep time. Moreover, a short REM latency has been found to be associated with an increased risk of major depression beyond the familial risk associated with depressed proband (Giles et al. 1998). Among endogenous depressive symptoms, terminal insomnia, pervasive anhedonia, unreactive mood, and appetite loss are reported to be related to short REM latency in depressed patients (Giles et al. 1986). Recently, poor treatment outcomes have also been observed among patients who report poor sleep; who have increased amounts of REM sleep; who have increased numbers of eye movements during REM sleep; or who have an abnormal sleep "profile," including poor sleep efficiency, short REM sleep latency, and increased numbers of rapid eye movements (Buysse et al. 2001). These dysfunctions suggest that manipulations of REM may have therapeutic benefits for the depressed. Prolonged selective REM deprivation by awakenings has produced such beneficial effects (Vogel et al. 1980). To my knowledge selective REM deprivation has not been tried as a treatment for nightmares.

That the majority of antidepressant drugs, across several different categories, which exhibit robust suppression of REM sleep, appear to support therapeutic effects of REM deprivation. Others, however, such as bupropion and nefazodone, lack REM suppressant effects. Thus, it is still an unresolved issue whether REM sleep abnormalities are depressiogenic or whether early, prolonged, and more active REM sleep reflects an attempt to compensate for elevated levels of a waking depression (Cartwright and Lloyd 1994). In general, those who are severely depressed are reported to have poorer dream recall and blunted dream affect (Armitage et al. 1995). In contrast, those who are less severely depressed, particularly females, report higher rates of unpleasant dreams and nightmares than other psychiatric patients or normal subjects (Cartwright 1991).

Stage II NREM Nightmares

Some nightmares occur in association with NREM rather than REM sleep. Among these NREM nightmares are a small number that occur in Stage II NREM sleep (Dement and Kleitman 1957a, 1957b; Fisher et al. 1970; Foulkes and Vogel 1965; Vogel, Foulkes, and Trosman 1966). They are very much like REM nightmares but appear to cause more distress than REM nightmares.

Nightmares Associated with Narcolepsy

Narcolepsy is a sleep disorder that causes an individual to suddenly experience an overwhelming sleepiness. Such a "sleep attack" can be triggered by intense emotion. In addition the narcoleptic patient may experience terrifying sleep-onset (hypnagogic) or awakening (hypno-pompic) hallucinations that are like short nightmares. The original use of the term "nightmare" denoted the combination of sleep paralysis and hypnagogic hallucinations (Mahowald and Ettinger 1990). These hypnogogic hallucinations are usually associated with a degree of sleep paralysis and may include seeing simple visual forms changing in size or more elaborate images of animals or people engaging in threatening actions. Other terrifying nightmare images may occur when the individual is attempting to wake up. Sleep paralysis is an inability to move during the transition into or out of sleep. When you are just waking up but cannot move some terrifying images may come to you. This sort of nightmare imagery occurs in more than 33 percent of the general population (Partinen 1994).

Sleep and Suicide

Recurrent nightmare sufferers are thought to be at increased risk for suicidal ideation—though it is unclear whether the risk extends to actual attempts (Ağargün and Cartwright 2003). Ağargün et al. (1998) examined the association between repetitive and frightening dreams and suicidal tendency in patients with major depression. They reported that the patients with frequent nightmares, particularly women, had higher mean suicide scores and were more likely to be classified as suicidal. A prospective follow-up study in a sample drawn from the general population (Tanskanen et al. 2001) also reported that the frequency of nightmares was directly related to the risk of suicide. When researchers compare electroencephalographic (EEG) sleep characteristics of major depressives with or without a history of suicidal ideation, the patients with a history of suicidal ideation often evidence REM-NREM imbalances. They found suicide attempters had longer sleep latency, lower sleep efficiency, and fewer late-night delta wave counts than normal controls. They also demonstrated that nonattempters, compared to attempters, had less REM time and activity in the second REM period, but more delta wave counts in the fourth nonREM period. This EEG sleep profile is very similar to that seen in patients with recurrent nightmares.

Why might imbalances in the amount of REM versus SWS lead to nightmares or self-destructive impulses? If we assume that the experience of positive affect requires some sort of neurophysiologic balance between SWS delta activity and REM then it follows that alterations in mental activity (reductions in positive affect and enhancements in negative affect) will be associated with alterations in the balance between REM and SWS. The balance between REM and SWS was modeled by Borbély and Wirz-Justice (1982). Borbély formalized the insight that mammalian sleep involved a balance between sleep amount and sleep intensity and that sleep was therefore under homeostatic control. As discussed in an earlier chapter, in the two-process model of sleep regulation a sleep need process (Process S) increases during waking (or sleep deprivation) and decreases during sleep. This part of the model indexes restorative aspects of sleep and explicitly predicts that sleep is required for some restorative process of the brain or the body or both. Process S is proposed to interact with input from the light-regulated circadian system (Process C) that is independent of sleep and wakefulness rhythms. Slow-wave delta activity (SWA) is taken as an indicator of the time course of Process S because SWA is known to correlate with arousal thresholds and to markedly increase during the previous waking period and during the rebound period after sleep deprivation in all mammals studied. Once a threshold value of Process S is reached (i.e., once the appropriate amount and intensity of SWS is reached), Process C will be activated. Simulations using the model's assumptions show that the homeostatic component of sleep falls in a sigmoidal manner during waking and rises in a saturating exponential manner during sleep.

The two-process model predicts that both REM and NREM are under homeostatic control and mutually inhibit one another's expression. Too much REM is associated with reductions in SWS and vice versa. Borbély's model tells us how sleep intensity is adjusted depending on sleep need. If an animal goes without sleep for too long the urge to sleep builds up and once sleep is initiated the animal spends an inordinate amount of time in SWS and only after that is accomplished is REM sleep made up.

In the case of suicidal ideation and of nightmares, the REM/SWS balance is upset and so mood regulation is impaired. The individual is chronically sleep-deprived, chronically attempting to go into SWS, and chronically unable to experience normal amounts of pleasure. It is possible that a greater REM density and longer REM time earlier in the night displaces the appearance of NREM and thus the individual, despite being sleepy all the time, is actually sleep deprived. This situation means that the individual experiences a reduction in SWS delta counts later in the night. In short, too much REM leads to decreased SWS and enhanced unpleasant affect. This sleep imbalance leads to enhanced vulnerability to recurrent nightmares and when prolonged and extreme to suicidal ideation. Please note that none of this story is yet proved. At this point it is mere conjecture.

Nightmares and Post-Traumatic Stress Disorder (PTSD)

Recurrent nightmares occur in 40 percent to 56 percent of individuals with post-traumatic stress disorder or PTSD (Schreuder, Kleijn, and Rooijmans 2000). Nightmares can, in fact, be considered a hallmark feature of PTSD. Unlike typical nightmares, the content of disturbing dreams in PTSD is often linked to a specific memory of a traumatic incident in the person's life. The individual, in effect, relives the trauma with each nightmare. Nightmares related to PTSD may occur in a REM episode throughout the sleep period instead of being confined to late REM episodes as is the case with most nightmares (Nielsen and Zadra 2005). Polysomnographic studies in PTSD patients have shown that they have poor sleep maintenance, increased eye movement density, decreased percentage of REM sleep, and an increased tendency to have REM sleep at sleep onset (REM pressure). These data imply that they may also experience increased amounts of SWS, although this has not yet been demonstrated.

Trauma-related nightmares are associated with frequent awakenings (Germain and Nielsen 2003; Woodward et al. 2000) and are extremely distressing to the patient. One can only imagine how terrible it must feel to repeatedly undergo elements of a horrible traumatic experience like combat or rape. In some sufferers, these nightmares have been found to recur for decades with little or no change (Coalson 1995).

NIGHTMARES AND PSYCHOPATHOLOGY

Our review of the range of disorders associated with nightmares makes it clear that nightmares can co-occur with neuropsychiatric disorders. But that does not mean that nightmares are a sign of neuropsychiatric disorder. Association does not imply causal effect. Association simply implies that one process happens when another process happens and that may be because both processes share a third process—perhaps imbalances in REM and NREM. Many diseases can perturb sleep and when that perturbation is severe, REM and NREM balance will be disturbed, which in turn may give rise to nightmares. Other events besides disease can disrupt the balance between REM and NREM. There may be a genetic propensity for high amygdalar activation levels and for high REM levels for example. Or, there may be transient nondisease processes, exposure to drink or chemicals, for example, that temporarily inhibit REM or NREM expression. These transient inhibitory events would then upset the balance between the two sleep states yielding a greater propensity for nightmares and so on. There is, in short, no necessary link between nightmares and mental illness.

Chapter 7

 **Phenomenology of the Nightmare**

One clue to understanding any experiential state or process is to study its formal features—its phenomenology. The formal design features of any given cognitive process can reveal its potential functional features because design often, though not invariably, reveals function. A machine, a building, or a tool has the design features it does in order to accomplish the function for which it was designed.

So what are the design features of nightmares? Presumably they share some features with ordinary dreams but they must also exhibit their own unique properties—the characteristics that make them nightmares rather than ordinary dreams. In what follows, I will describe what I believe to be the distinctive properties of nightmares.

BASIC VISUAL FEATURES

Like ordinary dreams, nightmares are visual scenarios composed of affect-laden images and simulations of events that are perceptually and thematically organized into a narrative typically concerning the self/dreamer. Like dreams, nightmares exhibit greater clarity in the foreground of the dreamer's attention, while background details are vaguely represented. No one knows whether nightmares are in color. My sense is that they are though they do not display a range of colors. This chromaticity is part of their emotional vividness.

EMOTIONAL ATMOSPHERE

Unlike dreams, nightmares often carry a sense of foreboding and uncertainty for the dreamer. There is an air of dread and threat lurking in the background settings of nightmare scenarios.

AUTOMATICITY

Dreams automatically occur during REM sleep for most people. Whether we like it or not, dreams happen to us. We cannot shut them off. The same is true for nightmares. Indeed, no one chooses to have a nightmare and when we find ourselves in a nightmare no one chooses to keep it going. If anything nightmares are more difficult to terminate than a dream. Once triggered a nightmare proceeds regardless of our wishes.

COGNITIVE CONTENT ELICITS THE EMOTIONAL CONTENT

My own feeling is that nightmare content is not made up in order to explain more primary emotional experiences. Instead the cognitive content of the nightmare is what elicits the emotional experience. When a nightmare experience is triggered the cognitive system is reset and biased to access memory images that elicit unpleasant memories. In addition the driving motive of a nightmare is the striving (discussed in the chapter on content) of the dreamer to protect the self. When the self comes under attack, fear and other unpleasant emotions are unleashed. Once unpleasant emotions are triggered they may prompt further retrieval of unpleasant memory images, and they in turn facilitate more extreme surges of negative emotions. The triggering event is the retrieval of an unpleasant memory image and it is this cognitive content that then sets the nightmare machine in motion.

If the nightmare were a mere after-the-fact confabulation or rationalization for a series of decontextualized and unpleasant emotions, there would be no reason to expect consistent content across nightmares. After all we have no reason to expect that unpleasant emotions would prompt similar narratives in every individual who experiences negative emotions.

CREATIVITY

Like dreams, nightmares are associated with great cognitive creativity as they involve the production of sometimes quite elaborate imagery, stories, and background plots to understand the central narrative. Nightmares are almost gothic in their plots, characters, and subplots. We will see in a later chapter that nightmares are the source of some great stories and works of art. Nightmares are not mere reflections of waking consciousness, nor are they mere catalogues of floating memory fragments. They take specialized input (e.g., the retrieval of an unpleasant memory image or an attack the self-representation) and subject that input to elaborate and hyperassociative narrative constructions that terrify the dreamer and then compel her to share the narrative with anyone who will listen in the waking world.

"COMPELLINGNESS"

While we are having a nightmare, we believe in the reality of what we are dreaming. When we wake from a nightmare we often say to ourselves, "Thank heaven it was only a dream!" Like dreams, nightmares compel belief, so nightmares must activate whatever cognitive system supports belief fixation. In addition, nightmares are intensely moving or emotional experiences. The dreamer feels compelled to reflect on them and to share them with others.

NARRATIVE FORM

Nightmares satisfy requirements for being well-formed narratives. Narratives are composed of a plot or plots with goals and subgoals of a group of actors who strive to achieve these goals in the context of a setting and a plot. Typically, what drives the story line is conflict between the actors concerning their goals. Most stories end with some resolution of the conflict. This may not be the case with nightmares—especially those that wake the dreamer. Narratives are particularly good vehicles for revealing character traits or dispositions of the actors depicted in the story. How does each actor respond when faced with a struggle or conflict? Narratives reveal character. Nightmare narratives are especially potent in this regard.

SELF-IDENTITY

One constant feature of nightmares is that the self comes under attack by very powerful forces and the attack is terrifying. Nightmares, therefore, concern the shaping of a self-identity and its reputation. When an individual shares a nightmare with a conspecific he or she is sharing information that is hard to fabricate or fake about his or her ability to cope with or bear horrifying events. Herman and Shows (1984) showed that college students (n = 295 subjects, aged from their twenties to seventies) recalled an average of ten dreams per month. Dream recall declined steadily with age to an average of about five per month in the seventy-year-old group. Even if we assume that only one out of five dreams is shared with at least one other person over the course of a month then we can conclude that dream sharing is a normal part of a person's social experience.

We have seen that nightmares are very compelling experiences that virtually demand to be shared. We can assume that when nightmares are shared with another they to some extent change the way that the other views the self of the dreamer. It's hard to imagine more positive appraisals of the dreamer after a nightmare is shared. On the contrary, the dark, unpleasant mood associated with the nightmare may contaminate the interaction. The listener may walk away from the encounter feeling worse off then before and feeling also the same sense of the dread that the dreamer felt during his nightmare. The listener then evaluates the dreamer in this light: The nightmare sharer is someone who has experienced and who holds particularly significant, scary, even momentous information. We cannot expect positive appraisals of such a person but we can expect that he or she will be feared and to some extent held in awe.

LACK OF METAPHOR

Unlike dreams, nightmares are not particularly metaphorical. Metaphors, according to Lakoff (2001), are "ways of understanding relatively abstract concepts in terms of those that are more concrete" (165). The abstract, however, is not being confronted in the nightmare. Instead the nightmare deals with primal emotional energies and unadorned and terrifying imagery. This is not to say that images and themes in dreams cannot represent emotional themes in the life of the individual, only that such representational content is reduced relative to ordinary dreams.

SELF-REFLECTIVENESS

In ordinary dreams we uncritically accept many incongruous and improbable happenings. There seems to be a lapse in self-reflectiveness in ordinary dreams. In nightmares, on the other hand, things are more complicated. While there does seem to be uncritical acceptance of wildly improbable characters/beings such as aliens from another planet, there is also a heightened awareness of self and the fact that it is under threat and must respond either by fleeing or taking other action. The nightmare focuses the spotlight on the self under (admittedly imaginary) threat.

MIND READING

Many ordinary dreams involve the dreamer in interaction with at least one other being or person. To interact with another involves attributions or inferences about the other. Most fundamentally, we assume that the other person has a mind and possesses beliefs, desires, and goals just as we do. Therefore, dreaming must involve the attribution of intentionality toward other dream characters. To attribute intentionality to agents is to assume that they are motivated by beliefs, desires, intentions, hopes, fears, deceit, etc.

In nightmares this kind of "mentalizing" is performed by the dreamer but in a distorted form. Specifically the dreamer is interested in only one thing—the malignant intentions of the imaginary monster who is threatening the dreamer. To narrow the focus of the mentalizing process, the dreamer must inhibit the tendency of the theory of mind mechanism to ascribe complex or conflicting motives to the other—in this case the "monster."

Another characteristic of nightmares that contributes to this collapse of normal functions of the theory of mind mechanism is that the major nightmare characters are unfamiliar beings. They are beings with anomalous minds, so it will be difficult if not impossible for the dreamer to ascribe normal mental states to these unfamiliar characters.

SUMMARY OF FORMAL FEATURES OF NIGHTMARES

I summarize the formal features of nightmares in Table 7.1.

Why do nightmares have the formal properties that they do? Why has Mother Nature produced these narratives that do not resolve; that place the self under extreme distress and threat, that enhance the self's negative or awesome reputation when shared, that block the self's normal mind-reading abilities; that place the self in vivid imagistic foregrounds with dark sinister and unfamiliar background settings and then sets a monster of some kind after the dreamer? In short, why place the self in a dangerous situation with a dangerous being and then strip the self of its cognitive and emotional tools normally used to deal with dangerous situations?

For example, if nightmares represent a simple failure of normal dreaming mechanisms then why should they have these formal properties? If nightmares are a breakdown of normal dreaming processes why place the self under extreme threat with fewer resources to deal with the threat? A breakdown of normal mechanisms would yield more random and various content. No, these formal features point toward functional aims of Mother Nature.

So then what function? It cannot be a mood–regulatory function. Nightmares are dismal ways to regulate mood. Why would placing the self under extreme duress with few tools to meet the distress help one to regulate mood?

In short, we find that the formal properties of nightmares place constraints on theorizing about the nightmare. Specifically, theoretical models of the nightmare must be consistent with formal cognitive properties of the nightmare including all those listed in Table 7.1.

The formal properties of dreams also make clear that nightmares (at least REM nightmares) are a different species of cognition than that which occurs in the waking state. While many of the properties of nightmares can also be identified in the waking state, they form a

Table 7.1
Formal Features of Nightmares

Features (as compared to ordinary dreams)	Comments
Vivid imagery but darkened menacing background	The visual foreground is vivid while background settings are dark, unfamiliar, scary, and menacing
Increased automaticity	Hard to voluntarily terminate a nightmare
Not confabulatory	Narrative driven by cognitive content not rationalizations of emotional content
Triggered by retrieval of negative memory	This is an inference from examination of formal properties … it needs to be experimentally verified
Enhanced creativity	Nightmares have more complex narratives than ordinary dreams
Hyperassociative	Only with respect to negative memories and emotions
Increased focus on "self" under threat	The dreamer has intense consciousness of self
Problematic narratives	Nightmares are well-formed narratives but may never end with a resolution of a conflict
Compellingness	Must be shared with one others after awakening
Sharer of nightmare held in awe by others	When nightmares are shared after awakening the person who shares a nightmare is considered as supremely burdened
Decreased metaphoric imagery	Nightmares are raw cognitively and emotionally
Failure of mind reading	Characters in nightmares are not considered to have ordinary minds

unified product when they coalesce in the dream state. While offline simulations do occur in the waking state, they are not obligatory and they do not typically involve intense emotion or scenes of major duress. Daydreams, instead, are focused on wishes, goals, and plans. They also are more often episodic and fleeting impressions rather than organized narratives.

We will explore these issues in the upcoming chapter on theoretical accounts of the nightmare.

Chapter 8

Theoretical Accounts of the Nightmare

In previous chapters, we examined existing knowledge about nightmares. We focused on cases of recurrent nightmares and cases of individuals who have frequent nightmares. We traced the development of the nightmare in children and its manifestation in adults. We examined the content of nightmares, biology of nightmares, and personality correlates of nightmares.

FACTS THAT MUST SERVE AS THE BASIS FOR NIGHTMARE THEORY

In this chapter, I will summarize reported facts about nightmares that any nightmare theory must address (see Table 8.1) and then discuss my own and others' theoretical accounts of nightmares and show how they lead to different predictions regarding the nature and treatment of nightmares.

Incidence and Content of Nightmares in Children

Nightmares are first reported by children and peak during late childhood and early adolescence. We compared children's nightmares with their ordinary dreams. We learned that children's dreams start out with a fair amount of "scenes" of passive interaction where the child witnesses some interaction with a parent or other important figure in the child's life. All too often children's dreams contain victimization themes, but these victimization scenarios decrease as children get older and their daily social interactions increase. Children's dreams also evidence high percentages of animals. Finally, children report hearing conversations and messages from adults, animals, imaginary figures,

Table 8.1
Facts That Must Serve as the Basis for Nightmare Theory

Characteristic	Comments
Incidence and content of nightmares in children	Nightmares are first reported by children and peak during late childhood and early adolescence. The combination of "victimization themes" and the presence of "supernatural agents" in children's dreams = nightmares.
Phenomenology and content of adult nightmares	Nightmares in adults have story lines that do not resolve; that place the self under extreme distress and threat, that enhance the self's negative emotions and images, that block the self's normal mind-reading abilities (it is difficult to understand the intentions of a space alien or monster for example); that place the self in vivid surrealistic foregrounds with dark sinister and unfamiliar background settings and then sets a monster of some kind after the self to hurt the self.
Emotional distress associated with nightmares	The presence of supernatural creatures in nightmares predicts the occurrence of a "major misfortune" in nightmares and thus predicts distress associated with nightmares
Personality characteristics of nightmare sufferers	"Thin boundaries", creativity, introversion, and perhaps a borderline schizotypal disposition
Nightmares and REM biology	Highly activated amygdala; deactivated dorso-prefrontal cortex; ANS storms; interactions with NREM delta activity

monsters, and counterintuitive supernatural agents in their dreams. It is this latter element—the presence and actions of supernatural agents including monsters—in dreams that distinguishes nightmares from ordinary dreams in childhood. Children who experience frequent nightmares may also be particularly open to belief in imaginary friends and supernatural agents.

Phenomenology and Content of Adult Nightmares

The situation is similar in some respects to adults who report nightmares. Adults also experience a high level of victimization themes and the presence of unnatural and malignant agents in both ordinary dreams and nightmares. Nightmares in adults have story lines that do not resolve, that place the self under extreme distress and threat, that enhance the self's negative emotions and images, that block the self's normal mind-reading abilities (it is difficult to understand the intentions of a space alien or monster for example), that place the self in vivid surrealistic foregrounds with dark sinister and unfamiliar emotional atmospheres and background settings, and that set monsters of some kind after the self to inflict harm.

The most consistent content difference between nightmares and garden variety dreams in adults is that nightmares contain the "unfamiliar" and the threatening. Characters are less familiar than in normal dreams; friends and family show up less often than in normal dreams; and the settings in which the dream action occurs is unfamiliar. In these unfamiliar settings aggressive interactions are very common. The sense of striving is extremely high in nightmares as well.

Emotional Distress Associated with Nightmares

The nightmare elements typically shared with others are the following: The dreamer finds himself in very strange and unfamiliar settings where there are high levels of aggression and threat and the dreamer is striving after some goal—presumably safety or escape but that has yet to be shown to be the case. As in the case of children's nightmares, the presence of a supernatural or unnatural being or monster in adult dreams is particularly salient. When such a supernatural agent appears in a dream it is more likely to be called a nightmare by the dreamer and a major "misfortune" is more likely to occur in the dream. The presence of supernatural agents in nightmares, therefore, predicts the degree of a nightmare's emotional distress.

The link between unnatural creatures and the occurrence of a "major misfortune" in nightmares may be extremely significant clinically as the presence of misfortune in dreams is very likely a causative factor in the emotional distress associated with the nightmare. The distress associated with some nightmares best predicts daytime clinical disturbances.

Personality Characteristics of Nightmare Sufferers

We have also learned that those adults who report frequent nightmares are a special group of people characterized by thin boundaries,

creativity, introversion, and perhaps a borderline schizotypal disposition. This ominous phrase simply means that these individuals pay
more attention to "intrapsychic" events than do other people and give
greater weight to fantasy, imagination, and ideas than do other people.
Of course, when one gives too much weight to fantasy over reality,
this tendency may become destructive. It is therefore irresponsible to
romanticize the schizotypal personality trait. Nevertheless, the correla-
tion between nightmare frequency and the schizotypal personality
trait may be due to the ability to deeply enjoy and appreciate fantasy
rather than to the inability to distinguish between the real and the
unreal.

PROPOSED FUNCTIONAL THEORY OF NIGHTMARES

Given all of these facts concerning nightmares, nightmares cannot be
considered mere random breakdowns of the normal dream or sleep
system. Why should nightmares occur at all? Does it make any sense to
suppose that nightmares might have a function? Just because their content and form is not random does not mean that they *must* have a function. Nevertheless, consistent form and content *suggest* design, and
design is one of the diagnostic criteria for a functional adaptation. Can
nightmares therefore be considered functional or even an adaptation?

Relation of Functional Design to Adaptation

Let us discuss for a moment the idea of an adaptation. Evolutionary
biologists and psychologists agree that to demonstrate that a trait is
adaptive there must be evidence that the trait exhibits "functional
design." What is functional design? Functional design refers to the
thing that features or working parts of a trait accomplish. If the features
of a trait seem to work together to produce a common effect that benefits the organism in some way, then that trait exhibits functional design.
A bird's wing exhibits functional design. Its features are designed for
insulation and flight. When activated, wings allow birds to fly, so they
confer a benefit of movement. When the bird is stationary, wings provide insulation and so confer additional benefit on birds. The individual
features of a wing work together to produce a benefit: flight and/or
insulation.

Or take a man-made artifact that we know was functionally
designed, a key, for example. Even if we did not know that keys were
in fact designed by human beings for a purpose we would be able to
deduce design by examining its properties. A key exhibits functional
design because its shape makes it manipulable—it fits with the hand

and fingers of an average person. The key's teeth interlock exactly into the gears of a lock and when the key is used in the proper manner it reliably turns the gears, releases the lock, and opens the door.

An adaptive trait is likely to be more complex than a nonadapted trait given that its features must mesh with and address some problem for an organism in the environment. The greater the specific fit of the trait to the problem the more likely that the trait was designed by natural selection to address that problem. The lesser the fit, and the lack of evidence of functional design, the more likely that the trait in question was not an adaptation but was instead a mere chance association or by-product from some other functional complex. By-products in turn could arise from mutation, or drift.

It is important to point out that evidence of functional design does not mean that the trait in question is always going to appear functional or create a "happy" organism. Because of their complexity, adaptations are often costly to operate. They require that the organism give something, expend some effort or energy to keep the trait operating in good condition. The brain for example, requires a tremendous metabolic investment on the part of the animal who "chooses" to build a brain—the more complex the brain the greater the metabolic investment and the greater the chance that other parts of the animal go without. The brain in turn will create all kinds of opportunities and all kinds of new costs for the animal.

Even very basic adaptations may not necessarily appear to be good for the animal. Fever, for example, creates a very uncomfortable organism that can barely move around or defend itself. Yet fever saves lives by making it difficult for pathogens to thrive in the host. Fever has high metabolic and operational costs—it speeds up the metabolic machinery of the host causing the body to utilize resources at a 20 percent faster rate than normal. The higher the fever, the more effective it is but at higher temperatures fever can produce delirium and physiologic collapse. Even at lower temps fevers can kill sperm and so produce temporary sterility in males. Here we have an adaptation that directly produces a short-term impairment in reproductive fitness.

Similarly, nightmares may appear to cause dysfunction but they may nevertheless be an adaptation if it can be shown that they exhibit functional design and that they benefit the individual (or more precisely that they benefited our ancestors).

As far as I can tell no one has ever looked for the benefits conferred on an individual by the nightmares he or she is having! This should not be surprising. It is counterintuitive to think that nightmares are functional in any way—yet that is what I am suggesting is the case. Nightmares are functional because they are adaptations—they benefited our ancestors.

Effects of Nightmares on Social Behaviors

Despite a paucity of studies on effects of nightmares on social behaviors of nightmare sufferers, there is evidence that nightmares have some beneficial effects for the individual who reports nightmares. First, although nightmares are associated with negative emotions, the sharing of a nightmare with others may have an effect on others that ultimately benefits the dreamer. For example, listeners may attempt to help the dreamer in some way or the listener may hold the individual in some respect or even awe. Nightmares are frightening experiences and to survive a nightmare and live to tell about it may elicit respect from others. Though less true in modern society this is what I believe occurred among our ancestral populations.

In conditions of tribal living before the advent of evidence-based science or modern comforts hearing about a nightmare would have been tantamount to listening to a terrifying religious vision. The individual telling the tale would have been treated as marked or sacred in some sense. This heightened status would have conferred both costs and benefits to the individual, with the benefits outweighing the costs, else the genes or proclivity towards experiencing and sharing nightmares would not have been passed down to present generations. Notice that the receipt of benefits depends upon the sharing of the nightmare vision with others. People who kept their nightmares to themselves would only experience the costs and the distress of the vision, not the social benefits. This latter observation suggests that nightmare sufferers should evidence relatively high verbal abilities; unfortunately, I know of no such evidence yet reported.

Triggers of Nightmares

To further the case that nightmares are functional and that they addressed some fitness-linked problems or opportunities for our ancestors it would help to show that nightmares can be reliably elicited under specific triggering conditions that resemble or replicate the conditions that our ancestors faced when they "decided" to share nightmares. Evidence that nightmares are preferentially and reliably elicited by specific and selective triggers and not others may provide further evidence of functional design. We know trauma can trigger nightmares but trauma-related nightmares are atypical nightmares that often occur outside of REM sleep. We want to know what triggers the more typical REM nightmares.

Although I know of no controlled studies on the issue, anxiety over social relationships appears to be a reliable trigger of nightmares in modern populations. *Most specifically anxiety about one's own identity or sense of self is a reliable trigger of nightmares.* What about for our ancestors? The available evidence, reviewed in a previous chapter, from studies of premodern tribal cultures, suggests that nightmare sharing was linked with changes in identity and social status. For example, a child who shared a nightmare in some compelling way might be marked for later training to become a shaman, with the nightmare serving as evidence for the child's worthiness for such training. Similarly in adults, special dreams or nightmares in which the dreamer was visited and gifted by a spirit being would have identified that individual as a spiritual specialist. If, instead, an individual reported being attacked in a nightmare by the spirit being, the dreamer could gain enhanced prestige as long as the dreamer emerged from the attack intact or even better off. The dream experience was taken as evidence that the individual could handle battles with malevolent spirit beings.

Adaptive Function of Nightmares

As suggested in earlier chapters, a potential adaptive function of nightmares was to provide an opportunity for the dreamer to change his or her social identity and status, and to enhance his or her prestige by sharing the nightmare in a compelling way. You cannot share nightmares in a compelling way unless you really experience them and you cannot really experience and gain practice at sharing them unless they occur on a regular basis—thus the phenomenon of recurrent nightmare sufferers. The aim was to provide evidence that the individual interacted in a successful way with the spirit world. Dreams and nightmares were considered reliable and unfakeable evidence, since they were involuntary products of the mind or soul.

Role of Prestige in Development of Self and in Evolution of Human Societies

I have presented arguments for the claim that the sharing of nightmares among ancestral populations enhanced the prestige of the individual sharing the nightmare. As noted above and in previous chapters, the sharing of dreams and nightmares among premodernized tribal cultures was common and did indeed enhance the prestige of the sharer, particularly if the dream or nightmare vision was shared compellingly. Why was social prestige so important to our ancestors? It still is important to us of course.

Prestige is central to the evolution of social order in human societies. Individuals who gain prestige are positioned to become tribal leaders and to thereby increase their share of the resources in the tribe. The sense of self is built on the sense of being valued by others. Evidence of being valued by others comes from two sources: kin and non-kin. When one is loved by kin, then one knows one is valued by them. What about non-kin? Prestige is the best evidence that one is valued by non-kin.

Prestige fundamentally derives from what has been called "information and resource holding potential." Individuals who can convince others that they know something important or have access to something important will automatically receive deferential treatment. If a low-status individual gains an opportunity to observe a high-status individual over a period of time and establishes the reliability of the high-status individual's "information", then the high status individual will receive more resources. One of the crucial factors that confers prestige on an individual is that person's ability to convince others that he or she has something important to share. As the capacity for language-based communication evolved in humans, good storytelling abilities and rhetorical skills became prime signals of information-holding capacity and thus of prestige. For example, a tribal leader who could give a good speech before the tribal assembly was given deference in tribal councils. The greater the evidence that a given speaker has special knowledge or is holding special information of some kind, the more prestigious and charismatic that individual becomes. The sharing of a terrifying and awe-inspiring nightmare could convince others of one's special abilities and knowledge, particularly with respect to dealing with the realm of the supernatural. Thus, charismatic teachers would become particularly successful.

There is abundant anthropological and archeological evidence (Mumford 1966; Rappaport 1999; Weber 1946; Durkheim 1995) that points to the generative potential of charismatic teachers (and by implication, students) for the roots of cooperation, particularly in the forms of religious ritual. The religious behaviors of premodern tribal peoples often involved identification of individuals who were thought to possess charisma, manna, or power and their subsequent elevation to shaman status or to leadership roles in the tribal councils.

Given the fact that the shaman had to be a person of exceptional intelligence or social abilities, the generation of dream and nightmare-inspired tribal religious practices and mythologies would theoretically enhance cooperation among individuals within the group and thus increase its overall fitness.

Role of the Dream/Nightmare in the Skill Set of Spiritual Specialists

What was the role of the dream specialist, spirit specialist, or the shaman? Could or did the shamans teach their fellows anything worthwhile or did they simply enhance levels of superstitious nonsense among ancestral populations? Why would they persist through the modern era in so many societies if they were causing harm to their kinsmen? Winkelman (2000) and others (Eliade 1951/1972; Harner 1982; Krippner 2000; McClenon 1997a, 1997b) have suggested that shamans and related religious specialists were able to heal real ailments and illnesses via the production of trance in their patients. Shamans helped ancestral populations at the price of increasing the genes that allowed for production of trance in individuals.

Theoretically, the ability to learn from individuals such as the shamans, who display anomalous or superior cognitive abilities, would lead to increased chances for obtaining better resources and thus increased reproductive success. Natural selection will therefore favor development of special propensities to seek, detect, predict, and become receptive to extraordinary mental qualities such as the ability to go into and to produce trance in others.

Signals Used to Identify Supranormal Abilities and Exceptional Individuals

How did our ancestors choose the best teachers? While simple observation of "the one who has the resources" will factor into such an assessment; better assessments, particularly for long-lived social primates with prolonged juvenile dependency periods like ourselves, demand identification of the one who will *consistently be successful* in acquiring resources over long periods of time.

One way to identify a potential shaman or religious specialist or leader would be to choose someone already identified as such by others. Once again prestige and reputation become important. But reputation is not enough. Reputation needs to be backed up by information about the individual that is reliable and cannot be faked. If you saw someone treated with extreme deference and ritual displays of praise and homage you would conclude that the person was probably an exceptionally gifted person. Thus, *ritual itself* would advertise the identification of exceptional individuals. Another way to identify exceptional individuals was whether or not they had experienced events that would prepare them for the leadership role they would one day assume. In both children and adults the experience of terrifying dreams might mark the individual out for special consideration. In adolescents and adults the ability to speak compellingly about his dream visions in social interactions would mark the individual off as a potential leader.

In this way, dream visions would intersect with forces driving the evolution of speech and language functions. Linguists have asserted that many of the formal properties of language use flow from the principle of relevance (Sperber and Wilson, 1995, 2002). This basic principle of human communication states that in order for a speaker's contribution to a conversation to be well-formed or felicitous, it should pertain to or add information to the matter at hand or to the topic currently under discussion. The speaker's contributions should have high information content where the value of the information is measured in terms of relevance to the listener's concerns. Dessalles (1998) summarizes the relevance principle this way: "An utterance must either refer to a problematic situation or attempt to reduce the problematicity of a situation" for the listeners (133). If a speaker can bring to a conversation information that is valuable to the listeners, he will gain prestige and deference from the listeners. Thus, getting access to valuable information and sharing it in a relevant and compelling way was vitally important to our ancestors as it was a route to prestige and leadership.

Evolution of Language Skills, Dreaming Skills, and Reputation

The information-driven component of the relevance criterion presumably created some degree of competition among speakers allowing relevance to become linked to speaker quality. The person who could acquire the greatest quantity of relevant information would thereby increase his prestige, the number of his followers, and the number of cooperative alliances he could form. Because relevance became linked to "resource-holding potential" the competition to attain relevance likely became and remained intense in early human communities. Relevant information had to be updated and enhanced constantly, precisely in order to remain relevant and to stay ahead of the competition. Information derived from dreams, visions, and nightmares was relevant information since it concerned the healing, religious, ritual, and mythopoetic practices of the tribe. Individuals would therefore require impressive dream experience and dream-interpretation abilities. These in turn would contribute to the tribe's mythic and religious lore—a lore that all tribal members had to learn.

Although the relevance constraint likely led to greater overall and generalized forms of intelligence in early humans (particularly among leaders), the relevance criterion likely led to specialized forms of expertise as well. The relevance criterion is inherently context-sensitive. For information to be relevant it must help solve a specific problem in a specific place and time. Take for example, the problem of illness. There is a child who is feverish, dehydrated, and dying. You could be highly intelligent with large stores of tribal lore and wisdom and even be considered a tribal leader, but if you could not help ameliorate the child's illness, your contributions to discussions about the child would be considered irrelevant. The lowliest tribesman with an herbal remedy or a shaman with his terrifying visions, incantations, and ability to induce trance would possess greater prestige in this situation than would the tribal leader. The link between technical intelligence, relevance, and prestige would therefore make its contribution to the rise of such intelligence among early humans. Nightmares are "relevant" because they are compelling.

Once listeners used relevance as a factor in identifying persons of quality, relevance likely became a criterion people used when deciding with whom they would affiliate, cooperate, and follow. As relevance grew in importance so did rhetoric or the ability to display relevance in an eloquent speech, story, or communication. Pursuit of information (and with it relevance) created competition among would-be leaders. The competition was to become the most relevant person in the tribe. Individuals who could demonstrate the greatest intelligence, the greatest eloquence, the greatest story-telling ability, or the greatest technical know-how would possess the most relevant information content and therefore prestige. He who could best convey valuable information most efficiently and/or eloquently to listeners would attain high status and prestige. To stay on top (to stay relevant) however, the leader would have to update his informational sources and content continuously. In the case of shamans and religious specialists, only those with the most compelling dreams and visions and the greatest intelligence could succeed consistently.

The relevance criterion imposes strong constraints on the very structure of language itself. It says that messages must convey an optimal amount of (relevant) information in a given unit of time if they are to satisfy the relevance constraint. To do so, language displays a structure dependence so that listeners can quickly identify the agent and patient role in a sentence. The basic units of a language are the information packets we call sentences. Each sentence uses thematic roles or slots to reveal who did what to whom. A listener who has learned a particular language knows that certain types of information (e.g., agents) come before other types of information (patients). This, "who did what to whom" is the kind of information that a social species like ours would find so valuable—so relevant. At some point in the emergence of anatomically modern humans, relevance became linked with prestige. That link both facilitated the rise of specialists including specialists in dreams and dream interpretation or individuals others would defer to, and shaped the evolution of the language faculty itself.

Storytelling Skills and Prestige or Reputation

I believe I have offered a plausible answer to the question of what sort of benefit something as unpleasant as a nightmare could possibly confer on our ancestors. It helped particular individuals address the problem or opportunity of acquiring prestige but only if the dreamer was willing to share the nightmare with others. To share the dream visions with others in a compelling way, the dreamer had to obey the relevance constraint and had to become a fluent speaker and a good storyteller. If he became a specialist in religious and healing practices, he had to develop yet other abilities such inducing trance states in others, or telling amazing and compelling stories. For that he needed to acquire yet more prestige for which dreams and nightmares would act as a veritable treasure trove of new images, information, spirit helpers, and other affect-laden and social elements potentially useful in healing rituals.

Biological Contributions to Signaling "Quality"

So far we have developed an evolutionary approach to nightmares and nightmare content but we now need to consider the role REM played in this evolutionary scenario. The social pressure to acquire prestige made dreaming potentially useful if the individual was willing to share dreams with others. Given that the source of dreams and nightmares was REM sleep, REM sleep itself would indirectly be influenced by the individual's need to signal and impress others. How did the social context within which dreaming and nightmares developed influence REM physiology? Presumably, those individuals whose physiology was more able to produce REM dreams that were compelling and relevant for ancestral populations were favored. Gradually REM sleep physiology became more efficient at producing bizarre or compelling visionary experiences. In short, REM sleep itself was recruited to become a signaling device—a device to produce costly, unfakeable, and compelling signals that could be shared socially.

Nightmares first and foremost are a species of REM dreams. Not all dreams and not all of the content of REM-related dreams are due to REM physiology alone (Nielsen 2000; Solms 2000). Nevertheless, it is likely that a significant portion of the content of REM-related dreams, especially nightmare content, is a direct result of various components of REM physiology (Dement and Kleitman 1957a, 1957b; Goodenough 1991; Hobson, Pace-Schott, and Stickgold 2000; Schonbar 1961). For example, when ponto-geniculo-occipital (PGO) spikes occur during a REM episode, one is more likely to get dream reports that contain rapid plot shifts and greater amounts of bizarre imagery. In addition, the limbic brain activation patterns that occur during REM very likely account for dreams containing emotionally charged social interactions (Maquet et al. 1996). In short, it is not unreasonable to treat dream reports that occur in temporal relation with REM episodes as part and parcel of REM physiology itself. To construct a full theory of the nightmare it is reasonable to bring in an account of REM physiology and to try to see elements of REM physiology as contributions to a signaling behavior.

COSTLY SIGNALING THEORY (CST)

If nightmares were used by our ancestors to signal special abilities or characteristics, then the biology producing those nightmares might also exhibit some evidence of signaling capacity. One approach to understanding nightmare phenomenology and REM physiology as signaling functions draws on that part of evolutionary theory known as Costly Signaling Theory (CST) (Bliege-Bird and Smith 2005; Bradbury and Vehrencamp 1998; Grafen 1990; Maynard-Smith and Harper 2003; Zahavi 1975; Zahavi and Zahavi 1997). CST is concerned primarily with understanding animal signaling behaviors. The basic idea is simple: For signals between two parties to be workable or believable by both parties they must be reliably unfakeable. Only signals that can't be faked can be trusted to carry honest information. Unfakeable signals are those signals that are metabolically, motorically, or behaviorally difficult to produce (costly). Their production costs or costliness is their certification of honesty. Costly signals are preferred by animals under conditions where the animals are capable of deception but require reliable and honest signaling between the parties (e.g., between the two sexes during mating season).

Costly signaling theory or CST first emerged in the context of sexual selection theory (Zahavi 1975). Sexual selection theory suggests that some sex-related traits such as large breasts in human females may have evolved because they signal reproductive fitness. Large breasts might indicate that the woman in question has more than enough metabolic resources available to handle both the necessary production of milk to raise young *and* even more—an overabundance of milk for young.

Other traits such as large antlers might indicate the presence of parasite-resistance genes in a reindeer or an elk. Large antlers in effect advertise the presence of these "good genes." This, in turn, creates selective pressures for displaying and enhancing such advertisements. Males without the parasite-resistant gene will be unable to display large antlers, as they will not be able to metabolically grow and maintain the antlers without paying a metabolic cost that in turn will make them more vulnerable to parasite infestation. Thus, large antlers, although costly to produce and thus an expensive handicap, nevertheless constitute an honest signal of good genes, and thus, honest communication between potential mates will be possible. In short, costly signaling makes communication possible under adverse conditions, that is, conditions in which the parties have partially conflicting interests.

According to CST, a signal is defined as a behavior, expression, or phenotype produced by one individual (the signaler) that aims to influence the behavior of a second individual (the receiver). A shared nightmare certainly fits this definition, especially if the person, say a child, who shares the nightmare is then marked off as a potential candidate for leadership or shaman roles within the tribe (as demonstrated above and in previous chapters). Extensive modeling and empirical studies in CST (Bliege-Bird and Smith 2005; Bradbury and Vehrencamp 1998; Grafen 1990; Maynard-Smith and Harper 2003; Zahavi 1975; Zahavi and Zahavi 1997) have demonstrated that any trait at all can function as a costly signal as long as it: 1) can convey reliable information about inter-individual variation in the underlying quality being advertised and 2) imposes a cost on the signaler that is linked to the quality being advertised. Certainly nightmares satisfy condition two: They impose a cost on the individual who experiences them which is measured in the level of emotional distress the individual undergoes both during the nightmare and afterwards when images linger. What about condition one? Do nightmares convey reliable information about inter-individual variation in the underlying quality being advertised by nightmares? Let us suppose that the quality being advertised is "resilience" or the ability to bear and get through distress. If that is the case then nightmares satisfy the first condition as well. Many other signals are designed to do the same. Trials of initiation, scarifications, and a number of psychological traits such as fortitude, patience in suffering, stories about overcoming trials and suffering also signal the ability to bear and overcome distress. Accounts of nightmares can do the same. In short, nightmares have the characteristics that allow them to be used in a CST game. That should not be surprising; many traits have such characteristics.

Under conditions of genetic conflict (we will discuss genetic conflict more thoroughly in another chapter), the two parties in a communication game may be motivated to transmit nonveridical, deceptive information in order to obtain an advantage. If one individual can gain an advantage from another by concealing information or by sending misleading information, he or she will do so. In the short run, at least, using deception would sometimes have advantages. But fundamentally, communication requires that signals be honest and reliable, at least on average. If they were not reliable, the intended receivers would evolve to ignore them. Costly signals appear to have evolved in order to guarantee the reliability and honesty of a communication system. Communication will be stable when the signaler and receiver pursue strategies that together comprise a signaling equilibrium such that neither party gains from unilateral defection to deception or change in strategy. To keep both signaler and receiver in the game, hard-to-fake signals must be utilized and hard-to-fake signals are those that cost something to the signaler, a cost that deceivers are unwilling to bear.

Humans, of course, engage in a range of signaling behaviors, but can REM sleep, dreams, and nightmares plausibly be considered signaling behaviors? Human signaling behaviors include everything from speech and language exchanges to emotional displays, body-language (e.g., clothes, postures, tattoos, etc.) and other nonverbal behaviors. My basic claim with respect to nightmare phenomenology is that nightmare experiences and content can function as signals that can influence a person's reputation. The signal in question is that the dreamer or nightmare sufferer can bear distress and thus must have good genes. How do nightmares signal that the sufferer can bear distress?

Dreams and nightmares can also facilitate production of signals when they produce some daytime effect such as a memory or a mood (or both) or a behavior that communicates a message to an observer. A person, for example, who awakens from a disturbing dream or a nightmare may behave differently during the night and during the day from a person who awakens from, for example, an erotic dream or a bizarre dream. Many dreams, even unremembered dreams create background moods and behavioral dispositions that linger through much of the subsequent daytime period (Kramer 1993). While it is difficult to demonstrate that unrecalled dreams can influence daytime mood and behavior, we know that depriving a person of his or her REM/dream sleep can significantly alter daytime mood states, at least in some vulnerable individuals (see Bonnet 2005; Dinges, Rogers, and Baynard 2005; Moorcroft 2003; Vogel 1999).

It is easier to demonstrate that recalled dreams can influence daytime mood and behavior. We know from personal experience that this is the case. A bad dream or nightmare can color one's mood throughout the day. Most people have had such experiences. Kuiken and Sikora (1993) for example, found that 13 percent of 168 respondents to a questionnaire on dream recall reported that at least twelve times in the past year, they had had dreams that significantly influenced their daytime mood; 25 percent of respondents indicated that they had had such dreams at least four times in the past year, and 44 percent at least twice in the past year. Like any other mood state, these dream-related dispositional and mood states, we claim, can be "read" by observers as informational about the internal states and quality of the dreamer. Dreams can also affect daytime mood and behavior by being shared with others.

I contend that many of the signals produced by the nightmare can be and should be construed as costly signals—emotions or mental simulations that produce daytime behavioral dispositions that are costly to the dreamer and that signal "quality" (or ability to bear distress/resilience) in the dreamer (McNamara and Szent-Imrey 2007). For example, often the dreamer will appear in the nightmare as handicapped in some way (i.e., under attack, being chased, having difficulty escaping attack, grappling with supernatural beings, etc.). The dreamer, during waking life, is then influenced by the carry-over effect of the unpleasant dream content. The informational and affective content of the dream creates a mental state in the dreamer that operates during the daytime to facilitate signaling behaviors. The subtle signaling effect might be via display of the intense emotions or physical demeanor that had first appeared in the dream.

Let's take the example of an individual living in an ancestral hunter-gatherer tribe, who has a nightmare involving a spirit attack. This individual awakens from the nightmare still having difficulty catching his breath and so forth. When that individual then carries on with his day, he will surely be influenced by what he considered, nay what he experienced, as an attack on his life by a spirit being. After a while he may share the nightmare with others and revel in the fact that he survived the attack and thus his social prestige will be enhanced accordingly. First, the mood induced by the nightmare-induced distress of having been attacked is subtly conveyed to others in the tribe. This mood is a costly signal which is being conveyed to others. When the nightmare is shared with others, these others then begin to understand why the dreamer was behaving as if he had been attacked. The information spreads around the tribe that the individual had survived an attack by a malicious spirit and his prestige is correspondingly enhanced. Note that it is crucial that the individual ensure that the dream/nightmare is interpreted in such a way that is favorable to him. If the attack dream is interpreted in a negative way then he will be marked as someone controlled by malevolent spirits and his prestige will be correspondingly diminished. Thus, dream interpretation becomes a political enterprise and a focus of social competition. This competition will fuel the production of ever more costly forms of dreaming and signaling.

A costly signaling approach to nightmare expression is broadly consistent with both the formal properties of nightmares and with dream content (discussed in previous chapters). It predicts that dream recall will vary as a function of communicative need. Typical dreams that are recalled and shared are like mild nightmares. They involve unpleasant emotions and scenes that place the dreamer in a victim role or under some handicap (naked, disoriented, without identification, unable to move, etc.).

While REM sleep may be in a position to influence a person's waking mood state (via production of emotional states and dreams), it is not at all clear which REM period is most operative in that influence. We have seen that nightmares generally occur in the later REM periods. Most healthy individuals will experience between three and five REM periods per night. As the night progresses, activation patterns become more intense, culminating in the long dreams characteristic of the final REM period of the night. The early REM researchers, who were influenced by psychoanalytic theory, presented evidence that all REM episodes contribute to the emotional processing that occurs during sleep the results of which are summarized in the final REM episode of the night (French and Fromme 1964; Trosman et al. 1960).

Trosman and colleagues (1960), and French and Fromme (1964) suggested that dreams at the beginning of the night would announce an emotional wish or emotional conflict that dreams later in the night would pick up and work with in an attempt to contain or resolve the emotional conflict. These investigators presented several case studies involving collection of dreams across the night that seemed to support the claim.

In addition to the satisfaction of formal criteria for application of CST, there is *prima facie* evidence that REM sleep dreams and physiology participate in some sort of signaling function for the individual. First, REM biology is associated with those paradigmatic human signaling displays—the emotions. The intense activation of the limbic and amygdalar regions (Maquet and Franck 1997) in the absence of dorsal prefrontal inhibitory effects (Hobson, Stickgold, and Pace-Schott 1998) during REM ensures intense emotionality during and after a REM episode. In short, the brain region responsible for emotional signaling during the waking period undergoes intense and repeated activation during REM. This fact is consistent with an emotional signaling function for REM and nightmares.

REM-related nightmares are eminently capable of handicapping an individual—a frequent working definition of a costly signal. REM biology is demonstrably—even extravagantly—costly. This costly physiology makes sense if one assumes that its purpose is to handicap the individual. Although this claim sounds paradoxical, much in biology is paradoxical. The aim is to produce enough of a handicap to convince the receiver that the sender is honest, but too much of a handicap will only impair the individuals from functioning effectively. Thus, CST theory predicts that REM biology should to some extent have negative, even injurious, effects on the health (but not the reproductive fitness) of the individual. There is in fact abundant evidence that this is so (McNamara 2004a).

We have now presented an evolutionary approach to nightmare production. We linked the production and sharing of nightmares to strategic attempts at enhancing the dreamer's prestige. We then showed that REM physiology itself, particularly late REM episodes, facilitate production of brain states that allow for signaling of emotional states during the daytime. REM-related signaling in turn was shown to be of a particular kind—costly—as REM-related dreams and nightmares are, of course, unpleasant and terrifying experiences. The individual who experienced and shared recurrent nightmares in ancestral contexts (of small tribal hunter-gather groups, for example) would signal his ability to consistently bear emotional and physical distress, including tremendous and terrifying visions that carried potentially vital information for the tribe. Individuals sharing their nightmares would, if done correctly, gain social prestige, which would translate into enhanced reproductive fitness.

How does this theoretical approach compare to other theories of the nightmare? Most other theories of the nightmare suggest that nightmares involve some sort of breakdown of normal mood regulatory functions of the dream.

FREUD'S VIEW OF NIGHTMARES

Freud's original dream theory postulated that the dream helped the sleeping person stay asleep as it allowed the person to hallucinate satisfaction of desires and wishes while still asleep. Thus dreams protected sleep. Nightmares were hard to understand from these original Freudian premises concerning dream function. Beginning with Freud himself, various attempts have been made to argue that nightmares are really wishes, but masochistic in content and thus just like any other dream. They function to satisfy a wish. But this approach seems forced and nonfalsifiable. Given the fact that many people awaken from a nightmare it seems hard to argue that nightmares protect sleep via hallucinated wish fulfillment.

FISHER'S VIEW OF NIGHTMARES

In one of the earliest theories of REM dreaming as mood regulation, Fisher and colleagues (1970) noted that nightmares occurring spontaneously in the laboratory were characterized by low or even absent autonomic nervous system (ANS) activation (heart rate, respiratory rate, etc.) during REM sleep. One would think that reduced ANS activation would diminish chances for a nightmare, but Fisher and his colleagues argued that the lowered ANS he documented in some REM nightmares paradoxically suggested that the normal function of REM was to "desomatisize" or decouple ANS activation from emotional surges during REM. Nightmares result when the anxiety exceeds a certain threshold and the REM desomatization mechanism breaks down, allowing autonomic activation to occur. Yet Fisher and his colleagues themselves documented cases of nightmares where no ANS activation occurred.

KRAMER'S VIEW OF NIGHTMARES

Kramer (1993) too believed that dreaming evidenced mood regulatory functions, but he and his colleagues argued that ANS and brain activation increased across the night until some emotional conflict was adequately addressed in the dreams associated with late REM periods. As in the case of Hartmann's contextualizing images, Kramer argued that dream content—especially in the form of various characters—could contain rising emotional levels as the emotional conflict is processed throughout successive REM periods. Nightmares would represent a breakdown in this mood regulatory mechanism.

HARTMANN'S VIEW OF NIGHTMARES

Hartmann et al. (1987) pointed out that nightmare patients exhibit certain personality characteristics that might help us to understand nightmares. He reported that frequent nightmare sufferers were characterized by "thin boundaries" such that they did not discriminate internal from external events as strongly as did individuals with thick boundaries. They therefore experienced more difficulty screening out irrelevant cognitive and emotional intrusions which, during dreaming, can lead to nightmares.

Hartmann has proposed that nightmares serve the function of contextualizing, or framing, overwhelming emotional experiences which can then be subjected to processes of emotional integration. For example, a dream image of an oncoming tidal wave may turn an overwhelming emotion of helplessness and fear into a vivid image that can be worked within the dream. The CST approach to nightmare content described above is entirely consistent with the presence in dreams and nightmares of images and metaphors that depict emotional states in a way that facilitates use of the dream by the dreamer for individual and social aims.

NIELSEN AND LEVIN'S VIEW OF NIGHTMARES

Recently, Nielsen and Levin (2007) have proposed an affect and network model (AND) of nightmare production. It stipulates that nightmares result from dysfunction in a network of affective processes that, during normal dreaming, serves the adaptive function of *fear memory extinction*.

It is interesting that most extant theories of the nightmare assume a mood regulatory function for dreams and then dysfunction of this to account for the nightmare. If we consult Table 8.1 consisting of the list of the characteristics that any theoretical account of nightmares must address we see that these mood regulatory theories of the dream certainly address many of these characteristics. Presumably nightmares occur in children more frequently because they are not practiced mood regulators. Thin boundaries make it more difficult to regulate mood and so forth. What these mood-regulatory approaches do not account for is why the presence of supernatural agents should be so consistently associated with the nightmare.

THEORY AND TREATMENT STRATEGIES

How does all this theorizing help to treat the distress associated with REM nightmares? Two things might reduce nightmare frequency, intensity, and distress: 1) a reduction in activation levels of the amygdala, and 2) a focus on working cognitively and imagistically with the content variables ("supernatural agents" and "misfortunes") of nightmares that are linked with nightmare distress. Cognitive-behavioral techniques such as monitoring, relaxation, and exposure therapy can accomplish the latter and pharmacologic agents the former. A combination of pharmacologic and cognitive-behavioral treatment interventions are likely to be most powerful.

Several cognitive-behavioral techniques are effective in decreasing nightmare frequency. Monitoring nightmares, relaxation therapy, and exposure exercises decreased nightmare frequency and the nightmare induced fear (Miller and Di Palato 1983). Exposure treatment typically includes the following steps. The patient is given a self-help manual and instructed to write down the nightmare after awakening and to re-experience it in imagination. The re-experiencing under controlled conditions is thought to enable the patient to learn that he has some control over the frightening imagery he experiences in nightmares.

To supplement exposure exercises and to increase the patient's sense of mastery over the frightening nightmare content, the therapist can utilize cognitive restructuring techniques. With these restructuring techniques the patient takes the story line or the images (or both) of the nightmare and rewrites it, sometimes literally. I would recommend taking the images of the supernatural beings and to work with them as it is these images that apparently carry most potency in terms of being linked to the distress within the dream itself.

Krakow et al. (2000) studied effects of imagery rehearsal therapy (IRT) on sexual assault survivors with PTSD and post-traumatic nightmares. These patients received two three-hour sessions of IRT at one-week intervals and a one-hour follow-up session three or six months later. In the first session, patients practiced pleasant imagery exercises and cognitive-restructuring techniques for dealing with unpleasant images associated with nightmares and the original trauma. In the second session, participants were instructed to write down a self-selected nightmare that was not too intense (preventing too much exposure) and to rewrite the story line of the nightmare in any way they wished. They had to keep rehearsing the new story line "mentally" at home. Results of the treatment showed that relative to baseline assessments of the patients, IRT significantly reduces the number of nightmares per week and PTSD symptoms. Krakow and his group have shown that improvements after IRT are maintained for up to thirty months after treatment (Krakow, Kellner, and Pathak 1995). One limitation of these IRT studies is that the control-group of most studies consisted of a group of patients on a waiting list. In other words IRT has not yet been tested against a placebo condition. A randomized controlled trial is needed to investigate the efficacy of cognitive-behavioral interventions for nightmares.

In recent years, new pharmacologic studies have appeared that are targeted at reducing either nightmare distress or the frequency of nightmares. The only pharmacologic agent that has demonstrated any convincing success however is Prazosin, an alpha-1 adrenergic antagonist. This drug is typically used to treat hypertension. In a placebo-controlled study (Raskind et al. 2006), forty combat veterans with chronic PTSD and distressing trauma nightmares and sleep disturbance were randomized to evening Prazosin (13.3 $+/-$ 3 mg/day) or placebo for eight weeks. Results showed that Prazosin was significantly superior to placebo for reducing trauma nightmares and improving sleep quality and global clinical status with large effect sizes. Prazosin shifted dream characteristics from those typical of trauma-related nightmares toward those typical of normal dreams. The beneficial effect was not due to reduction of high autonomic reactivity, as the authors found that blood pressure changes from baseline to end of study did not differ significantly between Prazosin and placebo. This result strengthens the argument that Prazosin works at the level of the forebrain to reduce nightmare distress. As reviewed above one central forebrain structure that is involved in PTSD-related nightmares is the amygdala.

While everyone has experienced a nightmare, there is a portion of the population that experiences them frequently—even in the absence of other medical or neuropsychiatric conditions. These are children and a select few adults. Individuals who suffer frequent nightmares most likely carry a genetic predisposition to do so. These individuals are likely to evidence thin boundaries, an introverted disposition, and exceptional levels of creativity. The genetic endowment of frequent nightmare sufferers may increase the reactivity of the amygdala (possibly via an increase in noradrenergic synapses in the central nucleus)—a forebrain structure that is differentially activated every time the brain cycles into a REM sleep episode.

The amygdala specializes in mediation of fear and other unpleasant emotions. Prolonged and elevated levels of activation in the amygdala are more likely to occur in late-stage REM and that is why we see nightmares arising out of this stage of sleep. Nightmares in both children and adults typically involve the dreamer in unfamiliar settings with unfamiliar characters. Nightmares have unusually high levels of striving and most importantly, confrontations with a supernatural being of some kind. When these supernatural beings appear in a dream, misfortunes for the dreamer are much more likely to occur and these in turn eventuate in a nightmare.

We have argued that nightmares can be considered functional and even may be adaptations. Nightmares exhibit functional design in that they have a specific brain physiology, specific mental content, and occur in a specific segment of the population. They are nonrandom mental processes. When shared with others in a compelling way, they have been shown to enhance the social prestige of individuals in premodern societies and cultures, funneling these creative individuals into spiritual and healing "professions." Thus they "solved" a problem—the problem of how to achieve social prominence and prestige in order to increase one's fitness. Finally, nightmare content variables and resultant nightmare distress, when shared in a social context, can to some extent be understood as costly signaling behaviors and profitably be analyzed within the costly signaling theoretical evolutionary framework.

Chapter 9

Nightmares and Popular Culture

Nightmares are intense and therefore memorable experiences. Sometimes they are literally unforgettable. It is this latter element, the unforgetability of nightmares, that makes them potent cultural phenomena when used in the arts. Artists of all kinds—painters, musicians, novelists, short-story writers, and moviemakers—love to use nightmares in their tales and in their images. Nightmares are fantastic combinations of tales and images. As we have seen previously, the most frightening of nightmares often contain fantastic supernatural beings, bizarre and terrifying supernatural characters that appear in strange and unfamiliar settings. What artist could resist such raw material? We have also seen that adult nightmares have story lines that do not resolve; that place the self, the hero in an artist's tale, under extreme distress and threat, that enhance the hero's negative emotions and images, that block the hero's normal mind-reading abilities, and that place the hero in vivid combat with some supernatural monster. These are the kinds of tales and images that myths are made of, and myths are the generative spiritual material out of which whole cultures are born. It's no wonder that artists turn to nightmares to fashion their creations.

It is worth taking a closer look at how artists use nightmares to create a work of art in order to see whether the ways in which artists use nightmares can tell us anything interesting about nightmares themselves. I will focus on the example of spirit possession, since it is a constant theme in nightmares and a popular theme in artistic productions that utilize nightmares.

MOVIES, NIGHTMARES, AND SPIRIT POSSESSION

Moviemakers are the modern equivalents of the bards, storytellers, and mythmakers of the ancient world. Movies both reflect the culture's ethos and shape the culture's mores. Nightmares enter into the movies in both implicit and explicit ways. Take for example William Friedkin's *The Exorcist* (1973) based on a 1971 novel of the same title by William Peter Blatty. Here was a tale about an innocent, spiritually receptive ("thin boundaries") teenage girl (the paradigmatic female child nightmare sufferer) who undergoes a dramatic and prolonged spirit possession. As we have seen in previous chapters, nightmares were understood by tribal peoples as potentially dangerous because they often involved the potential for spirit possession. When the spirit was malignant or difficult to control, it could take possession/control of the host whose reputation, health, and standing in the community could suffer accordingly. Spirit possession as a result of a bad dream was considered disastrous by most premodern peoples. Nightmares, in short, were and are considered a portal through which spirit possession could occur.

NIGHTMARE-RELATED SPIRIT POSSESSION IS A UNIVERSAL PHENOMENON

Demonic possession, in particular, is thoroughly documented throughout Asia, Africa, Latin America, South America Oceania, and Europe (Cohen 2007). In one study that surveyed available ethnographic materials on 488 cultures, possession in one form or another was documented clearly in 437 of those cultures (Bourguignon 1973). Both the data and the testimony from tribal informants suggest that spirit possession was, and is, intimately linked with dreams and nightmares. It was often through the dream where a helper or benevolent spirit first contacted the dreamer and it was in a nightmare where the demon first attempted to take possession of the dreamer.

The term "nightmare" itself reflects this link between bad dreams and demonic spirit possession. Nightmares were widely considered to be the work of demons and more specifically incubi, which were thought to sit on the chests of sleepers. In Old English the name for these demonic spirits was "mare" or "mære" from a proto-Germanic "marōn." One of the most famous paintings of the relationship between bad dreams and spirit possession was Swiss painter Henry Fuseli's *The Nightmare* (Fuseli 1781). Freud apparently kept a print of this painting in his study. The painting depicts a young woman asleep or in a swoon on her divan or bed, with her arms swung above her head; her head and arms falling off the side of the divan. A disgusting-looking demon sits astride the woman's chest next to her bosom like a small animal. He looks out impudently toward the viewer, in satisfied, leisurely, contemplation. His pointed ears are shadowed against the red drapery. On the left of the canvas, as if pushing through the drapery, a horse's head with glowing eyes and a mindless grin on its face intrudes onto the scene. The tabletop in the foreground has what appear to be bottles of medicines, drink, or perhaps laudanum, the narcotic mixture of alcohol and opium that was a reliable producer of nightmares and in wide use in Fuseli's time.

More than 55,000 people in London went to the exhibition of this painting when it first appeared in 1782, this when the population of London was only about 750,000. The painting, in short, deftly summarizes what we now know to be true about nightmares: Young women and girls are more vulnerable to nightmares than any other demographic group. Nightmares are particularly distressful when they are associated with the appearance of a supernatural monster/being in the dream content. Many types of drugs enhance the chances for a nightmare experience. If one starts to awaken from a nightmare one may experience both a malignant presence in the room and/or a weight upon the chest that makes breathing difficult. This parasomniac state, when one transitions between sleep and waking consciousness, forces the dreamer to experience elements of REM consciously while one wakes from REM. Specifically, one experiences the paralysis of REM along with the respiratory distress associated with REM all in the process of waking up. Why one should also experience the sense of a malignant presence is still unknown. Presumably, the mind confabulates a malignant presence in order to explain the paralysis, fear and difficulty breathing. Yet, this explanation is unsatisfactory at best since it is not clear that confabulation is what is happening during the awakening. Instead elements of the dream-nightmare may still be at play during the awakening and we have seen that those elements typically involve attack by a malignant being. So, the dreamer, instead of making up an ad hoc story to explain his predicament, carries on the dream-nightmare story line into waking life, at least for a few minutes while the paralysis wears off.

In any case, the link between bad dreams, nightmares, and spirit possession is ancient, universal, and potent. Spirit possession is defined by experts as any altered state of consciousness that is understood by locals to be due to the influence of an alien spirit. It occurs in two major forms: 1) malevolent or demonic possession, and 2) benevolent or holy spirit possession. Demonic possession is linked to nightmares while holy spirit possession is linked to intense and emotionally moving dreams. Demonic possession is involuntary, lasts a long time (on the order of months unless an exorcism ritual is preformed), and involves profound physiologic changes. Holy spirit possession is voluntary, requiring the consent of the dreamer/individual, is transient, and also involves profound physiologic changes. With demonic possession, body motor changes are particularly intense. The possessed will twitch, writhe, or shake uncontrollably and babble profusely. Obscenities are

Table 9.1
Characteristics of Demonic Possession versus Holy Spirit Possession
in Nightmares

Demonic Possession	Holy Spirit Possession
Heralded by nightmares; dreamer feels drained, terrified, and demoralized by the nightmare	Premonitions of the experience may come in dreams that leave the dreamer feeling moved and elevated
Nightmare content involves confrontation with the demon and a feeling that strength is being drained	Dream content involves communications with the holy spirit and a feeling of peace and elevation
Identity of individual is subsumed by the demon over long periods	Identity of individual is subsumed by the spirit only transiently
The experience is involuntary	Consent is required from the subject before the spirit will take possession
Fugue states come and go	No loss of memory
Personality of dreamer is impaired	Personality of dreamer is enriched
Physiological changes involve autonomic lability; nausea and vomiting; weight loss; focus on self to exclusion of others	Physiologic changes involve enhanced sensory capacities; heightened awareness of others
Motor tics and writhing	Few or no motor changes
Obscenities	Silence or glossolalia (i.e., uttering unintelligible speechlike sounds)

not uncommon. With holy spirit possession motor changes are less marked but can occur. Obscenities never occur, although babbling and glossolalia may occur. (See Table 9.1 above for a comparison of the characteristics of demonic possession with holy spirit possession.)

In a typical demonic possession experience, a victim awakens from a bad dream and does not remember who he or she is. This fugue state then eventuates in fluctuating states of consciousness with the person sometimes quite lucid and other times going into a trance state. The trance state however, is not the kind we usually think of where the individual is relaxed and almost asleep. Instead the trance state involves the suspension of the individual's identity and the emergence of a new identity. The individual now speaks in the voice of the new identity. The scene in *The Exorcist* (Blatty and Friedkin 1973) where the demonically possessed twelve-year-old Regan MacNeil (played by Linda Blair), is hypnotized by an unwitting psychiatrist portrayed the emergence of the new identity quite dramatically. After entering into a trance the voice of the innocent twelve-year-old Regan was replaced by the growling of a dog and the voice of the demon. As is common in real cases of possession, when brought out of the trance, Regan had no memory of what she had said during the trance state.

Many movies have taken up the theme of the nightmare as a portal to the realm of evil spirits who are out to take possession of or to harm human beings. A *Nightmare on Elm Street,* written and directed by Wes Craven (1984) became a wildly popular movie with teenage and young adult audiences when it was released in the early 1980s. It affords a special ability to nightmares: They are uniquely able to mediate evil— supernatural evil—to the human world. In this movie, a particularly evil mind/person/being, "Freddy Kruger" enters the nightmares of a group of teenagers. He haunts, terrifies, and pursues the individual dreamer in the nightmare. If the dreamer believes that the nightmare is real then Kruger has the power to harm, even kill, the dreamer. Kruger had been a child murderer during his real life. In the nightmares, Kruger is transformed into a supernatural demon. Kruger's face is hideously disfigured, gnarled, and burnt. He wears a trademark glove with fingertip blades. His murders of children led a group of parents to kill him by burning him alive, thus the disfigured face. Kruger, in death, can now only get to children through their nightmares. Student Nancy Thompson keeps staving off sleep so she can avoid Kruger.

David Hufford has studied variants of sleep-related "spirit" phenomena (Hufford 1982). While a young man still in college, he himself had a vivid experience of being visited by a demonic presence during or after awakening from a nightmare. He heard the sound of his bedroom door creaking open and then footsteps moving toward his bed. He then felt an evil presence. He was aware of not being able to move, being consumed by terror. He apparently was half awake as his eyes were wide open. He next felt the demon on his chest restricting his breathing. He later told others that he felt he was going to die. Then suddenly the paralysis melted away and Hufford seized the moment to jump out of bed and ran several blocks to be with others in the student union.

Hufford became sufficiently interested in his experience to later begin a scholarly investigation of it. He found that the experience was common. Virtually everyone had had it and found it unforgettable. He then documented its frequent occurrence and its associated folklore in the special cultures of Newfoundland and Nova Scotia. In those cultures, the evil presence is conceived of as a hag or witch who targets young women in order to prevent a pregnancy or to steal a soul.

Fuseli's *The Nightmare* (mentioned earlier) appears to capture these sorts of nightmarish awakenings, depicting a demon sitting on the chest of a terrified and paralyzed victim. Modern sleep researchers distinguish these sorts of experiences from nightmares proper. The experience of awakening with paralysis is known as sleep paralysis. Yet, the paralysis is only one part of the experience. The terrifying part of the experience is the sensing of an evil presence and the respiratory difficulties. Surely these parts of the experience are carry-overs from a nightmare that the dreamer was having before he started awakening. After all, one can experience sleep paralysis without the accompanying terror. Many people have experienced the sensation of not being able to move even though they were awake. Although puzzling and maybe even a bit scary, it is not usually associated with terror or the sense of an evil presence. It is when these latter two elements accompany the experience that you get the syndrome Hufford is talking about (Hufford 1982). I would argue that the syndrome is a conscious experience of the tail end of a night-mare. The crucial ingredient once again, the ingredient that creates the terror, is the presence of the demon or evil presence. J. Allan Cheyne of the University of Waterloo in Canada has collected more than 28,000 tales of sleep paralysis (2007). Cheyne runs a Web site (http://watarts.uwater-loo.ca/~acheyne/S_P.html) where visitors fill out surveys about their experiences during sleep paralysis.

ALIEN ABDUCTION

Spirit possession related to nightmares has also been linked to modern claims of "alien abduction." Accounts of space alien encounters typically begin with the abductee waking in the night while sensing an intruder. The person can't move but senses a presence that is somehow touching or operating on the person. The person may also experience a sense of floating or of losing control of his or her own mind. All of these symptoms or experiences are consistent with a sleep paralysis event or an incomplete awakening from a REM-related nightmare involving an attempt by a nonhuman being to take possession of the dreamer's mind. Later individuals with these sleep paralysis experiences can make sense of the experience by supposing alien abduction into a spaceship. Despite their fantastic claims, investigations of the mental status of "abductees" show that they are psychiatrically and cognitively normal. The best explanation we have for their experiences is the sleep-paralysis/awakening from REM nightmare.

Yet, that explanation is unsatisfactory. Why don't all people who experience sleep paralysis also experience alien abduction? Nor can we assert that claims of alien abduction are just the modern equivalents of the claims of spirit possession of old. The phenomenologies of the two experiences are quite dissimilar. In spirit possession the identities of the dreamers are subsumed under the new identity of the demon or spirit who takes possession of the dreamer's personality. Dramatic personality changes do not occur in abductees. Nor do abductees experience any profound physiologic or motoric changes. Instead they experience varying degrees of post-traumatic stress disorder.

The link between nightmares and the alien abduction experience was highlighted in the science fiction TV miniseries *Taken,* which first aired on the Sci-Fi Channel in 2002. *Taken,* executive-produced by Steven Spielberg, was a multigenerational story spanning five decades and four generations, centering on three families: the Keys, Crawfords, and Clarkes (Spielberg 2002). World War II veteran Russell Keys is plagued by nightmares of his abduction by extraterrestrials during the war. Throughout the TV series, nightmares continually are referred to as heralds of alien influence. The unhappily married Sally Clarke is impregnated by an alien night visitor. The aliens regularly abduct individuals from these families, experiment upon them, and then release them to study. The abductees are partially amnestic for the abduction but nightmares encode vague memories of the experience. As the decades go by, the members of each generation of these three unfortunate families are affected by the goals and intentions of the aliens, culminating with the birth of Allie Keys, who is the final product of the aliens' experimentation to create an alien-human hybrid—a human fully possessed by and incorporating an alien mind.

BOOKS, NIGHTMARES, AND SPIRIT POSSESSION

Certainly one of the most popular writers in the present generation to have mined the horrifying tales that generate nightmares is Stephen King. Nightmares are a persistent theme throughout his works. Nightmares are also a source for some of his finest stories. Take *The Shining* (1977) for example. *The Shining* was made into a movie by film director Stanley Kubrick in 1980. The film stars Jack Nicholson as tormented writer Jack Torrance; Shelley Duvall as his wife, Wendy; and Danny Lloyd as their son, Danny (Kubrick 1980). The idea for the novel came to King when he and his wife stayed in a mountain resort hotel in the Colorado Rockies that was closing down for the season. They were the only two guests in the hotel during their stay. After his wife Tabitha had gone to sleep in their hotel room, King took a walk around the empty hotel. He ended up in the bar and was served drinks by a bartender named Grady. He also then went to bed.

That night I dreamed of my three-year-old son running through the corridors, looking back over his shoulder, eyes wide, screaming. He was being chased by a firehose. I woke up with a tremendous jerk, sweating all over, within an inch of falling out of bed. I got up, lit a cigarette, sat in a chair looking out the window at the Rockies, and by the time the cigarette was done, I had the bones of the book firmly set in my mind. (Beahm, 1998)

King's *The Shining* (both the novel and the film) portrays several nightmare-related themes now familiar to us. Most prominent perhaps is the theme of possession; the disintegration of one personality and the slow emergence of another, more evil, malignant, and murderous personality. In this case the identity of the possessing demon is left ambiguous. It is more the spirit of a place—the genius loci of the Overlook Hotel and the Indian burial grounds upon which it was built. Jack Torrance, a former prep-school teacher who wants to be a writer, accepts a job as a winter caretaker at the large, isolated Colorado resort hotel high in the mountains. He moves into the hotel with his wife and child Danny, who is telepathic and sensitive to supernatural forces. The ability to read minds and to send messages telepathically is called "shining."

Danny, via his telepathic abilities, understands the malevolent nature of the spirit of the place and the hotel. He has nightmares about the place and begins seeing ghosts and violent scenes connected to the hotel's past. Eventually, Jack becomes possessed by the demon spirit connected to the hotel, which attempts to use him to kill his wife and Danny in order to absorb Danny's psychic abilities.

Expressions of popular culture utilize the nightmare to produce compelling stories that scare the hell out of us! In particular, the theme of being pursued, chased, or assaulted by a supernatural being who wants to possess us or abduct us for experiments and so forth rather then kill us per se is ubiquitous in books, stories, paintings, and movies. This is a powerful confirmation of the potent impact nightmare phenomenology has on popular culture. In short the supernatural monster is central to both nightmares and popular culture. Who is this monster? And why is the monster so central to nightmares? We will turn to these issues in the next chapter.

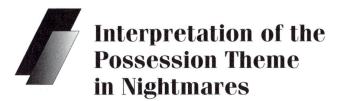

Chapter 10

Interpretation of the Possession Theme in Nightmares

For most of human history, nightmares were widely considered to be the work of demons and more specifically incubi, or evil spirits, which were thought to seek to control of and possess the soul of the dreamer. In Old English, the names for these demonic spirits were "mare" or "mære" from a proto-Germanic "marōn"; eventuating, of course, in the word "night-mares." Nightmares, in fact, are particularly distressful when they are associated with the appearance of a supernatural monster or demon in the dream content. Both within a nightmare and when one starts to partially awake from a nightmare, one may experience a malignant presence in the dream if asleep or in the room if one is half awake. If you read hundreds of nightmares experienced by hundreds of individuals across many cultures as I have, you find that this evil being/presence, whether in the form of a demon, or dangerous animal or intruder/stranger or alien, is out to get the dreamer. If the evil presence is supernatural or a spirit being, then in most cases the dreamer's soul or personality will be the target of the demon's attack.

It is this latter case, an attempt by an evil spirit to take over control of the mind or personality of the dreamer that I would like to analyze further in this chapter. The reason why this is so important an issue is that the presence of an evil spirit who is out to possess or own the dreamer's mind is experienced as particularly distressing by the dreamer. These are the paradigmatic nightmares. These are the nightmares that really torment nightmare sufferers and these are the nightmares that hold the key to potential interpretations of nightmare content.

We have seen that demonic possession in premodern societies occurred via nightmares, was involuntary, lasted a long time (on the order of months unless an exorcism ritual was performed), and involved profound physiologic changes. With demonic possession, motoric changes are particularly intense. The possessed will twitch, writhe, or shake uncontrollably and babble profusely. Obscenities are not uncommon.

My interest here, however, is not in daytime possession phenomena per se but in how the demon takes possession of the mind/personality of the dreamer in the nightmare. What does the demon represent that he can in some cases actually seize control of the personality? Presumably, prior to the advent of the scientific age, such a seizure would result in full-fledged "possession" phenomena. In the modern age, one sees various symptoms ranging from extreme distress to full-fledged personality change or dissociative identity disorder. It thus behooves us to explore the dynamics of those nightmares that involve a dream character/demon who is out to control the dreamer's essence or selfhood.

SELECTION OF NIGHTMARES WITH SPIRIT POSSESSION THEMES

To study these dynamics, I will analyze a collection of nightmares that involve demon characters in one capacity or another. These nightmares were collected semi-randomly from public Internet Web sites that archive dreams and nightmares donated or posted by individuals who simply wanted to share their dreams with others and perhaps get some feedback on their meaning. These nightmare reports have been de-identified so the only data we have about the dreamers are age and sex. To select nightmares (with demons in them) for analysis, I simply searched Web sites for nightmares containing the word demon in them. I then randomly eliminated all but about 15 such nightmares as I had space to comment on only about that many. Note that I could have cast the net more widely by including such keywords as devil, aliens, monsters, and so forth. These nightmare characters also threaten the dreamer's ego or self in varying degrees and sometimes even seek to control or possess the dreaming self, but the relationship is weaker than in the case of demons. So I stuck with "demon" as my key word.

CAVEATS IN THE INTERPRETATION OF NIGHTMARES AND STANDARD EXPLANATIONS OF THE POSSESSION THEME

In the following discussion it should be understood that I will be using shorthand when I refer to the word "demon" and when I ascribe intentional states to it. As scientists we have to assume that demons do not exist and do not exhibit intentional states. The characters and beings that populate dreams are, accordingly, products of the dreamer's own mind. So if we stick with this "standard" reductionist assumption,

I believe that most psychologists, in order to explain dream characters like the demon, would subscribe to some sort of story like the following: The demon complex is a symbol or metaphor for some sort of underlying emotional threat. Some sort of psychic-emotional complex is surfacing in the unconscious mind of the dreamer and is being experienced as an overwhelming threat to the psychic or cognitive integrity of the dreamer's ego-complex or "self-complex." In short, there is some internal memory or emotional storm that is threatening the psychic balance of the dreamer's self-identity. The dreamer experiences this as a threat of annihilation or worse. The threat is personified as an evil demon.

There are, however, several problems with this story as an explanation for the demon-possession theme in nightmares. First, not every nightmare sufferer has an emotional memory or trauma that is threatening his or her ego integrity. You can have nightmares without having any significant history of physical or emotional trauma. It is therefore unlikely that emotional storms of some sort can account for the ubiquity of the demon-possession theme in nightmares. The demon cannot be reduced to emotional storms in all persons who experience nightmares. Second, even in cases where there is a history of emotional trauma, the ego nevertheless is not always perceived as being under threat nor is it weak in any sense. You can have a history of emotional trauma and *not* have weak ego defenses. Third, even if we assume that emotional trauma is present in a nightmare sufferer, it is not clear why it must be symbolized with a demon. Why not some other symbol of threat? There are millions of threats out there. Many are not considered "evil." Instead they are considered dangerous but dumb. What is interesting about nightmares that cause distress is that they have characters in them that *intend* the dreamer harm. Yet the dreamer knows very little else about the evil demon other than this bare fact. The dreamer's ability to read the mind of the evil demon starts and stops with his ability to understand that the demon intends overwhelming harm to the dreamer's essence, not just to the dreamer's physical body. Animals can harm the body and attacks by animals in dreams rarely cause a full-fledged nightmare. Instead you need the presence of a demon to produce a really terrifying nightmare. A final problem with the emotional trauma story as an account of the nightmare possession theme is that it is odd to claim that the demon (or any other character in a dreamer's dreams except for the dreamer himself) represents another part of the dreamer's mind because it suggests that one part of the mind "wants" to take control of the "self" part of the mind. Why should this be? If the demon was part of the dreamer's ego, then presumably it already possesses the dreamer's mind/personality, so there is no need for it to take over the dreamer's mind. Yet that is manifestly what it intends to do. Thus, for all these reasons the demon as symbol of the dreamer's emotional conflicts is not satisfactory.

So if emotional trauma or memories are not the source of the threat to the dreamer's essence or personality then what is the source? The answer is that we just do not know. Our best strategy to discover the answer is to stay true to the phenomenology of the nightmare itself until we come up with a reasonable explanation for that phenomenology.

RECURRING PATTERNS IN THE SPIRIT-POSSESSION THEME

If you analyze hundreds of nightmares you eventually begin to discern a pattern in the demon-possession-themed nightmare. The demon patiently works to take control of the dreamer's mind and personality and uses cunning, guile, seductive wish-fulfillment images, and finally outright violence to do so. The demon announces himself first in a barely discernable voice or via a barely discernable touch or a barely discernable but ominous presence in the dream. Then the demon may attack individuals who are important to the dreamer in waking life—family members and such. Once the demon gets close to the dream-ego and obtains the dreamer's trust, an attack ensues. The demon will brave a short, swift, spasmodic attack on the dreamer often in the form of a small animal or some other small creature that attacks the dreamer. The dreamer realizes that this attack is serious even though the creatures are small and relatively easy to deal with. Next the demon will take on more formidable forms like large animals, space aliens, zombies, or actual demons and now the dreamer runs for it. The demon gives chase and may or may not catch the dreamer. Eventually the dreamer allows the demon to get close to him in the dream. The demon usually accomplishes this by tricking the dreamer. The demon pretends to be someone whom the dreamer trusts. By the time the dreamer realizes the mortal danger he is in the demon has succeeded in getting a kind of spiritual or emotional hold on the spirit of the dreamer and thus the dreamer is especially vulnerable in these dreams/nightmares.

Eventually, the demon makes a full-scale attempt to take over the dreamer's identity. This attempt may occur in a hundred different ways depending on the personal idiosyncrasies of the dreamer. The common denominator in these nightmares is that the dreamer becomes unsure of his or her identity and the experience is unwelcome and terrifying. Note that there are some individuals who enjoy playing around with identities in their fantasies and dreams and these people are not in danger of "possession" or dissociative disorder. In nightmares, on the other hand, the sudden loss of identity is frightening and deeply disturbing to the dreamer.

Once the demon attempts to take over the dreamer's identity, the dreamer must respond—either fight back or lose out to the demon. Losing out to the demon means increased vulnerability to daytime psychopathology, so a fight is recommended.

I will now illustrate some of these possession themes in a collection of dreams downloaded from various Web sites dedicated to dreams and nightmares. Naturally the reader should take the following analysis with a big dose of skepticism, as I know next to nothing about the people who posted or donated these dreams. Precision and accuracy are simply not possible here. Instead my claim is that the possession theme is universal across individuals and cultures and thus should be reflected in any random selection of nightmares one cares to select. If you select enough nightmares you will eventually come across examples of each of the stages of the possession phenomena I mentioned above. My purpose here is simply to illustrate the kind of material I have in mind when speaking of the possession theme in nightmares.

Let us begin with dreams where the demon announces his presence.

Demon Announces Himself as Ominous Presence

The Nightmare Project Dream #023

I dreamt that I could see myself sleeping. I lay on my left side in the middle of the bed, as I normally do when I fall asleep. It felt like an out-of-body experience more than a dream. I started to hear a whispering at the foot of my bed. It sounded like an older man or demon whispering my name over and over again, very slowly. I asked out loud, ''Who's there?'' Immediately, I was thrown off my bed by some very powerful force and started spinning around on the floor very, very rapidly. As I screamed as loud as I could, terrified, I looked up to see my ceiling fan spinning as fast as I was.

I woke up all of a sudden, but still in the position I had dreamt I was in. I turned on the lights and couldn't fall back to sleep for hours. (Posted at the Nightmare Project Web site, www.nightmareproject.com on 09/14/2001 by a twenty-two-year-old female about a nightmare she had had when she was 16.)

In this dream, the demon announces himself in a barely audible whisper. Also, by vocalizing the name of the dreamer, he hints at his intention—to take over the dreamer's identity. The dreamer, instead of trusting and allowing the demon into her consciousness, responds forcefully and demands to know ''Who's there?'' Thus the demon is stopped in his tracks. From the point of view of the memory complex theory of the possession theme, what is happening here is that the personified threat arising from the emergence of painful or unacceptable emotions or memories seeks to insinuate itself into the consciousness of the dreamer but the dreamer prevents this from happening by treating the "intruder" as an alien and hostile being. From my point of view, that of a neutral phenomenologist, the dreamer made the correct and healthy choice by excluding the memory complex, demon, or whatever you want to call it, from her consciousness. From the trauma/memory complex view (i.e., the standard view), the dreamer should have attempted to integrate this threatening material into her consciousness. Thus, we have two diametrically opposed assessments on the meaning and interpretation of nightmare content: the phenomenologist versus the standard psychological/clinical assessments.

Now what is the meaning of the dreamer being thrown out of her bed and spun around like a top on the floor of her room? From a physiologic point of view, it sounds like a mini-seizure or even an attack of vertigo of some kind. From the point of view of the dynamic meaning of the content of the dream, the demon was the powerful force who threw her out of bed and spun her around. Who knows why he did this. We would need to interview the dreamer to get a reasonable handle on the event. In any case the demon did not give up after being rebuffed by the dreamer. "Demons" never give up without a fight; they relentlessly pursue the dreamer. We will see in the next dream that when the dreamer allows the demon into the dreamer's personal space the demon gains power over the dreamer. In the following dream the demon has the power to partially paralyze the will and the behavioral system of the dreamer who will be followed, hounded, and chased by these malignant presences in the dream until the dreamer decisively rejects the demon.

Hall and Van de Castle Norms: Male: #0237

The dream took place on the first landing of the stairs in the house we last lived in. It seemed that it was about 11 o'clock at night and pitch black. I was standing alone but I felt someone walking up the stairs behind me. Hard as I tried, I couldn't yell out or move as the person came closer. He came closer and closer but in the darkness I couldn't see who it was. As he reached for me I woke up shaking and in a cold sweat (Schneider and Domhoff 2005; www.dreambank.net).

In this dream, the demon has gotten close to the dreamer so he has the power to paralyze the dreamer's ability and even will to shake off the intruder.

The Nightmare Project Dream #002

I used to live in a peculiarly-shaped apartment, not the kind everyone thinks of. My bed faced a closet, large and dark, with huge wooden doors. As I dreamt one night, a demon burst through the apartment door, and called me by a name I do not go by, but still I recognized it as mine. When the demon saw that

I recognized this name, his already demonic appearance grew far more evil, and he let out the most bloodcurdling roar I have ever heard. The demon chased me around the apartment, and cornered me in my bedroom. I jumped in bed, under the blankets, knowing for some reason that this was a safe zone.

The demon came into the room and waited in the closet for me to get out of bed. It tired of waiting, and let out another horrifying scream. It scared me so badly that I woke up, lying in my bed, staring at the closet. The door was half-open, as the demon had left it. The feeling of pure evil was still so real, I was positive the demon was in the closet. I was petrified until daylight. To this day, it still makes me wonder. (Posted to The Nightmare Project Web site, www.nightmareproject.com, 02/24/2000, by a twenty-nine-year-old male about a nightmare he had when he was 18 years old.)

Here the dreamer finds a safe zone that allows him to exclude or prevent the demon's influence over him. Like kids everywhere the safe zone is under the blankets! Psychically speaking the important point here is that there is a way to prevent the demon from hurting the dreamer. Initially it is finding a safe zone or some part of the mind that is off-limits to the demon. The demon will respond by attempting to invoke fear in the dreamer. Often this will work but in this case it apparently did not. Another interesting thing about this nightmare is the lingering feeling of pure evil upon awakening. Now what kind of domain of experience can that refer to? If we exclude religious conceptions of evil then it can only refer to predator-prey experiences perhaps? Distant infantile memories of dimly perceived threats? Neither of these fanciful explanations seem to capture the phenomenology of the demon experience in nightmares. The demon-possession theme carries too much cognitive content to be reduced to primitive or infantile reflexes. The theme is about high-level identity issues; the construction of self-hood and the control of attentional awareness and other cognitive functions of the self.

Demons Attack Dreamer's Familiar Others

The Nightmare Project Dream #009

This dream made a huge impact on me. It involves my mother, to whom I am incredibly close. She and I were in a very small town when we found a cave. We, along with everyone else in the town, decided to explore it together. In the cave we found two demons, each with the body of a goat and the head of a dog, and cloven feet and hands. At random, they started ripping out and eating the hearts of the townsfolk. Some of the victims died. Some didn't.

Then the demons escorted us out of the cave and into the sun. At this point, they turned into beautiful women with long, black hair and blood-red lips. They asked my mom and me to take them somewhere in our car, and got into the back seat. My mom looked at me over the top of the car and said, "One of us has to survive this."

Those were her last words. I did not see the demon women rip out my mother's heart, but it was understood. (Posted at the Nightmare Project Web site, www.nightmareproject.com, on 09/02/2000 by a nineteen-year-old female who had had the nightmare a year earlier when she was eighteen.)

A psychoanalytic interpretation of this nightmare would likely claim that the dreamer wished harm to the mother but this would miss the essential action of the nightmare: the mother's self-sacrificial act on behalf of her daughter. The mother apparently sacrificed herself so that her daughter would survive the attack of the demons. Since the nightmare is the dream of the daughter and not the mother the demons are there to possess the dreamer, not the mother or the townsfolk. The demons presumably can more easily attack the dreamer if they first take out the dreamer's allies. In any case people close to the dreamer help to construct the dreamer's identity and so if the dreamer's identity is at issue in the nightmare then the foundational "others" who help to make up the dreamer's identity are suddenly no longer available to buttress that identity. As the threat to the dreamer's identity becomes more pronounced, symbols of the foundation of that identity become progressively more unavailable. Another interesting aspect of this dream is that the demons can appear in beautiful and appealing guises. They do not necessarily have to be hideous. Indeed they may be more dangerous to the dreamer in instances when their true nature is hidden.

In the following nightmare from Barb Sanders, whom we have met in a previous chapter, many of these themes are especially clear. Sanders is an especially savvy dreamer and she therefore comments on many images in her dreams which help us to understand the images from the point of view of the dreamer (not necessarily the waking Barb Sanders). The dreamer's point of view is precisely the perspective we need to get a valid first-person phenomenological picture of the dream/nightmare themes. I will therefore first present the nightmare report here in its entirety so that the reader can get the gist of the narrative. I will then comment on individual themes to bring out the richness of the report for our analyses on the possession theme in nightmares (Schneider and Domhoff 2005; www.dreambank.net).

Barb Sanders: Dream #0225

A nightmare. Entities or souls or creatures from other planets are coming to meld with humans and take our spirits away. I am very frightened. The children are the first to go and then the adults. It's a terrible feeling of the fear of losing myself as through death or absorption into another. They come, three of them. The one coming for me is a big man in a chicken hawk suit with red and blue fluffy feathers. He talks like an English pirate (irate)? We meld and a transparent form of my body is tucked under his wing and off we fly. What a ride.

I can feel my stomach lurch as we go zipping up to the cosmos and down again. It's like a jet plane. We get to their planet. Then a man gets shot and falls. I'm surprised because I thought, "1.) No one dies here, and 2.) ugly, mean people don't exist here." They take the body of a two-year-old baby and this shot man's soul goes into the baby. His face is only softened and rounded like a baby. I'm appalled because they had told me we were just being borrowed. Now I know we were being lied to. I feel awful. I tell Nate to run. "I'm sorry I got you into this mess." (Posted on 01/06/81 on the Dreambank.net Web site)

Now I will reprint here individual themes of Barb Sanders' nightmare and comment on them accordingly.

"A nightmare." Sanders calls this report a nightmare; we could have guessed that it was simply by noting that possession themes are prominent in the dream.

"Entities or souls or creatures from other planets are coming to meld with humans and take our spirits away. I am very frightened." The dreamer here is very aware of the intentions of the creatures from other planets. They are coming to possess the spirits of humans. They want control of the minds of humans. Demons often travel in packs it seems. The dreamer understands the seriousness of the threat as she says "I am very frightened."

"The children are the first to go and then the adults." The demons always target the more vulnerable ones first. We have seen that they target foundational persons for the dreamer's identity. In this case it is the children.

"It's a terrible feeling of the fear of losing myself as through death or absorption into another." Sanders very clearly states what is at stake in these sorts of nightmares—loss of identity and control to another.

"They come, three of them." There may be some significance to the inverted trinity theme here.

"The one coming for me is a big man in a chicken hawk suit with red and blue fluffy feathers. He talks like an English pirate (irate)?" The demon does not appear in his terrifying aspect. Instead he appears in an almost farcical form talking like a caricature of an evil person—a pirate. It is as if the dreamer is no longer threatened by a real evil presence. The demon is tamed for the time being.

"We meld and a transparent form of my body is tucked under his wing and off we fly." Sander's identity is melded into that of the demons. Note that the dreamer's identity is not lost here. There is a melding or fusion of the two. So alienation has not yet occurred. Instead the dreamer seems to not to take the threat seriously anymore. She senses that the threat is empty.

"What a ride. I can feel my stomach lurch as we go zipping up to the cosmos and down again. It's like a jet plane. We get to their planet. Then a man gets shot and falls. I'm surprised because I thought, 1.) No one dies here, and 2) ugly, mean people don't exist here." On the demon's planet she expected ugly mean people but instead finds that it is a lot like Earth where people die, etc. The dreamer's guard is down.

"They take the body of a two-year-old baby and this shot man's soul goes into the baby. His face, is only softened and rounded like a baby. I'm appalled because they had told me we were just being borrowed. Now I know we were being lied to. I feel awful.

I tell Nate to run. 'I'm sorry I got you into this mess.'" The dreamer, after witnessing a macabre form of possession, now feels betrayed and threatened again. She tells a friend to run for it. We see here how the demons trick the dreamer into trusting them; then they insinuate themselves further into the dreamer's awareness or trust until it is too late and all that one can do is run for it. If measures are not taken by the individual, the identity of the individual will come under pressure.

We will see in the next nightmare (another one from Barb Sanders) an elaboration of the theme of trusting to demons and then regretting it. Once again I will first reprint the nightmare in full and then comment on several subthemes.

Barb Sanders: Dream #0478

A frightening dream. I went to a party. Everyone is drinking, laughing, and frenetic. I hesitate to join them. They swirl around me, encouraging me to join them. Darryl sits across from me. He teases me and says something about a girl he used to know. I feel the same old distance from him (placed by him). I call him Howard and feel embarrassed. A lot of people disappear. The party seems to have moved on down the street, maybe to Aunt Elaine's house. I belatedly want to join them now. I drink some wine. I feel slightly high. Instead, I end up in my living room. An uncle and a cousin are there. I greet them. I laugh at my cousin because he carries a rifle on his shoulder everywhere he goes. I say, "How silly, you are getting carried away." A man then appears at the door. He's smiling gently and wants me to join the party. I feel a desire and a fear to go. There is some danger to me if I go. I clutch my cousin and say, "Look at my hand. See the bullet wounds?" He looks. He says, "There is poison here, you've been poisoned." The man beckons me to come to the party. I realize then that they've gotten their poison into me, but not quite enough. I still can resist. I say, "I don't want to be a part of your project." It is hard for me to say because the drug makes me want to go. I say it several times and he just stands there waiting for me, because he knows the drug is powerful. I'll be sucked into another being like in the *Invasion of the Body Snatchers*. I run to my "dad" and plead with him, telling him I don't want to, and to please help! I'm trying to but I'm growing weaker. "Please help me!" He doesn't respond to me other than to weakly smile at me to acknowledge that he has heard me. I grab my cousin, who before I had seen as weak and silly and cling to him, hugging him hard, hanging on like he was my anchor to that room. Then a fat lady, mostly naked is dancing at a party. Her husband picks her up off the floor and makes love to her. He is detached, fully clothed, and his back is to me. She is fully exposed. I see her vagina. I see her face clearly. A prim blonde woman sits rigidly beside them. I am shocked. This is on T.V. After he's done, the man sticks a fat piece of paper in the blonde woman's mouth. She is disgusted. It's a symbol of a large penis. Her red lipstick forms an "o" around it. Then I am upstairs in my bedroom. I wake up from a nightmare. I run downstairs, crying, "The little men are inside my stomach!" I'm crying. My uncle or grandfather soothes me. He says, "No, it isn't possible. I've been barricading the stairs for you all night." I am not comforted. I go back upstairs. I sit on the bed and hug my nanny. She is an old square robot, and not very sophisticated. I ask it, "Why aren't there any nice men for me?" It says, "Look, there are," and shows me two of them (on a screen on its chest). I say, "But if I take them, what will be left for my brother!" Nanny laughs and shows me many women for Dwight. I am still worried. Then I'm at a dance, watching the musicians. One can't find his banjo. Then he finds it and sees that something has eroded the outside. I realize that what ever "they" touch, corrodes like that and that "they" are there. I turn and the man is standing there, smiling. He says, "It's so close. We almost had you." I try to resist. (Posted on 09/09/81 on the Dreambank.net Web site.)

"A frightening dream. I went to a party. Everyone is drinking, laughing, and frenetic. I hesitate to join them. They swirl around me, encouraging me to join them." It will become clear later in the dream that the "they" she refers to are "demons" or beings who want to possess and control her mind. They use things that might entice Barb Sanders: an exciting party atmosphere and words of encouragement.

"Darryl sits across from me. He teases me and says something about a girl he used to know. I feel the same old distance from him (placed by him). I call him Howard and feel embarrassed." Daryl is incorrectly called Howard by the dreamer ... a blurring of identities. These two are men that are apparently important, emotionally or sexually, to Sanders, identity.

"A lot of people disappear. The party seems to have moved on down the street, maybe to Aunt Elaine's house. I belatedly want to join them now. I drink some wine. I feel slightly high. Instead, I end up in my living room. An uncle and a cousin are there. I greet them. I laugh at my cousin because he carries a rifle on his shoulder everywhere he goes. I say, "How silly, you are getting carried away." Sanders gets in deeper as she drinks some wine and her judgment is now impaired. She wants to trust them but something in her calls up from memory, some protective force against them—her cousin. Her cousin, apparently was not a very trusting guy. He was not so gullible. Yet the dreamer wants to let them in so she denigrates the cousin who carries around a rifle on his shoulder, presumably to deal with threats.

"A man then appears at the door. He's smiling gently and wants me to join the party. I feel a desire and a fear to go. There is some danger to me if I go." The demons appear friendly in order to seduce the dreamer into joining with them. But, the dreamer finally senses danger.

"I clutch my cousin and say, "Look at my hand. See the bullet wounds?" He looks. He says, "There is poison here, you've been poisoned." Now the dreamer fully realizes that she has been infiltrated ... some poison has seeped in via a wound. The "silly" but now reliable cousin is the source of her information and strength at this point.

"The man beckons me to come to the party. I realize then that they've gotten their poison into me, but not quite enough. I still can resist. I say, "I don't want to be a part of your project." This is the decisive moment of the nightmare. The dreamer struggles to reject the fusion attempt with the aliens/demons.

"It is hard for me to say because the drug makes me want to go. I say it several times and he just stands there waiting for me, because he knows the drug is powerful.

I'll be sucked into another being like in the Invasion of the Body Snatchers.'' The demons do not give up easily. They rely on the power of the drug/poison. The dreamer needs to call in more help.

"I run to my 'dad' and plead with him, telling him I don't want to, and to please help! I'm trying to but I'm growing weaker. 'Please help me!' He doesn't respond to me other than to weakly smile at me to acknowledge that he has heard me." She turns to foundational sources for her identity but they are weak at best.

"I grab my cousin, who before I had seen as weak and silly and cling to him, hugging him hard, hanging on like he was my anchor to that room." She returns to the cousin who has displayed strength in the past.

"Then a fat lady, mostly naked is dancing at a party. Her husband picks her up off the floor and makes love to her. He is detached, fully clothed, and his back is to me. She is fully exposed. I see her vagina. I see her face clearly. A prim blonde woman sits rigidly beside them. I am shocked. This is on T.V. After he's done, the man sticks a fat piece of paper in the blonde woman's mouth. She is disgusted. It's a symbol of a large penis. Her red lipstick forms an 'o' around it." Now the dreamer is shown the full consequences of an alliance with, or fusion with, the demons. There will be degradation and a loss of self.

"Then I am upstairs in my bedroom. I wake up from a nightmare." Here we have a dream within a dream. The possession theme is often associated with these sorts of amazing switches in consciousness during a dream. The dreamer thinks she wakes up but is not really awakened. If the dreamer believes that she has awakened then she becomes more trusting and more easily "poisoned" or controlled.

"I run downstairs, crying, 'The little men are inside my stomach!' I'm crying. My Uncle or grandfather soothes me. He says, 'No, it isn't possible. I've been barricading the stairs for you all night.' " The demons want to persuade the dreamer that the threat is gone, that she is now safe.

"I am not comforted. I go back upstairs. I sit on the bed and hug my nanny. She is an old square robot, and not very sophisticated. I ask it, 'Why aren't there any nice men for me?' It says, 'Look, there are,' and shows me two of them (on a screen on its chest). I say, 'But if I take them, what will be left for my brother!' Nanny laughs and shows me many women for Dwight.''

As the dreamer struggles to protect her identity the bizarreness levels of the images increase. She once again attempts to draw upon old foundational persons relevant to her identity, in this case a nanny. The nanny, like all the other characters in the dream, except crucially the cousin, tries to convince her that the danger has passed.

"I am still worried." The nanny's ploy does not work. The dreamer remains concerned and therefore vigilant.

"Then I'm at a dance, watching the musicians. One can't find his banjo. Then he finds it and sees that something has eroded the outside." The dreamer finds herself at another festive event and then finds more evidence of the infiltration of the demons … a violin has been touched by them and the violin has been damaged.

"I realize that what ever 'they' touch, corrodes like that and that 'they' are there. I turn and the man is standing there, smiling. He says "It's so close. We almost had you.' "

This is a fascinating turn of events in the dream as the demons come right out and admit that they are trying to possess her, the dreamer, and almost succeeded! Will the dreamer now let down her guard?

"I try to resist." The fight is not over and the dreamer continues to resist. All forms of guile and trickery have not managed to persuade the dreamer to let down her guard and let the demons in. They will need to mount a more violent attack in situations like this.

Demon Chases Dreamer, in Form of Animal Alien, or Zombie

I will not provide a nightmare report here to illustrate the attack theme in dreams and nightmares as it is too commonly known to bene-fit from illustration here. When the chase ends the dreamer has a choice to make: to continue to resist or to deal with the ones chasing him. If the dreamer attempts to destroy the demon they will revert to guile to protect themselves.

Demon Tricks Dreamer by Assuming Trusted Identity

Nightmare Project Dream #007

It would start out as a fairly ordinary nightmare (I suffered frequent nightmares in my youth). Generally some demonic, evil thing would be chasing me, or some such scenario. Knowing at some level that it was a bad dream, I would try my best to wake up from it by calling out or making some sound. Finally, after much effort, I would wake up screaming.

My sister, to whom I have always been extraordinarily close, would then enter the room to comfort and console me. She would embrace me and pat my back, and tell me that I was all right, that it was only a dream.

But, just as I would calm down, with my heart and breathing gradually returning to normal, my sister would suddenly break away from me. Leveling me with a piercing, evil stare, she would slowly back away and begin laughing in a cruel, maniacal way. I would then realize that I had not woken up at all, that it was a false awakening. In reality I was still dreaming, still in the night-mare, not yet released from my frightening night-visions. Again, more desper-ately now, I would struggle and struggle in a vain effort to awake while my dream-sister continued to cackle.

Then I would suddenly awake, sweating and screaming. My dear sister would rush to my side, only to back away again and laugh ... This loop might be repeated four or five times before I would actually wake up. Of course, when my sister truly came to comfort me when the episode really *did* end, I would be nearly hysterical with fear, not trusting that she was actually my true sister! (Posted at the Nightmare Project Web site, www.nightmareproject.com on 08/06/2000 by a thirty-year-old female who was fourteen when she had the nightmare.)

Here we have several of the themes we covered when discussing Barb Sanders' nightmares. The demon comes in the form of someone we trust or are attracted to in order to obtain the dreamer's trust. Once that trust is obtained the dreamer can be infused with the poison of the demons and thus made more weak and tractable. In the above dream we also have the phenomenon of awakening from a dream within a dream. Once again we see that the demons use this as a ploy to gain the trust of the dreamer—to make her believe that she is now safe. In this case the aim appears to have been to drive a wedge of fear and distrust between the dreamer and her "dear sister." Presumably the sister was a foundational source for the dreamer's identity and had to be undermined in order to gain control of the dreamer's identity.

Demon Attempts to Take Over the Dreamer's Identity

Nightmare Project Dream #023

I had this dream a couple of times during puberty. I went into the forest surrounding my home. The light of day was waning. I waded through red and yellow autumn leaves on the forest floor, heavy from the previous rain shower. As I walked, a soft breeze caught my hair. When I turned to face the wind, I noticed an ancient cottage standing amidst the trees.

I knocked on the wooden door, and my teacher opened it. Later, I found myself facing a mirror. As I sat staring into it, I told him about my problems. He said, "Take a closer look. Do you see who you really are?" And as I looked, my true identity revealed itself as the most horrendous, demonic visage I have ever seen. I awoke screaming and found that I could not stop. I ran to my older sister, waking her with my screams. I didn't dare sleep for weeks, only finding rest when exhaustion claimed me. (Posted at the Nightmare Project Web site, www.nightmareproject.com, on 02/04/2002 by a twenty-six-year-old male about a nightmare he had when he was fifteen.)

Here we have the dreamer approaching a trusted individual, an old "teacher" but in an unfamiliar and perhaps an eerie setting. Instead of supporting the true identity of the dreamer, the teacher tries to convince him that he is demonic, already possessed. Teachers are particularly powerful influences on developing individuals—people searching for their true identities. Part of the function of a teacher is to reveal to the individual their hidden talents and thus their true identities. In the nightmare above this function of the teacher is inverted. Instead of revealing a true identity, the teacher tries to convince the dreamer of an untrue identity—an alienated identity.

In the next dream, the dreamer allowed demonic influences into her trust via a drug experience.

Nightmare Project Dream #003

I went to my room and shut the door in order to get away from my family. My walls are normally light blue, but in the dream they were white and the light from the window shone so perfectly as I lay down on top of my bed. The radio was playing a song that went, "I'm going out for awhile so I can get high with my friends, don't wait up 'cause I won't be home." I felt peaceful and content as I closed my eyes.

I felt my body begin to float, which didn't bother me until I realized that I couldn't get down and had lost control. Suddenly I heard a demon's voice, and as I looked in the mirror across from my bed I saw a devil-like creature. I was still floating, but now thought I would fall. I frantically tried to get down. Hearing this demon's voice frightened me so much I began to pray for help from God, but found I couldn't speak. I kept trying, but I couldn't get up enough breath. Finally, I managed to get out the words, "Help me, help me." I fell back onto my bed, and right then I woke up. (Posted to the Nightmare Project Web site, www.nightmareproject.com, 03/25/2000 by a 15-year-old female who was 14 at the time she had the nightmare.)

In this dream, the dreamer found a way to stop the dissolution of her will and identity: she called on God for help. The experience of loss of will and identity is vividly described in this dream. It feels like weightlessness; not being rotted in the earth. When she looked in a mirror she sees herself as already possessed by a demon. She then realizes her acute danger and she calls for help. The call succeeded.

In the next nightmare no such happy ending occurs.

Nightmare Project Dream #005

I had this dream while in graduate school. I was walking back to my dormitory on a winter night, just after sunset. The street lamps bathed the scene in an orange light. Suddenly, a thick, pea soup, London-type fog descended. Unable to see at all, people froze in place. For me, that was the corner of my dorm and the main street. People called to each other trying to get their bearings. Among them, I heard some friends. I called out to them, "I'm in front of Henry Hall. If you follow my voice, you can get home." "Okay," they responded. And then, just as I knew my friends were approaching, I began to change into a hideous monster. I could feel my fangs and claws growing, and was sure my eyes were turning red. I felt demonic, and knew that as soon as my friends found me, I would kill them. I have dreamt of turning into a monster or demon many times. (Posted at the Nightmare Project Web site, www.nightmareproject.com, on 05/27/2000 by a forty-two-year-old female about a nightmare she had when she was twenty-eight.)

One feels that this dreamer may have already succumbed to the demons as she experiences the dream from the point of view of the demon, the one who wants to consume identities. She uses guile to gain people's trust and then she "knows" that she will kill them. On the other hand perhaps this dreamer is particularly powerful and able to resist possession by an "alien" being or character. In that case her experiences would be invaluable as she could get into the mind of the agent attempting to destroy others. This is the kind of person who would have become a candidate sorcerer or shaman in premodern societies.

In the next dream the dreamer tries to resist the loss of his identity to the demons but seems to partially fail, as he was just a child when the assault came.

Nightmare Project Dream #021

One stormy night, I was wakened by thunder and went to my parent's bed. After I went back to sleep, I had this dream. I am wearing a mask depicting the face of a demon. Naturally, I remove it, but behind it is another demon mask, and behind that another. I can never get all the masks off my face. I awoke in a cold sweat. Hanging on the wall of the bedroom were the masks I had worn in the dream. Needless to say, I woke up my parents. (Posted at the Nightmare Project Web site, www.nightmareproject.com on 09/10/2001 by a twenty-seven-year-old male about a nightmare he had when he was eight.)

Perhaps the dreamer's parents found a way to protect the true identity of the dreamer as he apparently psychically survived the attack when he was just a child. His strategy of physically tearing off the false identity is a good one but a difficult one for a child as there is no strong identity yet in place that can replace the false one.

Dreamer Must Fight Demon or Lose Identity

Losing out to the demon means increased vulnerability to daytime psychopathology. So a fight is recommended. But how do you fight them? We have seen that some dreamers, particularly children, know how to find a safe zone in their minds. They can hide there for a while. Other individuals, adults, can use their memories to call up trusted characters or personages to help them in their struggles with the "demons." Yet other more religious dreamers can call upon God for help and this strategy seems to be particularly effective even for nonbelievers. In the final sample report we look at a successful strategy to resist an assault on the dream ego during a nightmare.

DreamBank Dream #2878

I am in some mad nightmare where tremendous forces of hate and violence are coming at me and I must fight it off by sending back blasts of intense love. People come at me, wanting to kill me and I send back intense love, trying not to succumb to the hate and violence. It is pretty overwhelming. (Posted on 10/31/95 to www.Dreambank.net by Barb Sanders.)

Chapter 11

Conflict Theory and the Nightmare

Like any other dream the nightmare contains characters that interact in a variety of ways with the dreamer. One of the distinctive things about nightmares is that the two main characters are the dreamer and some being who is threatening the dreamer. When that being or character is a supernatural being like a demon, the dreamer is more likely to report extreme duress, fear, and terror as part of the nightmare. Now as we have seen in previous chapters most investigators of the nightmare consider the "demon" (or any other character for that matter) as a kind of "stand-in" or symbol for the dreamer's emotional complexes. While this suggestion is plausible, there are many problems with it. To recapitulate briefly what we have already discussed, it is odd to claim that the demon (or any other character in a dreamer's dreams except for the dreamer himself) represents some other part of the dreamer's mind if we consider the dreamer's mind a unity. If the mind is a unity then it should not be able to entertain, simultaneously two different desires, beliefs, or intentions. But as we have seen in the nightmare this is precisely what happens. The monster or demon in a nightmare virtually always intends the possession of the dreamer's self, mind, soul, or personality. If the demon was part of the dreamer's ego then presumably it already is in possession of the dreamer's mind/personality so there is no need for it to attempt to take over the personality/mind of the dreamer. Yet that is precisely what it intends to do. If the mind is a unity how can it be both threatened and the threatener? Both victim and victimizer? Both dreamer and demon?

MIND IS NOT A UNITY

In this chapter I will entertain the proposition that the mind is not a unity and that the nightmare reveals the disunity in mind like no other psychological process. Many dreams involve the dreamer in interaction with at least one other being or person. To interact with another involves attributions or inferences about the other. Most fundamentally, we assume that the other person has a mind and possesses beliefs, desires, and goals just as we do. Therefore, dreaming must involve the attribution of intentionality toward other dream characters. To attribute intentionality to agents is to assume that they are motivated by beliefs, desires, intentions, hopes, fears, deceit, and so on.

This kind of mentalizing is performed by the dreamer in relation to other dream characters. This is a remarkable fact if we assume that the mind is a unity: The dream self is mind-reading the "minds" of characters the dreamer himself has created! Given that the dreamer conjured up these characters from his own memory networks, it must be that the dreamer already "knows" what his created characters will think, believe, or desire. The dreamer, here, is in much the same position as the author of a novel. He creates a character and watches how that character's subsequent actions and interactions with others unfold over time. Even when a dreamer dreams that he is being pursued by strangers, animals, or demons that intend to do him harm, he is attributing mind to those pursuers.

PARADOX OF MIND READING IN DREAMS: THE ROLE OF THE "STRANGER"

How does a dreamer "read" the minds of other dream characters if these characters are already part of the dreamer's mind? If dream characters are already part of the dreamer's personality would they perhaps be experienced as familiar to the dreamer? In a study of 320 dream reports from thirty-three adults, Kahn et al. (2000) reported that less than half (48 percent) of the characters in dreams were familiar to the dreamer. The average report length in this study was 237 words and contained an average of 3.7 characters. In the studies by Strauch and Meier (1996), familiar characters tended to be colleagues, coworkers, and friends from the dreamer's circle of acquaintances. To a lesser degree, parents and siblings were also represented in these dreams. In these cases the dreamer is perhaps conjuring up episodic memories of his or her acquaintances and then personifying them or treating them as if they were more than just memories. In the Hall and Van de Castle norms, 12 percent of male dreams and 19 percent of female dreams contained family members (Hall and Van de Castle 1966; Domhoff 1996). About a third of dreams (both male and female) contain friends of the dreamer. All of these data imply that perhaps as many as half of the characters that appear in dreams are familiar to the dreamer and half are strangers.

It is these strangers or unfamiliar characters in dreams that are particularly interesting from the point of view of nightmares, since they constitute a disproportionately high percentage of the characters in nightmares. Even in some dream series, up to 80 percent of characters are unknown to the dreamer. Almost all of the unknown characters in dreams or nightmares however are thought by the dreamer to be males who are somehow threatening the dreamer!

Noting that up to 80 percent of characters in dreams may be unknown to the dreamer, Kavanau (2002) suggested that they were epiphenomenal expressions of faulty or "incompetent" synaptic circuits. But this suggestion predicts that unknown characters would not show any particular patterns of expression. Incompetent circuitry, for example, would not be expected to clothe its unknown characters in male garb or confront unknown characters that mostly function as threatening, aggressive personages. Indeed, one might instead predict, as Kavanau himself seems to, that incompetent circuitry would give rise to relatively undefined or vague characterizations and relationships. Yet empirical analyses of the properties and relationships of unknown characters in dreams reveals that they are most often male, threatening, and aggressive.

In an early study of more than one thousand dreams, Hall (1966) reported that: 1) strangers in dreams were most often male, 2) aggressive encounters were more likely to occur in interactions with an unknown male than with an unknown female or with a familiar male or female, and 3) unknown males appeared more frequently in dreams of males than of females. Using the Hall and Van de Castle system, Domhoff (1996) looked at the role of "enemies" in dreams. Enemies were defined as dream characters that typically interacted (greater than 60 percent of the cases) with the dreamer in an aggressive manner. Those enemies turned out to be male strangers and animals. Interactions with female strangers are predominantly friendly in the dreams of both males and females. Schredl (2000) reports that almost all murderers and soldiers in dreams are male. Domhoff (2003b) has shown that when male strangers appear in a dream, the likelihood that physical aggression will occur in that dream far exceeds what would be expected on the basis of chance. In short, male strangers signal physical aggression. Strauch and Meier (1996) do not comment directly on the role of strangers in dreams, but they too reported that half of the characters they scored in their sample of dreams were unfamiliar to the dreamer. In fact, in about every third dream, the dreamer encountered only strangers. In short, male strangers in dreams (both those of men and women) are a constant feature of dream life. Male strangers appear to reliably signal threat or aggression vis-à-vis the dreamer. When they appear in nightmares, of course, they are associated with great distress and fear. Interestingly when demons appear in nightmares as they frequently do, they too are considered to be male.

MALE STRANGERS AND AGGRESSION IN DREAMS

What does the link between male strangers and aggression in dreams tell us about the unity of mind in dreams. It suggests that no such unity exists in dreams. If there was one mind creating the dream scenario then most of the characters would be familiar to the dreamer as they would be called up from memory and personified accordingly. Also if strangers in dreams simply reflected daily interactions with strangers in waking life then one would expect a more balanced distribution between males and females, but as we have just seen strangers in dreams are usually male. No, some other mind exists in dreams and it is signaled by dangerous male characters in the dream or nightmare.

On the face of it, the only other minds in the universe other than humans are animal minds. More recently empirical investigation of mental breakdown in the clinic has suggested to some that there may be several minds within a single person. The *Diagnostic and Statistical Manual of Mental Disorders, 4th Edition (Text Revision)* (DSM IV-TR) of the American Psychiatric Association (2000) recognizes a syndrome known as dissociative identity disorder (DID), formerly known as multiple personality disorder (MPD). In DID, a single patient appears to possess and manifest two or more distinct identities (a "host personality" or "host" and one or more "alter egos," "alters," or "ego states") that alternate in control over conscious experience. Indeed many modern models of the self consider the self as composed of at least two major and distinct subpersonalities or agents with distinct interests that compete for control over the individual's attentional resources and decision-making capacities. Once again one can see this duality of mind very clearly at the level of the dream.

REM-NREM DISSOCIATIONS IN THE DREAMING MIND

My colleagues and I (McNamara et al. 2005) recently published evidence (deriving from an analysis of more than five hundred mentation reports from the REM, NREM, and waking states) that REM and NREM exhibit processing specializations in the kinds of cognitive operations they perform and in the kinds of social interactions they simulate. Mentation reports from REM, for example, exhibited greater numbers of simulations of aggressive social interactions than NREM, and NREM exhibited greater numbers of simulations of friendly interactions than REM. Indeed, there were absolutely no (zero) simulations of aggressive interactions in NREM reports. We (McNamara et al. 2005) investigated

Table 11.1
Hall and Van de Castle Social Interaction Percentages in Scored Dreams

	REM	NREM	WAKE	REM versus NREM	REM versus WAKE	NREM versus WAKE
Aggression/ friendliness %	65%	33%	23%	0.026*	0.001**	0.456
Befriender %	54%	90%	76%	0.043*	0.192	0.354
Aggressor %	52%	0%	100%	0.0001**	0.014*	0.0001**
Physical aggression %	25%	18%	0%	0.540	0.007**	0.043*

*p = <.05
**p = <.01
Note: Aggression/friendliness % = Dreamer-involved aggression / (Dreamer-involved aggression + Dreamer-involved friendliness); Befriender % = Dreamer as befriender / Dreamer as befriender + Dreamer as befriended); Aggressor % = Dreamer as aggressor / (Dreamer as aggressor + dreamer as victim); Physical aggression % = Physical aggressions / All aggressions
Source: McNamara, P., D. McLaren, D. Smith, A. Brown, and R. Stickgold, 2005. A "Jekyll and Hyde" within: Aggressive versus friendly social interactions in REM and NREM dreams. *Psychological Science*, 16(2), 130–36.

potential REM versus NREM processing specializations by studying one hundred REM, one hundred NREM, and one hundred wake reports that had been collected in the home from eight men and seven women using the "Nightcap" sleep/wake mentation monitoring system. The Nightcap system reliably identifies episodes of REM and of Stage II NREM. Using the standardized Hall and Van de Castle dream scoring scales (described above), we scored these reports for number and variety of social interactions. We found that: 1) social interactions were more likely to be depicted in dream than in wake reports; 2) aggressive social interactions were more characteristic of REM than NREM or wake reports (Table 11.1); and 3) dreamer-initiated friendliness was more characteristic of NREM than REM (Table 11.1 and Figure 11.1). It is important to note that dreamer- initiated aggressive interactions were reduced to zero in NREM dreams, while dreamer-initiated friendly interactions were nearly twice as common in NREM as in REM. These data suggest that REM and NREM may exhibit specializations in processing routines for emotional material with NREM preferring pleasant emotional material and REM preferring unpleasant material. We will directly test this hypothesis in studies proposed here.

These findings need to be replicated and explored. These results concerning social interactions of characters in REM and NREM dreams suggest that characters in dreams can operate independently of the will of the dreamer. When the dreamer is under attack from some other

Figure 11.1
Dreamer-Initiated Aggression/Befriending Percentages Out of Total Number of Social Interactions in REM, NREM, and Waking Reports

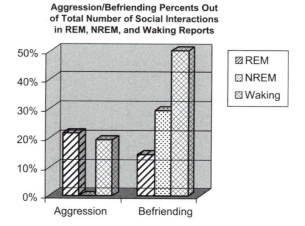

Note: Aggression P-Values: REM versus NREM < .0001; REM versus Waking < .1; NREM versus Waking < .0001; Befriending p-values: REM versus NREM < .09; REM versus Waking <.001; NREM versus Waking <.15. Roughly equal numbers of subjects (either six or seven) contributed to results depicted in each of the six columns (except for the NREM aggression column).
Source: McNamara, P., McLaren, D., Smith, D., Brown, A., and Stickgold, R. 2005. A "Jekyll and Hyde" within: Aggressive versus friendly social interactions in REM and NREM dreams. *Psychological Science,* 16(2): 130–36.

character, the dreamer never wishes it were so. Instead the dreamer does everything he can to flee the aggression. Characters in dreams therefore are not mere inventions of the dreamer. They are to some extent independent of the dreamer's will. Do they therefore satisfy criteria for being mental agents in and of themselves?

DREAMING AND CONSCIOUSNESS

Norman Malcolm (1956, 1959) argued that reports about dreaming are not publicly verifiable even in principle. Malcolm asserted that the notion of conscious awareness in sleep was contradictory on purely logical grounds. "If a person is in any state of consciousness it logically follows that he is not sound asleep" (Malcolm 1956, 21). According to Malcolm, dreams are not experiences at all (see also Dennett 1976). Malcolm and Dennett, however, are not giving due weight to the fact that dreaming is an active mental process as neuroimaging studies have now convincingly shown.

The interesting question, from a philosophical point of view, is not so much whether or not dreams are conscious experiences at all. Rather, one must ask about the theoretical status of other characters or minds in dreams. The criterion for the mental has usually been "intentionality." Does the agent in question exhibit intentional states such as beliefs, desires, and thoughts? Dream characters surely satisfy this criterion for the mental. But dream characters are peculiar and cannot be considered full-fledged mental agents. After all they do not persist past the dream they appear in as far as we know. Occasionally, we get reports that a character that appeared in one dream reappears in another some time later, but this is a rarity to say the least. On the other hand, the same characters can appear and reappear in recurring dreams and in so-called dream series that unfold over the course of a single night.

In any case dream characters do exhibit intentional states and thus must be considered in some sense "real" or causally effective intentional agents.

DREAM AGENTS/CHARACTERS CAN REPRESENT GENOMES WITHIN THE INDIVIDUAL

Where do these unusual agents come from? I believe that one possibility is that they are expressions of particular genomes within the individual. Individual organisms are composed of multiple genetic entities that obey varying transmission or inheritance patterns that create the context for intragenomic conflict (Partridge and Hurst 1998; Pomiankowski 1999) between two associated or antagonistic genes or genomes. The phenomenon known as genomic imprinting (Nicholls 2000; Tycko and Morison 2002; Verona, Mann, and Bartolomei 2003) is considered by many to be an example of intragenomic conflict. In this case, the genomes in conflict are paternally and maternally derived alleles, as imprinting involves the inactivation or silencing of one allele of a gene, depending on its parental origin. Expression of the associated allele likewise depends on whether it was inherited from the father or the mother. Haig's (2002) game theoretic models of the ways in which these genomes interact to produce a normal baby suggest that the paternally derived alleles enhance growth of a developing fetus or child regardless of its effects on the mother or siblings of the child, and that maternally derived alleles act to restrain transfer of resources to any given offspring. In this chapter, I examine the evidence for effects of genetic imprinting on sleep biology.

EFFECTS OF IMPRINTED GENES ON PHYSIOLOGIC SYSTEMS IMPLICATED IN GROWTH

Use of knockout mice models has revealed how intimately these imprinted genes shape internal physiologic systems supporting growth and reproductive behaviors. The paternally expressed genes Peg1 and Peg3, for example, are both expressed in the hypothalamus and influence regulation of CNS and neuroendocrine functions. Female heterozygous mice that inherited the knocked-out Peg1 gene from their father failed to build nests and to retrieve and care for pups. Peg3 knockouts not only failed to retrieve and care for pups but also could not effectively suckle their pups. Histological examination of the brains of these mothers revealed a significant reduction in oxytocinergic neurons in the hypothalamus. Given that oxytocin release is required for milk letdown in mice, offspring of these Peg3 knockout mice failed to gain weight and grow normally. These results are consistent with the idea that paternally expressed genes function to promote growth by controlling reproductive and parenting behaviors of mothers. Specifically, Peg1 and Peg3 appear to influence oxytocinergic circuits of the hypothalamus involved in care and nursing of pups.

Sleep state activation is linked with these hypothalamic oxytocinergic circuits. Activation of NREM SWS in the mother, for example, is required for oxytocin release (in rats and presumably in mice as well). Infant rats, on the other hand, prefer to nurse while they are in active sleep or AS/REM sleep. The AS/REM state, apparently, facilitates transfer of relatively large volumes of milk from the mother to the pup (Lorenz 1986; Lorenz et al. 1998). Thus, nursing in the rat may typically occur when all parties (mother and pups) are asleep, but in different sleep states: the mother in NREM SWS and the pup in AS/REM. Imprinted genes (Peg1 and Peg3) play a key role in this nocturnal interchange by influencing hypothalamic circuits that promote both wake-related and nursing-related maternal behaviors in the mother.

EFFECTS OF IMPRINTED GENES ON FUNCTIONAL BRAIN SYSTEMS IMPLICATED IN SLEEP PROCESSES

Keverne, Martel, and Nevison (1996) showed that functionally distinct regions of the brain may reflect the distinct contributions of the maternal and paternal genomes. They examined embryological development in mice possessing only maternal (parthenogenetic, PG) or paternal (androgenetic, AG) chromosomes. They produced a chimeric mouse containing a mixture of cells with either the single parent or normal complement of chromosomes (wild type). When they compared AG to PG wild types, they found that the distribution of PG and AG cells formed strikingly reciprocal patterns. Whereas PG cells were concentrated in cortical and striatal structures but excluded from hypothalamic, septal, basal forebrain, and preoptic areas, AG cells showed the opposite pattern. These data may have implications for sleep state biology, as REM sleep is associated with activation in hypothalamic, preoptic, basal forebrain, and limbic areas (i.e., areas with high paternal-line AG cell concentrations), and deactivation in selected cortical structures (i.e., areas high in maternal PG cell concentrations).

In summary, imprinted genes shape internal CNS physiologic systems concerned with growth, reproduction, and related behaviors. Given that both REM and NREM directly influence release and levels of a number of growth-related factors including GH, SS, and gonadal steroids (Inoue et al. 1999; Obal and Krueger 2003; Van Cauter et al. 1998), it seems reasonable to suppose that imprinted genes might exert a significant impact on selected properties of REM and NREM.

GENOMIC IMPRINTING AND SLEEP-STATE BIOLOGY

Before summarizing evidence for links between imprinted genes and sleep state biology, we need to briefly review key aspects of sleep state biology. REM sleep is promoted by cholinergic neurons originating within the LDT/PPT. REM sleep may be inhibited by noradrenergic and serotonergic neurons in the locus coeruleus and dorsal raphe, respectively. Activation of cholinergic REM (including phasic REM) is related to removal of inhibition exerted by these aminergic efferents on cholinergic cells in the LDT/PPT. When the aminergic neurons decrease their firing, cells of the LDT/PPT are released from inhibition and increase their firing. The release of acetylcholine from terminals of LDT/PPT cells triggers the onset of REM by activating brain regions that control various components of REM, including brain stem sites, hypothalamus, the limbic system, amygdala, and the basal forebrain. Cholinergic collaterals to the locus coeruleus and dorsal raphe nuclei exert an indirect excitatory effect on aminergic cell groups in these nuclei. As REM proceeds, this excitatory effect eventually reaches a threshold wherein their activation results in a feedback inhibition on REM-on cells of the LDT/PPT, thus ending the REM period. The initiation of NREM sleep may be a GABA-ergic-mediated process characterized by loss of wake-related alpha waves and slowing of EEG frequency.

Several imprinted sleep-related disorders and sleep-related genes can be documented. At 15q11-13:PWS and Angelman syndrome are neurodevelopmental syndromes that exhibit opposite imprinting profiles and opposite sleep phenotypes. PWS is associated with maternal additions or paternal deletions and exhibits a hypersomnic profile with REM abnormalities. Angelman syndrome, by contrast, is associated with paternal addition or maternal deletions, frequent night wakings, and insomnia with probably enhanced REM. These data are consistent with a genetic conflict model of sleep regulation where REM is aligned with patriline genetic influence and interests.

Genes that code for GABA B receptors are found at 15q11. What little evidence exists suggests that they are paternally expressed. Evidence summarized above (Amici et al. 2004) implies that maternally expressed 5-HT2A receptors mediate aminergic inhibition of REM-on cells in the PBL region, but that paternally expressed GABA B receptors may mediate inhibition of these aminergic inhibitory effects on REM, thus facilitating REM expression. Thus these data are consistent with a conflict model of sleep, again aligning REM with patriline interests.

At 20q13.2 there are genes that likely contribute to both REM and NREM expression. GNAS1 is crucial for expression of the whole series of G-protein receptors and thus neuroendocrine functions. The GNAS locus contains both paternally expressed and maternally expressed alleles. Franken, Challot, and Tafti (2001) identified a quantitative tract loci (QTL) that is implicated in regulation of the need for SWS. The disorder of loss of alpha EEG is linked to 20q13.2, as is nocturnal frontal lobe epilepsy and Ondine's curse, which involves sleep-related respiratory and ANS dysfunction. These data are neutral with respect to conflict model predictions except insofar as they confirm large-scale imprinting effects on sleep.

At 11p15.5 are several genes that code for growth regulatory factors. IGF2 is paternally expressed. Insulin may be paternally expressed. Beckwith-Widemann is an overgrowth syndrome involving duplication of the IGF2 gene. Given that IGF2 and INS are paternally expressed, and that they stimulate NREM, these data are not consistent with the conflict model, which aligns REM with patriline interests.

Serotonin, of course, is implicated in REM sleep regulation, and at least one 5-HT (serotonin) receptor is imprinted. The 5-HT2A receptor gene is maternally expressed. The Amici et al. (2004) study described above suggested that 5-HT2A receptors in the PBL mediated aminergic inhibition of REM expression. Given that the 5-HT2A receptor is maternally expressed, these data suggest that matriline genes act to inhibit REM, and thus these data are consistent with a conflict model wherein NREM expression is aligned with matriline genes, while REM is aligned with patriline genes.

These genetic effects on REM and NREM physiologies would be expected to give rise to markedly differing and opposing or antagonistic physiologic phenomena associated with each of the two sleep states and that is exactly what we find: Brain activation patterns are significantly different for REM and NREM, with REM demonstrating high activation levels in limbic/amygdaloid sites and deactivation of dorsolateral prefrontal cortex sites (Braun et al. 1997; Hobson, Stickgold, and Pace-Schott 1998; Maquet and Franck 1997; Maquet et al. 1996; Nofzinger et al. 1997), and NREM/SWS associated with deactivation of thalamic functions and emergence of synchronized wave activity throughout neocortical sites.

Hobson and Pace-Schott (2002) and Steriade and McCarley (1990), and others have presented a great deal of experimental evidence which suggests that regulation of the REM/NREM sleep cycle is governed by two major neural ensembles that act in an antagonistic fashion to turn on or turn off REM. Briefly, REM is generated by cholinergic neurons originating within the peribrachial regions known as the laterodorsal tegmental and pedunculopontine tegmental (LDT/PPT) nuclei, and is inhibited by noradrenergic and serotonergic neurons in the locus coeruleus and dorsal raphe, respectively. Activation of cholinergic REM is due to removal of inhibition of cholinergic cells in the LDT/PPT normally sustained by aminergic efferents. In sum, expression of the REM-NREM cycle is regulated, in part, by antagonistic cellular groups within the brainstem with aminergic cell groups inhibiting expression of REM (with emergence of NREM) and cholinergic groups promoting expression of REM. When cholinergic REM-on cells are activated, aminergic REM-off cell groups are inhibited, and vice versa.

Rapid-eye-movement (REM) and NREM sleep may also be regulated by separate sets of genes. Tafti and Franken (2002) have shown that inbred mice strains C57BL and C57BR are associated with increased REM and short SWS episodes, while the BALB/c strain is associated with short REM and long NREM episodes, indicating separate genetic influences on REM and NREM sleep amounts. Electrophysiologic measures of sleep in humans are also influenced by genes. Studies of sleep EEG in twins reared apart show separable genetic effects on REM versus delta waves of NREM as well as stronger correlations of EEG indices of sleep among monozygotic twin pairs as compared to dizygotic twin pairs (Linkowski 1999; Tafti and Franken 2002; Taheri and Mignot 2002). These data on imprinting and sleep state biology suggests that REM and NREM are regulated by opposing sets of imprinted genes. If so we should see antagonistic cognitive-emotion specializations associated with the two sleep states.

Rapid-eye-movement (REM) sleep and NREM do exhibit antagonistic cognitive processing specializations, particularly with respect to emotions. Spontaneously recalled dreams are typically filled with emotion. Between 75 percent and 95 percent of spontaneously recalled dreams (likely REM dreams) contain at least one emotion (Domhoff 1996; Merritt et al. 1994). Merritt and colleagues (1994) asked their subjects to specifically indicate, on a line-by-line basis, the presence of one or more specific emotions associated with the content of their spontaneously recalled dreams. Using this method, Merritt et al. found that 95 percent of all their dream reports (N = 200 reports) contained emotions and that each dream report averaged about 3.6 emotions per dream. Early reports of content differences between REM and NREM suggested that REM dreams were more emotional than NREM dreams. NREM dreams were characterized as being less vivid and more thought-like than REM dreams. Strauch and Meier (1996) comment that in their dream series, "barely every second NREM dream featured the dream self emotionally related to the dream situation, whereas four out of every five REM dreams involved the dreamer emotionally in its events" (138). Revonsuo (2000) presented a large amount of evidence suggesting that the majority of REM dreams involve unpleasant emotional states wherein the dreamer experiences some sort of physical or emotional threat in the dream.

Smith, Nixon, and Nader (2004) scored both REM and NREM reports for emotion content from twenty-five dreamers. They identified eight emotions that they then divided into positive and negative categories. The positive emotion category consisted of joy/elation and love, while the negative emotion category consisted of anger, anxiety/fear, sadness, and shame. They found that negative emotions were significantly more intense in REM than NREM, whereas positive emotions were not. Thus, although the available evidence indicates greater emotionality in REM dreams (and even perhaps an excess of negative emotions in REM dreams), NREM dreams are not without emotion. The question of specializations in emotional processing by REM and NREM, however, still needs to be investigated.

In short, what little evidence exists suggests that selected aspects of expression of REM and NREM are regulated by separate sets of genes. Some of these regulatory genes may be imprinted with paternally derived alleles influencing REM expression more than NREM and maternally derived alleles influencing expression of NREM more than REM. REM and NREM exhibit opposing processing specializations from the cellular right up to the cognitive level. Thus the conflict model of REM and NREM is consistent with all of these data. But it has to be admitted that the evidence for this kind of a conflict model of REM and NREM expression is weak and only correlative. Nevertheless it is consistent with the model of dual expression of agents in dreams and nightmares I outlined above where one set of agents is in conflict with another set of agents, or where one character is threatening another or the dream ego itself.

GENETIC CONFLICT AND DREAM PHENOMENOLOGY

If we assume that some sort of genetic conflict model, even if it is not the imprinted gene model, will eventually help to account for dream and nightmare phenomenology, then how are conflicts expressed and dealt with in nightmares? On the face of it conflict is what nightmares are all about, with the dream ego in direct war with other dream characters who are out to harm the dream ego. Are these conflicts ever resolved? If not, why not? If yes, how?

Nightmares "prefer" to occur in the later REM periods. There are between three and five REM periods per night in most healthy individuals. As the night progresses, activation patterns become more intense and culminate in the long dreams characteristic of the final REM period of the night. The early REM researchers, who were influenced by psychoanalytic theory, presented evidence that all REM episodes contribute to the emotional processing occurring during sleep but that results of all this processing are only summarized in the final REM episode of the night (French and Fromme 1964; Trosman et al. 1960).

These authors (French and Fromme 1964; Trosman et al. 1960) suggested that dreams at the beginning of the night (we now know that these would be NREM dreams) would announce an emotional wish or emotional conflict that dreams later in the night would pick up and work with in an attempt to contain or resolve the emotional conflict. These investigators presented several case studies involving collection of dreams across the night that seemed to support the claim.

For example, as mentioned above, Offenkrantz and Rechtschaffen (1963) studied the sequential sleep patterns and dreams of a patient in psychotherapy for 15 consecutive nights. They noted that scenes from childhood memories never occurred early in the night but did occur on eight of the fifteen nights in dreams occurring after 4:30 A.M. They also noted that all the dreams of a night tended to be concerned with the same emotional conflict or a small number of such conflicts. They also claimed they found evidence that the organization of a particular dream depended on the results of the dream work of the preceding dream, such that dream wishes required less and less disguise as the night progressed.

Offenkrantz and Rechtschaffen (1963) studied sequential NREM-REM dreams within a single night in three subjects who had previously demonstrated good dream recall from NREM sleep. They restricted themselves to noting only obvious connections between dreams in sequence rather than analyzing "latent" content or asking for the dreamer's associations to his or her dreams. They found repeated instances of dream elements recurring throughout the dream sequence. For example, the image of a street corner appeared in the first NREM dream of the night. It later appeared as the place where the dreamer met a girl. Other repeating elements noted in dream sequences of other subjects included: riding a bicycle, looking at a photograph, attending an outing, picnic, or camping trip, taking exams, sensing a sunny day, and so on. These elements, settings, or themes recurred throughout dream sequences and often framed emotional encounters in later dream images.

Many authors have suggested various ways in which NREM interacts with REM in processing of memories. Giuditta et al. (1995)

suggested that NREM selects memories that will be consolidated, and then consolidation occurs under REM. Fosse, Stickgold, and associates have drawn on the work of Buzsaki (1996) and their own empirical findings in analyses of dream content (Fosse et al. 2003) to suggest that one can "see" aspects of the process of memory consolidation as a function of REM-NREM interactions by looking at dream content. It was hypothesized that during slow-wave NREM sleep, memories of life episodes and events are consolidated into episodic memories and transferred to the cortex for storage. During REM sleep, hippocampal outflow to the cortex is blocked. Instead, the hippocampus receives information from cortical networks, thus preventing transfer of newly consolidated episodic memories to the cortex. Thus, one should not see instances of fully formed episodic memories in REM dreams, and in fact that is what Fosse et al. (2003) found. Instead, semantic and procedural aspects of memories are thought to be processed during REM. Consistent with the Stickgold et al. model, Cavallero, Cicogna, and Bosinelli (1988) elicited dreams from the onset phase, from NREM and REM sleep, and asked their subjects to freely associate to individual dream segments. Associations to REM dreams were more often related to general knowledge, whereas dream onset and NREM dreams were more closely related to memories of life episodes.

CONCLUDING REMARKS

While most students of the nightmare have treated nightmares as symptoms of breakdown or disorder in the person's neuropsychiatric system, I have broken with this tradition in this book. Instead I suggest that nightmares are like any other adaptive system. Nightmares exhibit functional design and solved a problem or addressed an opportunity for ancestral human populations. Functional adaptations need not be pleasant to be helpful. Nightmares, in fact, can be compared to a fever: unpleasant but adaptive and even life-giving.

What problem or opportunity did nightmares address for ancestral populations? I do not know for sure but I suggest that the suite of problems addressed by the experience and sharing of nightmares had to do with the individual's identity, reputation, and prestige in the group. Nightmares always involve an attack on the self or identity of the dreamer and nightmares most often occur in individuals whose identities are in flux or under duress.

Nightmares are first reported by children and peak during late childhood and early adolescence. In adults, nightmares occur in individuals "under pressure" of some kind or those with "thin boundaries" or those experiencing unusual stress. When children's dreams include the presence of "supernatural agents," including of course monsters, who evince some sort of hostile intention toward the child/dreamer, the dream is more likely to cause distress and to be called a nightmare. Children who experience frequent nightmares may also be particularly open to belief in imaginary friends and supernatural agents.

The situation is similar in some respects to adults who report nightmares. Nightmares in adults have story lines that place the self under extreme distress and threat, that enhance the self's negative emotions and images, that block the self's normal mind-reading abilities (it is difficult to understand the intentions of a space alien or monster for example); and sets a monster of some kind after the self to hurt or "possess" or control the self.

When a monster, demon, or some other unnatural creature appears in a dream or nightmare a "major misfortune" for the dreamer is much more likely to occur in the dream/nightmare. The link between the presence of supernatural agents in nightmares and disaster for the dreamer in the dream/nightmare may be extremely significant clinically as the presence of misfortune in dreams is very likely a causative factor in the emotional distress associated with the nightmare. It is the emotional distress associated with some nightmares that best predicts daytime clinical disturbances.

Nightmares, in short, are intensely compelling and memorable emotional experiences for most people where the individual's self is under attack and in danger of experiencing a major misfortune. Not surprisingly these nighttime experiences are likely to be shared with others. When you have a nightmare you most likely want to share it with someone else—especially moments after you awaken from a nightmare. The sense of dread lingers for a while after the nightmare. There is a need to be with someone rather than alone and a need to share the story and images associated with the nightmare.

When nightmares are shared with others in a compelling way, they have been shown to enhance the social prestige of individuals in premodern societies and cultures, funneling these creative individuals into spiritual, healing, or "shamanic" professions. Thus, they "solved" a problem—the problem of how to achieve social prminence and prestige in order to increase one's fitness. Finally, nightmare content variables and resultant nightmare distress, when shared in a social context, can to some extent be understood as costly signaling behaviors and profitably be analyzed within the costly signaling theoretical evolutionary framework.

Nightmares, then, should not be considered mere byproducts of some other system such as gastric upset (!) or emotional distress. Instead nightmares reflect an effort by the dreamer to respond to an intense assault on the dreamer's self or identity. The assault was believed in ancestral populations (and even today in some circles) to come from supernaturally destructive or demonic forces that were out to take possession of the dreamer's very soul. Much of the world's mythology and stories concerning spirit possession come from humanity's experiences with nightmares. The dreamer who experiences nightmares takes the unwelcome assault as an opportunity to "raise the stakes." He or she fights back against the assaulting entity and then attempts to promote healthy development of the sense of self or self-concept, usually in service to a change in social status or prestige of the individual.

Whatever the outcome of these self-related "strivings" or "battles" in nightmares, when nightmares become recurrent and unrelenting, the nightmare sufferer can and should seek help. Some treatment options have been mentioned in the text. The basic approach should be to strengthen the sense of self of the individual. With a little help from an experienced professional who affirms and supports the individual's sense of self, dreams and even nightmares can once again be experienced as sources for renewal, hope, and change.

Appendix: Additional Resources

REVIEW ARTICLES ON NIGHTMARES

Levin, R. and T. A. Nielsen. 2007. Disturbed dreaming, posttraumatic stress disorder, and affect distress: A review and neurocognitive model. *Psychological Bulletin.* 133 (3): 482–528.

Mellman, T. A., and M. M. Hipolito. 2006. Sleep disturbances in the aftermath of trauma and posttraumatic stress disorder. *CNS Spectrum.* 11 (8): 611–15.

Pagel, J. F., and P. Helfter. 2003. Drug induced nightmares—an etiology based review. *Human Psychopharmacology.* 18 (1): 59–67.

Phelps, A. J., D. Forbes, and M. Creamer. 2007. Understanding posttraumatic nightmares: An empirical and conceptual review. *Clinical Psychological Reviews.* Article in press.

Reading, P. 2007. Parasomnias: The spectrum of things that go bump in the night. *Practical Neurology.* 7 (1): 6–15.

Roldan, G., and R. C. Ang, 2006. Overview of sleep disorders. *Respiratory Care Clinics of North America.* 12 (1): 31–54.

Spoormaker, V. I., M. Schredl, and J. van den Bout. 2006. Nightmares: From anxiety symptom to sleep disorder. *Sleep Medicine Reviews.* 10 (1): 19–31.

van Liempt, S., E. Vermetten, E. Gueze, and H. Westenberg. 2006. Pharmacotherapeutic treatment of nightmares and insomnia in posttraumatic stress disorder: An overview of the literature. *Annals of the New York Academy of Sciences.* 1071: 502–7.

Zervas, I. M. and C. R. Soldatos. 2005. Nightmares: Personality dimensions and psychopathological attributes. *Internal Review of Psychiatry.* 17 (4): 271–76.

BOOKS ON NIGHTMARES

Belanger, Jeff. *The Nightmare Encyclopedia: Your Darkest Dreams Interpreted.* Franklin Lakes, NJ: New Page Books, 2005.

Bulkeley, Kelly. *Dreams of Healing: Transforming Nightmares into Visions of Hope.* Mahwah, NJ: Paulist Press, 2003.

Burgess, Mary, Isaac Marks, and Michael Gill. *Self-Help for Nightmares: A Book for Adults with Frequent Recurrent Bad Dreams*. Oxford, UK: Blue Stallion Publications, 2001.

Krakow, Barry and Joseph Neidhart. *Conquering Bad Dreams & Nightmares: A Guide to Understanding, Interpretation & Cure*. New York: The Berkeley Publishing Group, 1992.

NIGHTMARE/DREAM WEBSITES

Center for Sleep Medicine & Nightmare Treatment http://www.nightmare treatment.com/

Dream and Nightmare Laboratory http://www.jtkresearch.com/dreamlab/

DreamBank http://www.dreambank.net/

The Nightmare Project http://www.nightmareproject.com/

The Quantitative Study of Dreams http://dreamresearch.net/

Sleep Paralysis Page http://watarts.uwaterloo.ca/~acheyne/S_P

References

Achte, K., and T. Schakir. 1985. A study of the dreams of a group of bushmen. *Psychiatria Fennica*, Suppl. S26–S33.

Adams, K. 2005. Voices in my dream: Children's interpretation of auditory messages in divine dreams. *Dreaming*, 15 3: 195–204.

Ağargün, M. Y., A. S. Cilli, H. Kara, N. Tarhan, F. Kincir, and H. Oz. 1998. Repetitive frightening dreams and suicidal behavior in patients with major depression. *Comprehensive Psychiatry*. 39:198–202.

Albin, R. L., R. A. Koeppe, R. D. Chervin, F. B. Consens, K. Wernette, K.A. Frey, et al. 2000. Decreased striatal dopaminergic innervation in REM sleep behavior disorder. *Neurology*. 55 (9): 1410–12.

American Academy of Sleep Medicine. 2005. *International classification of sleep disorders: Diagnostic and coding manual.* 2nd ed. Chicago: American Academy of Sleep Medicine.

American Psychiatric Association. 2000. *Diagnostic and statistical manual of mental disorders*. 4th ed. (text rev.). Washington, D.C.: American Psychiatric Press.

Amici, R., L. D. Sanford, K. Kearney, B. McInerney, R. J. Ross, R. L. Horner, et al. 2004. A serotonergic (5-HT2) receptor mechanism in the laterodorsal tegmental nucleus participates in regulating the pattern of rapid-eye-movement sleep occurrence in the rat. *Brain Research*. 996 (1): 9–18.

Anders, T. F., A. Sadeh and V. Appareddy, 1995. Normal sleep in neonates and children. In *Principles and practice of sleep medicine in the child*, ed. R. Ferber and M. Kryger, 7–18. Philadelphia: W. B. Saunders.

Armitage, R., A. Hudson, M. Trivedi, and A. J. Rush. 1995. Sex differences in the distribution of EEG frequencies during sleep: Unipolar depressed outpatients. *Journal of Affective Disorders*. 34 (2): 121–29.

Asplund, R., and H. Aberg. 1998. Sleep and cardiac symptoms amongst women aged 40–64 years. *Journal of Internal Medicine*. 243 (3): 209–13.

Bach, V., F. Telliez, and J. P. Libert. 2002. The interaction between sleep and thermoregulation in adults and neonates. *Sleep Medicine Reviews*. 6 (6): 481–92.

Barrett, J. L., R. A. Richert, and A. Driesenga. 2001. God's beliefs versus mother's: The development of nonhuman agent concepts. *Child Development.* 72 (1): 50–65.

Barrett, L., R. Dunbar, and J. Lycett. 2002. *Human evolutionary psychology.* New York: Palgrave.

Basilov, V. 1997. Shamans and their religious practices from shamanism among the Turkic peoples of Siberia. In *Shamanic worlds: Rituals and lore of Siberia and central Asia,* ed. M. M. Balzar, 3–48. Armonk, NY: North Castle Books.

Bauer, D. H. 1976. An Exploratory study of developmental changes in children's fears. *Journal of Child Psychology and Psychiatry* 17 (1): 69–74.

Beahm, G. A. 1998. *Stephen King: America's best loved boogeyman.* Kansas City, MO: McMeel Press.

Beersma, D. G. M. 1990. Do winter-depressives experience summer nights in winter? *Archives of General Psychiatry.* 47:879–80.

Belicki, D., and K. Belicki. 1982. Nightmares in a university population. *Sleep Research.* 11:116.

Belicki, K. 1992a. Nightmare frequency vs. nightmare distress: Relations to psychopathology and cognitive style. *Journal of Abnormal Psychology.* 101:592–97.

Belicki, K. 1992b. The relationship of nightmare frequency to nightmare suffering with implications for treatment and research. *Dreaming.* 2:143–48.

Belicki, K., and D. Belicki. 1986. Predisposition for nightmares: A study of hypnotic ability, vividness of imagery, and absorption. *Journal of Clinical Psychology.* 42:714–18.

Benca, R. M. 2000. Mood disorders. In *Principles and practice of sleep medicine,* 3rd ed., ed. M. H. Kryger, T. Roth, and W. C. Dement, 1140–48. Philadelphia: W. B. Saunders.

Bixler, E. O., A. Kales, C. R. Soldatos, J. D. Kales, and S. Healy. 1979. Prevalence of sleep disorders in the Los Angeles metropolitan area. *American Journal of Psychiatry.* 136:1257–62.

Bjorklund, D. F., and A. D. Pellegrinni. 2002. *The origins of human nature: Evolutionary developmental psychology.* Washington, D.C.: American Psychological Association Press.

Black Elk, and Neihardt, J. 1932. *Black Elk speaks.* Lincoln, NE: University of Nebraska Press.

Blatty, W. P. 1971. *The exorcist.* New York: Harper and Row.

Blatty, W. P. 1973. *The exorcist,* film, directed by William Friedkin. Burbank, CA: Warner Bros. Pictures.

Bliege-Bird, R. and E. Smith. 2005. Signaling theory, strategic interaction, and symbolic capital. *Current Anthropology.* 46:221–48.

Blurton-Jones, N. G. 1993. The lives of the hunter-gatherer children: Effects of parental behavior and parental reproductive strategy. In *Juvenile primates: Life history, development and behavior,* ed. M. E. Periera and L. A. Fairbanks, 309–26. Oxford: Oxford University Press.

Boeve, B. F., M. H. Silber, C. B. Saper, T. J. Ferman, D. W. Dickson, J. E. Parisi, et al. 2007. Pathophysiology of REM sleep behaviour disorder and relevance to neurodegenerative disease. *Brain* 130 (11): 2770–88.

Bonnet, M. H. 2005. Acute sleep deprivation. In *Principles and practice of sleep medicine*, 4th ed., ed. M. H. Kryger, T. Roth, and W. C. Dement, 51–66. Philadelphia: W. B. Saunders.

Borbély, A. A. 1984. Schlafgewohnheiten, Schlafqualität und Schlafmittelkonsum der Schweizer Bevölkerung: Ergebnisse einer Repräsentativumfrage [Sleep habits, sleep quality, and sleeping drug consumption of Swiss population: Results of a representative inquiry]. *Schweizerische Ärztezeitung.* 65:1606–13.

Borbély, A. A., and Wirz-Justice, A. 1982. Sleep, sleep deprivation and depression: A hypothesis derived from a model of sleep regulation. *Human Neurobiology.* 1 (3): 205–10.

Bouchard, T. 2004. Genetic influence on human psychological traits: A survey. *Current Directions in Psychological Science.* 13:148–51.

Bourguignon, E. 1973. *Religion, altered states of consciousness and social change.* Columbus, OH: Ohio State University Press.

Bradbury, J., and Vehrencamp, S. 1998. *Principles of animal communication.* Sunderland, MA: Sinauer Associates.

Brauen, M. 1980. Feste in Ladakh [Festivals in Ladakh]. Graz, Austria: Academicshe Druk und Verlaganstalt.

Braun, A. R., T. J. Balkin, N. J. Wesenstein, M. Varga, P. Baldwin, S. Selbie, et al. 1997. Regional cerebral blood flow throughout the sleep-wake cycle. *Brain.* 120:1173–97.

Buysse, D. J., M. Hall, A. Begley, C.R. Cherry, P. R. Houck, S. Land, et al. 2001. Sleep and treatment response in depression: New findings using power spectral analysis. *Psychiatry Research.* 103 (1): 51–67.

Buzsaki, G. 1996. The hippocampo-neocortical dialogue. *Cerebral Cortex.* 6 (2): 81–92.

Cabana, T., P Jolicouer, and J. Michael. 1993. Prenatal and postnatal growth and allometry of stature, head circumference, and brain weight in Quebec children. *American Journal of Human Biology.* 5:93–99.

Calvo, J. M., S. Badillo, M. Morales-Ramirez, and P. Palacios-Salas. 1987. The role of the temporal lobe amygdala in ponto-geniculo-occipital activity and sleep organization in cats. *Brain Research.* 403 (1): 22–30.

Calvo, J. M., K. Simon-Arceo, and R. Fernandez-Mas. 1996. Prolonged enhancement of REM sleep produced by carbachol microinjection into the amygdale. *NeuroReport.* 7 (2): 577–80.

Carskadon, M. A., and W. C. Dement. 2006. Normal human sleep: An overview. In *Principles and practice of sleep medicine* 4th ed, ed. M. H. Kryger, T. Roth, and W. C. Dement, 13–23. Philadelphia: W. B. Saunders.

Carskadon, M. A., and A. Rechtschaffen. 2000. Monitoring and staging human sleep. In *Principles and practice of sleep medicine*, 3rd ed., ed. M. H. Kryger, T. Roth, and W. C. Dement, 1197–1216. Philadelphia: W. B. Saunders.

Cartwright, R. 1979. The nature and function of repetitive dreams: A speculation. *Psychiatry.* 42:131–37.

Cartwright, R., and S. Lloyd. 1994. Early REM sleep: A compensatory change in depression? *Psychiatry Research.* 51 (3): 245–52.

Cartwright, R. D. 1991. Dreams that work: The relation of dream incorporation to adaption to stressful events. *Dreaming.* 1:3–9.

Cavallero, C., P. Cicogna, and M. Bosinelli. 1988. Mnemonic activation in dream production. In *Sleep '86,* ed. W. P. Koella, F. Obal, H. Schulz, and P. Visser, 91–94. New York: Gustav Fischer Verlag.

Cheyne, J. A. 2007. Sleep paralysis and associated hypnagogic and hypnopompic experiences. Retrieved December 14, 2007, from http://watarts.uwaterloo. ca/~acheyne/S_P.html

Coalson, B. 1995. Nightmare help: Treatment of trauma survivors with PTSD. *Psychotherapy.* 32: 381–88.

Cohen, E. 2007. *The mind possessed: The cognition of spirit possession in an Afro-Brazilian religious tradition.* New York: Oxford University Press.

Craven, W. 1984. *A nightmare on Elm Street.* Film. Directed by Wes Craven. New York: New Line Cinema. www.newlinecinema.com

Crook, J. H. 1997. The indigenous psychiatry of Ladakh, Part I: Practice theory approaches to trance possession in the Himalayas. *Anthropology and Medicine.* 4 (3): 289–307.

Crook, J. H. 1998. The indigenous psychiatry of Ladakh, Part II: Narrative and metanarrative in the cultural control of dissociative states in the Himalayas. *Anthropology and Medicine.* 5 (1): 23–42.

Crook, J. H., and S. Crook. 1988. Tibetan polyandry: Problems of adaptation and fitness. In *Human reproductive behaviour: A Darwinian perspective,* ed. L. M. Betzig, M. Borgerhoff-Mulder, and P. Turke, 97–114. Cambridge: Cambridge University Press.

Datta, S. 1999. PGO wave generation mechanism and functional significance. In *Rapid eye movement sleep,* ed. S. Inoue, 91–106. New York: Marcel Dekker.

Day, S. E. 1989. *Embodying spirits: Village oracles and possession ritual in Ladakh, North India.* London: University of London.

Dement, W., and N. Kleitman, N. 1957a. The relation of eye movements during sleep to dream activity: An objective method for the study of dreaming. *Journal of Experimental Psychology.* 53 (5): 339–46.

Dement, W. and N. Kleitman. 1957b. Cyclic variations in EEG during sleep and their relation to eye movements, body motility and dreaming. *Electroencephalography and Clinical Neurophysiology.* 9 (4): 673–90.

Dennett, D. 1976. Are dreams experiences? *Philosophical Review.* 85:151–71.

Dessalles, J. 1998. Altruism, status and the origin of relevance. In *Approaches to the evolution of language,* ed. J. R. Hurford, M. Studdert-Kennedy, and C. Knight, 130–47. Cambridge: Cambridge University Press.

Dijk, D. J., B. Hayes, and C. A. Czeisler. 1993. Dynamics of electroencephalographic sleep spindles and slow wave activity in men: Effect of sleep deprivation. *Brain Research.* 626 (1–2): 190–99.

Dinges, D. F., N. L. Rogers, and M. D. Baynard. 2005. Chronic sleep deprivation. In *Principles and practice of sleep medicine,* 4th ed., ed. M. H. Kryger, T. Roth, and W. C. Dement, 51–66. Philadelphia: W. B. Saunders.

Domhoff, G. W. 1993. The repetition of dreams and dream elements: A possible clue to a function of dreams? In *The functions of dreaming,* ed. A. Moffitt, M. Kramer, and R. Hoffmann, 293–320. Albany: State University of New York Press.

Domhoff, G. W. 1996. *Finding meaning in dreams: A quantitative approach.* New York: Plenum Publishing Co.

Domhoff, G. W. 2003a. *The case against the problem-solving theory of dreaming.* Retrieved December 20, 2007, from http://dreamresearch.net/Library/domhoff_2004b.html

Domhoff, G. W. 2003b. *The scientific study of dreams: Neural networks, cognitive development, and content analysis.* Washington, D.C.: American Psychological Association.

Domhoff, G. W. 2005. The content of dreams: Methodologic and theoretical implications. In *Principles and practices of sleep medicine.* 4th ed., ed. M. H. Kryger, T. Roth, and W. C. Dement, 522–34. Philadelphia: W. B. Saunders.

Douglas, N. J. 2000. Respiratory physiology: Control of ventilation. In *Principles and practice of sleep medicine,* 3rd ed., ed. W. C. Dement, 221–28. Philadelphia: W. B. Saunders.

Dunbar, R. I. M., and L. Barrett, eds. 2007. *Oxford handbook of evolutionary psychology.* Oxford: Oxford University Press.

Dupras, T., H. Schwarcz, and S. Fairgrieve. 2001. Infant feeding and weaning practices in Roman Egypt. *American Journal of Physical Anthropology,* 115 (3): 204–12.

Durkheim, E. 1995. *Elementary forms of the religious life.* Trans. K. E. Fields. New York: Free Press.

Durston, P. J., M. Farrell, D. Attwater, J. Allen, H. J. Kuo, M. Afify, et al. 2001. OASIS natural language call steering trial. *Proceedings of Eurospeech 2001,* 1323–26. Aalborg, Denmark.

Freud, S. (1998). *The Interpretation of Dreams.* New York: Avon Books (original work published in 1900).

Eliade, M. 1972. *Shamanism: Archaic techniques of ecstasy.* Princeton: Princeton University Press. (Original work published 1951)

Estioko-Griffin, A. A. 1986. Daughters of the forest. *Natural History.* 95:36–43.

Fantini, M. L., and L. Ferini-Strambi. 2007. REM-related dreams in REM behavior disorder. In *The new science of dreaming: Vol. 1: Biological aspects,* ed. D. Barrett and P. McNamara, 185–200. Westport, CT: Praeger Publishers.

Ferman, T. J., B. F. Boeve, G. E. Smith, M. H. Silber, E. Kokmen, R. C. Petersen, et al. 1999. REM sleep behavior disorder and dementia: Cognitive differences when compared with AD. *Neurology.* 52 (5): 951–57.

Firth, R. 2001. Tikopia dreams: Personal images and social realities. *Journal of the Polynesian Society. 110* (1): 7–29.

Fisher, B. E., C. Pauley, and K. McGuire. 1989. Children's sleep behavior scale: Normative data on 870 children in grades 1 to 6. *Perceptual and Motor Skills.* 68:227–36.

Fisher, C., J. Byrne, A. Edwards, A., and E. Kahn. 1970. A psychophysiological study of nightmares. *Journal of the American Psychoanalytic Association.* 18: 747–82.

Fosse, M. J., R. Fosse, J. A. Hobson, and R. Stickgold, R. 2003. Dreaming and episodic memory: A functional dissociation? *Journal of Cognitive Neuroscience. 15:*1–9.

Foulkes, D. 1978. *A grammar of dreams.* New York: Basic Books.

Foulkes, D. 1982. *Children's dreams: Longitudinal studies.* New York: Wiley.

Foulkes, D. 1999. *Children's dreaming and the development of consciousness.* Cambridge, MA: Harvard University Press.

Foulkes, D., and G. Vogel. 1965. Mental activity at sleep onset. *Journal of Abnormal Psychology.* 70: 231–43.

Franken, P., D. Chollet, and M. Tafti. 2001. The homeostatic regulation of sleep need is under general control. *Journal of Neuroscience.* 21:2601–21.

French, T., and E. Fromme. 1964. *Dream interpretation: A new approach.* New York: Basic Books.

Fuseli, J. H., artist. 1781. *The nightmare.* [oil painting on canvas]. Detroit, MI: The Detroit Institute of Art.

Germaine, A., and T. A. Nielsen. (2003). Sleep pathophysiology in posttraumatic stress disorder and idiopathic nightmare sufferers. *Biological Psychiatry.* 54:1092–98.

Giles, D. E., D. J. Kupfer, A. J. Rush, and H. P. Roffwarg, 1998. Controlled comparison of electrophysiological sleep in families of probands with unipolar depression. *American Journal of Psychiatry.* 155 (2): 192–99.

Giles, D. E., H. P. Roffwarg, M. A. Schlesser, and A. J. Rush. 1986. Which endogenous depressive symptoms relate to REM latency reduction? *Biological Psychiatry.* 21 (5–6): 473–82.

Giuditta, A., M. V. Ambrosini, P. Montagnese, P. Mandile, M. Cotugno, Z. G. Grassi, et al. 1995. The sequential hypothesis of the function of sleep. *Behavioural Brain Research.* 69:157–66.

Goodenough, D. R. 1991. Dream recall: History and current status of the field. In *The mind in sleep: Psychology and psychophysiology,* 2nd ed., ed. S. J. Ellman and J. S. Antrobus, 143–71. New York: Wiley.

Grafen, A. 1990. Biological signals as handicaps. *Journal of Theoretical Biology.* 144: 517–46.

Gregor, T. 1981a. "Far, far away my shadow wandered …" The dream symbolism and dream theories of the Mehinaku Indians of Brazil. *American Ethnologist.* 8 (4): 709–20.

Gregor, T. 1981b. A content analysis of Mehinaku dreams. *Etho.,* 9 (4): 353–90.

Gregor, T. 2001. Content analysis of Mehinaku dreams. In *Dreams: A reader on the religious, cultural, and psychological dimensions of dreaming,* ed. K. Bulkeley, 133–66. New York: Palgrave.

Gurney, E., F. W. H. Myers, and F. Podmore. 1886. *Phantasms of the living.* 2 vols. London: Trubner.

Hagen, E. H. 2003. The bargaining model of depression. In *Genetic and cultural evolution of cooperation,* ed. P. Hammerstein, 95–123. Cambridge, MA: MIT Press.

Haig, D. 2002. *Genomic imprinting and kinship.* Piscataway, NJ: Rutgers University Press.

Hall, C. 1966. Strangers in dreams: An empirical confirmation of the Oedipus complex. *Journal of Personality.* 31:336–45.

Hall, C., and R. Van de Castle. 1966. *The content analysis of dreams.* New York: Appleton-Century-Crofts.

Halliday, G. 1987. Direct psychological therapies for nightmares: A review. *Clinical Psychology Review.* 7 (5): 501–23.

Harner, M. 1982. *The way of the shaman.* New York: Bantam.

Harner, M. J. 1972. *The Jivaro: People of the sacred waterfalls.* Garden City, NY: Doubleday.

Harris, I. R. 1948. Observations concerning typical anxiety dreams. *Psychiatry.* 11:301–9.

Hartmann, E. 1984. *The nightmare: The psychology and the biology of terrifying dreams.* New York: Basic Books.

Hartmann, E. 1987. *The sleep book: Understanding and preventing sleep problems in people over 50.* Washington, D.C.: American Association of Retired Persons.

Hartmann, E. 1998. Nightmare after trauma as paradigm for all dreams: A new approach to the nature and function of dreaming. *Psychiatry, Interpersonal and Biological Processes.* 61 (3): 223–28.

Hartmann, E., D. Russ, M. Oldfield, I. Sivan, and S. Cooper. 1987. Who has nightmares? The personality of the lifelong nightmare sufferer. *Archives of General Psychiatry.* 44:49–56.

Haynes, S. N., and D. K. Mooney. 1975. Nightmares: Etiological, theoretical, and behavioral treatment considerations. *The Psychological Record.* 25:225–36.

Heinze, R. I. 1991. *Shamans in the 20th century. Frontiers of consciousness series.* New York: Irvington Publishers.

Herman, S., and W. D. Shows. 1984. How often do adults recall their dreams? *International Journal of Aging and Human Development.* 18 (4):243–55.

Hewlett, S. A. 1991. *When the bow breaks: The cost of neglecting our children.* New York: Basic Books.

Hitchcock, J. T., and R. L. Jones, eds. 1976. *Spirit possession in the Nepal Himalayas.* Warminster, England: Aris and Phillips.

Hobson, J. A., and E. F. Pace-Schott. 2002. The cognitive neuroscience of sleep: Neuronal systems, consciousness, and learning. *Nature Reviews Neuroscience.* 3:679–93.

Hobson, J. A., E. F. Pace-Schott, and R. Stickgold. 2000. Dreaming and the brain: Toward a cognitive neuroscience of conscious states. *Behavioral and Brain Sciences.* 23:793–842.

Hobson, J. A., R. Stickgold, and E. F. Pace-Schott. 1998. The neuropsychology of REM sleep dreaming. *NeuroReport.* 9 (3): R1–R14.

Hofle, N., T. Paus, D. Reutens, P. Fiset, J. Gotman, A. C. Evans, et al. 1997. Regional cerebral blood flow changes as a function of delta and spindle activity during slow wave sleep in humans. *Journal of Neuroscience.* 17:4800–4808.

Hollan, D. 2003. The cultural and intersubjective context of dream remembrance and reporting: Dreams, ageing, and the anthropological encounter in Toraja, Indonesia. In *Dream travelers: Sleep experiences and culture in the western Pacific,* ed. R. I. Lohmann, 168–87. New York: Palgrave Macmillan.

Hublin, C., J. Kaprio, M. Partinen, and M. Koskenvuo. 1999. Nightmares: Familial aggregation and association with psychiatric disorders in a nationwide twin cohort. *American Journal of Medical Genetics.* 88:329–36.

Hufford, D. J. 1982. *The Terror That Comes in the Night.* (Publication of the Early American Folklore Society new series). Philadelphia, PA: University of Pennsylvania Press.

Hufford, D. J. 2005. Sleep paralysis as spiritual experience. *Transcultural Psychiatry.* 42(1): 11–45.

Inoue, S., K. Honda, M. Kimura, and S. Q. Zhang. 1999. Endogenous sleep substances and REM sleep. In *Rapid eye movement sleep,* ed. B. N. Mallick and S. Inoue, 248–63. New York: Marcel Dekker.

Jacobs, J., ed. 1990. *The Nagas: Hill peoples of northeast India.* London: Thomas and Hudson.

Jedrej, M., and R. Shaw, eds. 1992. *Dreaming, religion and society in Africa.* Leiden, Netherlands: E. J. Brill.

Jouvet, D., P. Vimont, F. Delorme, and M. Jouvet, M. 1964. [Study of selective deprivation of the paradoxical sleep phase in the cat]. *Comptes Rendus des Seances de la Societe de Biologie et de ses Filiale.,* 158:756–59.

Jouvet, M. 1999. *The paradox of sleep: The story of dreaming.* Cambridge, MA: MIT Press.

Kahn, D., R. Stickgold, E. F. Pace-Schott, and J. A. Hobson. 2000. Dreaming and waking consciousness: A character recognition study. *Journal of Sleep Research.* 9 (4): 317–25.

Kavanau, J. L. 2002. Dream contents and failing memories. *Archives of Italian Biology.* 140 (2): 109–27.

Kessler, R. C., O. Demler, R. G. Frank, M. Olfson, H. A. Pincus, E. E. Walters, et al. 2005. Prevalence and treatment of mental disorders, 1990 to 2003. *New England Journal of Medicine.* 352:2515–23.

Keverne, E. B., F. L. Martel, and C. M. Nevison. 1996. Primate brain evolution: Genetic and functional considerations. *Proceedings of the Royal Society of London, Series B, Biological Sciences.* 263: 689–96.

King, S. 1977. *The shining.* New York: Doubleday & Company.

Krakow, B. 2006. Nightmare complaints in treatment-seeking patients in clinical sleep medicine settings: Diagnostic and treatment implications. *Sleep.* 29 (10): 1313–19.

Krakow, B., M. Hollijield, R. Schrader, M. Koss, D. Tandberg, J. Lauriello, et al. 2000. Controlled study of imagery rehearsal for chronic nightmares in sexual assault survivors with PTSD: A preliminary report. *Journal of Traumatic Stress.* 13:589–609.

Krakow, B., R. Kellner, and D. Pathak. 1995. Imagery rehearsal treatment for chronic nightmares. *Behavioral Research Therapy.* 33:837–43.

Kramer, M. 1993. The selective mood regulatory function of dreaming: An update and revision. In *The functions of dreaming,* ed. A. Moffitt, M. Kramer, and R. Hoffmann, 139–96. Albany, NY: State University of New York Press.

Krippner, S. 2000. The epistemology and technologies of shamanic states of consciousness. *Journal of Consciousness Studies.* 7 (11–12): 93–118.

Krueger, J. M., J. A. Majde, and F. Obal. 2003. Sleep in host defense. *Brain Behavior and Immunity.* 17 (Suppl. 1): S41–S47.

Kubrick, S. and King, S. Film. 1980. *The Shining.* directed by S. Kubrick. Burbank, CA: Warner Bros.

Kuhn, A. S. 1988. *Heiler und ihre Patienten auf dem Dach der Welt. Ladakh aus ethnomedizinischer Sicht* [Healers and their patients on the roof of the world. Ladakh in ethnomedical perspective]. Frankfurt am Main, Germany: Peter Lang.

Kuiken, D., and S. Sikora. 1993. The impact of dreams on waking thoughts and feelings. In *The functions of dreaming*, ed. A. Moffitt, M. Kramer, and R. Hoffman, 419–76. Albany, NY: State University of New York Press.

Kupfer, D. J., and F. G. Foster. 1972. Interval between onset of sleep and rapid-eye-movement sleep as an indicator of depression. *Lancet*. 2 (7779): 684–86.

Lai, Y. Y., and J. Siegel. 1999. Muscle atonia in REM sleep. In *Rapid eye movement sleep*, ed. B. N. Mallick and S. Inoue, 69–90. New York: Marcel Dekker.

Lakoff, G. 2001. How metaphor structures dreams. The theory of conceptual metaphor applied to dream analysis. In *Dreams: A reader on religious, cultural and psychological dimensions of dreaming*, ed. K. Bulkeley, 265–84. New York: Palgrave.

Lancaster, J. B., and C. S. Lancaster, 1983. Parental investment: The hominid adaptation. In *How humans adapt: A biocultural odyssey*, ed. Donald J., 33–56. Washington, D.C.: Smithsonian Institution Press.

Ledoux, J. 2000. The amygdala and emotion: A view through fear. In *The amygdala*, ed. J. P. Aggleton, 289–310. Oxford: Oxford University Press.

Levin, R. 1994. Sleep and dreaming characteristics of frequent nightmare subjects in a university population. *Dreaming*. 4:127–37.

Levitan, H. L. 1976. The significance of certain catastrophic dreams. *Psychotherapy and Psychosomatics*. 27 (1): 1–7.

Lewis, I. M. 1971. *Ecstatic religion: An anthropological study of spirit possession and Shamanism*. Baltimore, MD: Penguin.

Linkowski, P. 1999. EEG sleep patterns in twins. *Sleep*. 8 (Suppl. 1): S11–S13.

Loevinger, J. 1976. *Ego development: Conception and theories*. San Francisco: Jossey-Bass.

Loevinger, J., R. Wessler, and B. Redmore, B. 1970. *Measuring ego development*. San Francisco: Jossey-Bass.

Lohmann, R. I., ed. 2003a. *Dream travelers: Sleep experiences and culture in the western Pacific*. New York: Palgrave.

Lohmann, R. I. 2003b. Dream travels and anthropology. In *Dream travelers: Sleep experiences and culture in the western Pacific*, ed. R. I. Lohmann, 1–17. New York: Palgrave.

Lohmann, R. I. 2003c. Supernatural encounters of the Asabano in two traditions and three states of consciousness. In *Dream travelers: Sleep experiences and culture in the western Pacific*, ed. R. I. Lohmann, 188–210. New York: Palgrave.

Lohmann, R. I. 2007. Dreams and ethnography. In *Cultural and theoretical perspectives*. Vol. 3 of *The new science of dreaming*. ed. D. Barrett and P. McNamara, 35–67. Westport, CT: Praeger Publishers.

Lorenz, D. M. 1986. Alimentary sleep satiety in suckling rats. *Physiology and Behavior*. 38:557–62.

Lorenz, D. M., C. J. Poppe, C. Quail, K. Seipel, S. A. Stordeur, and E. Johnson. 1998. Filling the gut activates paradoxical sleep in suckling rats. *Developmental Psychobiology*. 32:1–12.

MacFarlane, J. W., L. Allen, and M. P. Hoznik, 1954. A developmental study of the behavior problems of normal children between twenty-one and fourteen years. *Publications in Child Development, University of California, Berkeley.* 2:1–222.

Mahowald, M. W., and M. G. Ettinger. 1990. Things that go bump in the night: The parasomnias revisited. *Journal of Clinical Neurophysiology.* 7 (1): 119–43.

Mahowald, M. W., and C. H. Schenck. 2000. Diagnosis and management of parasomnias. *Clinical Cornerstone.* 2(5): 48–57.

Malcolm, N. 1956. Dreaming and skepticism. *Philosophical Review.* 45:14–37.

Malcolm, N. 1959. *Dreaming.* London: Routledge & Kegan.

Mannix, J. K. 2006. Dream recall. *Dissertation Abstracts International: Section B: The Sciences and Engineering.* 66:6930.

Maquet, P., and G. Franck. 1997. REM sleep and amygdale. *Molecular Psychiatry.* 2 (3): 195–96.

Maquet, P., J. M. Peters, J. Aerts, G. Delfiore, C. Degueldre, A. Luxen, et al. 1996. Functional neuroanatomy of human rapid-eye-movement sleep and dreaming. *Nature.* 38:163–66.

Maquet, P., and C. Phillips. 1999. Rapid eye movement sleep: Cerebral metabolism to functional brain mapping. In *Rapid eye movement sleep,* ed. B. N. Mallick and S. Inoue, 276–85. New York: Marcel Dekker.

Maynard-Smith, J., and D. Harper. 2003. *Animal signals.* Oxford: Oxford University Press.

McClenon, J. 1997a. Shamanic healing, human evolution, and the origin of religion. *Journal for the Scientific Study of Religion.* 36:345–54.

McClenon, J. 1997b. Spiritual healing and folklore research: Evaluating the hypnosis/placebo theory. *Alternative Therapies* 3 (1): 61–66.

McNamara, P. 2004a. *An evolutionary psychology of REM sleep and dreams.* Westport, CT: Praeger Publishers.

McNamara, P. 2004b. Genomic imprinting and neurodevelopmental disorders of sleep. *Sleep and Hypnosis.* 6 (2):100–108.

McNamara, P., R. Durso, and E. Harris. 2006. Life goals of patients with Parkinson's disease: A pilot study on correlations with mood and cognitive functions. *Clinical Rehabilitation.* 20 (9): 818–26.

McNamara, P., D. McLaren, D. Smith, A. Brown, and R. Stickgold. 2005. A "Jekyll and Hyde" within: Aggressive versus friendly social interactions in REM and NREM dreams. *Psychological Science* 16 (2): 130–36.

McNamara, P., and R. Szent-Imrey. 2007. Costly signaling theory of REM sleep and dreams. *Evolutionary Psychology.* 5 (1): 28–44.

Merritt, J. M., R. Stickgold, E. F. Pace-Schott, J. Williams, and J.A Hobson. 1994. Emotion profiles in the dreams of men and women. *Consciousness & Cognition.* 3:46–60.

Miller, W., and M. Di Palato. 1983. Treatment of nightmares via relaxation and desensitization: A controlled evaluation. *Journal of Consulting & Clinical Psychology.* 51: 870–77.

Mindell, J. A., and K. M. Barrett. 2002. Nightmares and anxiety in elementary-aged children: Is there a relationship? *Child: Care Health & Development.* 28:317–22.

Moorcroft, W. H. 2003. *Understanding sleep and dreaming.* New York: Kluwer Academic/Plenum Publishers.

Morrison, A. R. 1979. Brainstem regulation of behavior during sleep and wakefulness. In *Progress in psychobiology and physiological psychology,* ed. J. M. Sprague and A. W. Epstein, 91–131. New York: Academic Press.

Morrison, A. R., L. D. Sanford, and R. J. Ross. 1999. Initiation of rapid eye movement: Beyond the brainstem. In *Rapid eye movement sleep,* ed. B. N. Mallick and S. Inoue, 51–68. New York: Marcel Dekker.

Mueller, E., V. Locatelli, and D. Cocchi. 1999. Neuroendocrine control of growth hormone secretion. *Physiological Reviews.* 79 (2): 511–607.

Mumford, L. 1966. *Technics and human development: The myth of the machine.* New York: Harcourt, Brace and World.

Nicholls, R. D. 2000. The impact of genomic imprinting for neurobehavioral and developmental disorders. *Journal of Clinical Investigations.* 105 (4): 413–18.

Nielsen, T. 2000. A review of mentation in REM and NREM sleep: "Covert" REM sleep as a possible reconciliation of two opposing models. *Behavioral & Brain Sciences.* 23:851–66.

Nielsen, T. A., D. Kuiken, R. Hoffman, and A. Moffitt. 2001. REM and NREM sleep mentation differences: A question of story structure? *Sleep & Hypnosis.* 3 (1): 9–17.

Nielsen, T. A., L. Laberge, R. Tremblay, F. Vitaro, and J. Montplaisir. 2000. Development of disturbing dreams during adolescence and their relationship to anxiety symptoms. *Sleep.* 23:727–36.

Nielsen, T. A., and R. Levin. 2007. Nightmares: A new neurocognitive model. *Sleep Medicine Reviews.* 11:295–310.

Nielsen, T. A., and A. L. Zadra. 2005. Nightmares and other common dream disturbances. In *Principles and practice of sleep medicine.* 4th ed., ed. M. Kryger, N. Roth, and W. C. Dement, 926–35. Philadelphia: W. B. Saunders.

The Nightmare Project. Accessed on December 21, 2007, from http://www.nightmareproject.com. (Project Web site no longer available due to technical problems.)

Nofzinger, E. A., M. A. Mintun, M. B. Wiseman, D. J. Kupfer, and R. Y. Moore. 1997. Forebrain activation in REM sleep: An FDG PET study. *Brain Research.* 770:192–201.

Nutt, D. J., and A. L. Malizia. 2004. Structural and functional brain changes in posttraumatic stress disorder. *Journal of Clinical Psychiatry.* 65 (Suppl. 1): S11-S17.

Obal, F., Jr., and J. M. Krueger. 2003. Biochemical regulation of non-rapid-eye-movement sleep. *Frontiers in Bioscience.* 8:520–50.

Oberst, U., C. Charles, and A. Chamarro. 2005. Influence of gender and age in aggressive dream content of Spanish children and adolescents. *Dreaming* 15:170–77.

Offenkrantz, W., and A. Rechtschaffen. 1963. Clinical studies of sequential dreams. I. A patient in psychotherapy. *Archives of General Psychiatry.* 8:497–508.

Ohayon, M. M., P. L. Morselli, and C. Guilleminault, C. 1997. Prevalence of nightmares and their relationship to psychopathology and daytime functioning in insomnia subjects. *Sleep.* 20:340–48.

Olson, E. J., B. F. Boeve, and M. H. Silber. 2000. Rapid eye movement sleep behaviour disorder: Demographic, clinical and laboratory findings in 93 cases. *Brain.* 123:331–39.

Orem, J., and C. D. Barnes, eds. 1980. *Physiology in sleep.* New York: Academic Press.

Pagel, J. F., and P. Helfter. 2003. Drug induced nightmares: An etiology based review. *Human Psychology: Clinical & Experimental.* 18 (1): 59–67.

Paré, D., S. Royer, Y. Smith, and E. J. Lang. 2003. Contextual inhibitory gating of impulse traffic in the intra-amygdaloid network. *Annals of the New York Academy of Sciences.* 985:78–91.

Parmeggiani, P. L. 2000. Physiological regulation in sleep. In *Principles and practice of sleep medicine.* 3rd ed., ed. M. H. Kryger, T. Roth, and W. C. Dement, 169–78. Philadelphia: W. B. Saunders.

Partinen, M. 1994. Epidemiology of sleep disorders. In *Principles and practices of sleep medicine.* 2nd ed., ed. M. H. Kryger, T. Roth, and W. C. Dement, 437–52. Philadelphia: W. B. Saunders.

Partridge, L., and L. D. Hurst. 1998. Sex and conflict. *Science.* 281:2003–08.

Penfield, W., and T. C. Erickson. 1941. *Epilepsy and cerebral localization. A study of the mechanism, treatment and prevention of epileptic seizures.* Baltimore: C. C. Thomas.

Pennebaker, J. W., M. E. Francis, and R.J. Booth. 2001. *Linguistic inquiry and word count: LIWC.* Mahwah, NJ: Erlbaum Publishers.

Peters, L. G., and D. Price-Williams. 1980. Towards an experiential analysis of shamanism. *American Ethnologist.* 7:397–418.

Peters, R. W., R. G. Zoble, and M. M. Brooks. 2002. Onset of acute myocardial infarction during sleep. *Clinical Cardiology.* 25 (5): 237–41.

Phylactou, M. 1989. Household organisation and marriage in Ladakh, Indian Himalaya. PhD dissertation, London School of Economics and Political Science.

Pomiankowski, A. 1999. Intragenomic conflict. In *Levels of selection in evolution,* ed. L. Keller, 121–52. Princeton: Princeton University Press.

Rappaport, R. 1999. *Ritual and religion in the making of humanity.* Cambridge: Cambridge University Press.

Raskind, M. A., E. Peskind, D. Hoff, K. Hart, H. Holmes, D. Warren, et al. 2006. Parallel group placebo controlled study of Prazosin for trauma nightmares and sleep disturbance in combat veterans with post-traumatic stress disorder. *Biological Psychiatry.* 61 (8): 928–34.

Rauch, S. L., L. M. Shin, and E. A. Phelps. 2006. Neurocircuitry models of post-traumatic stress disorder and extinction.: Human neuroimaging research—past, present and future. *Biological Psychiatry.* 60:376–82.

Ray, K. 1992. Dreams of grandeur: The call to the office in northcentral Igbo religious leadership. In *Dreaming, religion and society in Africa,* ed. M. C. Jedrej and R. Shaw, 55–70. Leiden, Netherlands: E. J. Brill.

Rectschaffen, A., and A. Kales, eds. 1968. *A manual of standardized terminology, technique and scoring system for sleep stages of human subjects.* Bethesda, MD: HEW Neurological Information Network.

Reichel-Dolmatoff, G. 1997. *Rainforest Shamans: Essays on the Tukano Indians of the northwest Amazon.* Dartington, UK: Themis Books.

Resnick, J., R. Stickgold, C. D. Rittenhouse, and J. A. Hobson. 1994. Self-representation and bizarreness in children's dream reports collected in the
home setting. *Consciousness & Cognition*, 3:30–45.

Revonsuo, A. 2000. The reinterpretation of dreams: An evolutionary hypothesis
of the function of dreaming. *Behavioral & Brain Sciences*. 23:877–901; discussion 904–1121.

Riolo, S. A., T. A. Nguyen, J. F. Greden, and C. A. King. 2005. Prevalence and
treatment of mental disorders, 1990 to 2003. *American Journal of Public
Health*. 5:998–1000.

Robbins, J. 2003. Dreaming and the defeat of charisma: Disconnecting dreams
from leadership among the Urapmin of Papua New Guinea. In *Dream
travelers: Sleep experiences and culture in the Western Pacific*, ed. R. I. Lohmann, 18–41. New York: Palgrave.

Rösing, I. 2003. Trance, besessenheit und amnesie. Bei den Schamanen der
Changpa-Nomaden im lakakhischen Changthang [Trance, obsession and
amnesia. The shamans of Changpa-Nomaden]. Gnas, Austria: Weish-
aupt-Verlag.

Rowe, K., R. Moreno, T. R. Lau, U. Wallooppillai, B. D. Nearing, B. Kocsis, et al.
1999. Heart rate surges during REM sleep are associated with theta
rhythm and PGO activity in cats. *American Journal of Physiology: Regulatory, Integrative, & Comparative Physiology*. 277:R843–R849.

Sah, P., E. S. L. Faber, M. Lopez de Armentia, and J. Power. 2003. The amygdaloid complex: Anatomy and physiology. *Psychological Review*. 83:803–34.

Sally, D. 2003. Dressing the mind properly for the game. *Philosophical Transactions of the Royal Society of London, Series B, Biological Sciences*. 358 (1431):
583–92.

Salzarulo, P., and A. Chevalier. 1983. Sleep problems in children and their relationship with early disturbances of the waking-sleeping rhythms. *Sleep*.
6:47–51.

Sameroff, A. J., and M. M. Haith, eds. 1996. *The five to seven year shift: The age of
reason and responsibility*. Chicago: University of Chicago Press.

Samuel, G. (1993). *Civilized Shamans: Buddhism in Tibetan societies*. Washington,
D.C.: Smithsonian.

Sandner, D. 1979. *Navaho symbols of healing*. New York: Harcourt, Brace and
Jovanovich.

Schenck, C. H. and M. W. Mahowald. 1990. Polysomnographic, neurologic, psychiatric, and clinical outcome report on 70 consecutive cases with REM
sleep disorder (RBD): Sustained clonazepam efficacy in 89.5% of 57
treated patients. *Cleveland Journal of Medicine*. 57 (Suppl.): S9-S23.

Schenck, C. H., and M. W. Mahowald. 1996. REM sleep parasomnias. *Neurology
Clinics*. 14, 697–720.

Schneider, A., and G. W. Domhoff, 2005. DreamBank. Accessed on December
20, 2007, from http://www.dreambank.net/

Schneider, A., and G. W. Domhoff. 2007a. DreamSat: Automated Dream Data
Entry System and Statistical Analysis Tool. Accessed December 20, 2007,
from http://www.dreamresearch.net/DreamSAT/index.html/

Schneider, A., and G. W. Domhoff. 2007b. The quantitative study of dreams.
Accessed December 20, 2007, from http://www.dreamresearch.net/

Schneider, D., and L. Sharp. 1969. The dream life of a primitive people: The dreams of Yir Yoront of Australia. In *Anthropological studies*, ed. W. Goodenough, 1–11. Ann Arbor, MI: American Anthropological Association.

Schonbar, R. A. 1961. Temporal and emotional factors in the selective recall of dreams. *Journal of Consulting Psychology.* 25:67–73.

Schredl, M. 2000. Dream research: Integration of physiological and psychological models. *Behavioral and Brain Sciences.* 23:1001–3.

Schredl, M., and R. Pallmer. 1998. Geschlechtsspezifische Unterschiede in Angsttraummen von Schulerinnen und Schulern [Gender differences in anxiety dreams of school-aged children]. *Praxis der Kinderpsychologie und Kinderpsychiatrie.* 47: 463–76.

Schreuder, B., W. Kleijn, and H. Rooijmans. 2000. Nocturnal re-experiencing more than forty years after war trauma. *Journal of Traumatic Stress.* 13 (3): 453–63.

Sei, H., and Y. Morita. 1999. Why does arterial blood pressure rise actively during REM sleep? *Journal of Medical Investigation.* 46 (1–2): 11–17.

Sellen, D. W., and D. B. Smay. 2001. Relationship between subsistence and age at weaning in "preindustrial" societies. *Human Nature.* 12:47–87.

Shaw, R. 1992. Dreaming as accomplishment: Power, the individual, and Temne divination. In *Dreaming, religion, and society in Africa,* ed. M. C. Jedrej and R. Shaw, 36–54. Leiden, Netherlands: E. J. Brill.

Shirakawa, S., N. Takeuchi, N. Uchimura, T. Ohyama, H. Maeda, T. Abe, et al. 2002. Study of image findings in rapid eye movement sleep behavioural disorder. *Psychiatry & Clinical Neurosciences,* 56 (3): 291–92.

Simonds, J. F., and H. Parraga. 1982. Prevalence of sleep disorders and sleep behaviors in children and adolescents. *Journal of the American Academy of Child & Adolescent Psychiatry.* 21:383–88.

Smedje, H., J. E. Broman, and J. Hetta. 2001a. Associations between disturbed sleep and behavioural difficulties in 635 children aged six to eight years: A study based on parents' perceptions. *European Child & Adolescent Psychiatry.* 10 (1): 1–9.

Smedje, H., J. E. Broman, and J. Hetta. 2001b. Short-term prospective study of sleep disturbances in 5–8-year-old children. *Acta Paediatrica.* 90 (12): 1456–63.

Smith, C. T., M. R. Nixon, and R. S. Nader. 2004. Posttraining increases in REM sleep intensity implicate REM sleep in memory processing and provide a biological marker of learning potential. *Learning and Memory.* 11:714–19.

Solms, M. 1997. *The neuropsychology of dreams.* Mahwah, NJ: Lawrence Erlbaum.

Solms, M. 2000. Dreaming and REM sleep are controlled by different brain mechanisms. *Behavioral and Brain Sciences.* 23 (6): 843–50.

Sowell, E. R., P. M. Thompson, A. D. Tessner, and A. W. Toga. 2001. Accelerated brain growth and cortical grey matter thinning are inversely related during post-adolescent frontal lobe maturation. *Journal of Neuroscience.* 21 (22): 8819–29.

Sperber, D. and D. Wilson. 1995. *Relevance: Communication and cognition.* 2nd ed. Oxford: Blackwell Publishers.

Sperber, D. and D. Wilson. 2002. Pragmatics, modularity and mind-reading. *Mind & Language.* 17:3–23. Special Issue on Pragmatics and Cognitive Science.

Spielberg, S., exec. prod. 2002. *Taken TV Series*. Glenwood, CA: DreamWorks LLC and DreamWorks Television. www.dreamworks.com

Spoormaker, V. I., M. Schredl, and J. van den Bout. 2006. Nightmares: From anxiety symptom to sleep disorder. *Sleep Medicine Reviews*. 10 (1):19–31.

Stefanikis, H. 1995. Speaking of dreams: A social constructionist account of dream sharing. *Dreaming*. 5:95–104.

Steiger, A. 2003. Sleep and endocrinology. *Journal of Internal Medicine*. 254:13–22.

Stepansky, R., B. Holzinger, A. Schmeiser-Rieder, B. Saletu, M. Kunze, and J. Zeitlhofer. 1998. Austrian dream behavior: Results of a representative population survey. *Dreaming* 8:23–30.

Steriade, M., and R. W. McCarley. 1990. *Brainstem control of wakefulness and sleep*. New York: Plenum Press.

Sterpenich, V., G. Albouy, M. Boly, G. Vandewalle, A. Darsaud, E. Blateau, et al. 2007. Sleep-related hippocampo-cortical interplay during emotional memory recollection. *Public Library of Science Biology*. 5:1–14.

Strauch, I. 2005. REM dreaming in the transition from late childhood to adolescence: A longitudinal study. *Dreaming*. 15:155–69.

Strauch, I., and B. Meier. 1996. *In search of dreams: Results of experimental dream research*. Albany, NY: State University of New York Press.

Szymusiak, R., M. N. Alam, T. L. Steininger, and D. McGinty. 1998. Sleep-waking discharge patterns of ventrolateral preoptic/anterior hypothalamic neurons in rats. *Brain Research*. 803:178–88.

Tafti, M., and P. Franken. 2002. Invited review: Genetic dissection of sleep. *Journal of Applied Physiology*. 92:1339–47.

Taheri, S., and E. Mignot. 2002. The genetics of sleep disorders. *Lancet Neurology*. 1 (4): 242–50.

Tanskanen, A., J. Toumilehto, H. Viinamaki, E. Vartiainen, J. Lehtonen, and P. Puska. 2001. Nightmares as predictors of suicide. *Sleep* 24: 845–48.

Taupin, P., and F. H. Gage. 2002. Adult neurogenesis and neural stem cells of the central nervous system in mammals. *Journal of Neuroscience Research*. 69:745–49.

Tedlock, B. 1987. Zuni and Quiché dream sharing and interpreting. In *Dreaming*, ed. B. Tedlock, 105–31. Cambridge: Cambridge University Press.

Tedlock, B. 1992a. *Dreaming: Anthropological and psychological interpretations*. Santa Fe: School of American Research Press.

Tedlock, B. 1992b. The role of dreams and visionary narratives in Mayan cultural survival. *Ethos*. 20 (4): 453–76.

Tobler, I. 2005. Phylogeny of sleep regulation. In *Principles and practice of sleep medicine*, 4th ed., ed. M. Kryger, T. Roth, and W. Dement, 77–90. Philadelphia: W. B. Saunders.

Tonkinson, R. 1974. *The Jigalong mob: Aboriginal victors of the desert crusade*. New York: Holt.

Trosman, H., A. Rechtschaffen, W. Offenkrantz, and E. Wolpert. 1960. Studies in psychophysiology of dreams. IV: Relations among dreams in sequence. *Archives of General Psychiatry*. 3:602–7.

Tycko, B., and I. M. Morison. 2002. Physiological functions of imprinted genes. *General Psychiatry*. 3:602–7.

Ullman, M., and S. Krippner. 1973. *Dream telepathy*. New York: Macmillan Publishing Co.

Van Bork, J. J. 1982. An attempt to clarify a dream-mechanism. Why do people wake up out of an anxiety dream? *International Review of Psycho-Analysis.* 9:273–77.

Van Cauter, E., L. Plat, and G. Copinschi. 1998. Interrelations between sleep and the somatotropic axis. *Sleep.* 21 (6): 553–66.

Van de Castle, R. L. 1994. *Our dreaming mind*. New York: Ballantine.

Vann, B., and N. Alperstein. 2000. Dream sharing as social interaction. *Dreaming.* 10 (2): 111–20.

Vela-Bueno, A., E. O. Bixler, B. Dobladez-Blanco, M. E. Rubio, R. E. Mattison, A. and Kales. 1985. Prevalence of night terrors and nightmares in elementary school children: A pilot study. *Research Communications in Psychology, Psychiatry, & Behavior.* 10:177–88.

Verona, R. I., M. R. Mann, and M. S. Bartolemei. 2003. Genomic imprinting: Intricacies of epigenetic regulation in clusters. *Annual Review of Cell and Developmental Biology.* 19:237–59.

Vogel, G., D. Foulkes, and H. Trosman. 1966. Ego functions and dreaming during sleep onset. *Archives of General Psychiatry.* 14 (3):238–48.

Vogel, G. W. 1999. REM sleep deprivation and behavioral changes. In *Rapid eye movement sleep*, ed. B. N. Mallick and S. Inoue, 355-366. New York: Marcel Dekker.

Vogel, G. W., F. Vogel, R. S. McAbee, and A. J. Thurmond. 1980. Improvement of depression by REM sleep deprivation. New findings and a theory. *Archives of General Psychiatry.* 37:247-253.

Waterlow, J. C., A. Ashworth, and M. Griffiths. 1980. Faltering infant growth in less-developed countries. *Lancet* 2:1176–78.

Watson, D., and L. A. Clark. 1984. Negative affectivity: The disposition to experience aversive emotional states, *Psychological Bulletin.* 96 (3): 465–90.

Webb, W. B., and H. W. Agnew. 1971. Stage 4 sleep: Influence of time course variables. *Science.* 174:1354–56.

Weber, M. 1946. *Essay in sociology*. Ed. and trans. H. H. Gerth and C. W. Mills.. New York: Oxford University Press.

Whalen, P. J., L. M. Shin, L. H. Somerville, A. A. McLean, and H. Kim. 2002. Functional neuroimaging studies of the amygdala in depression. *Seminars in Clinical Neuropsychiatry.* 7 (4): 234–42.

Winikoff, B., S. Durongdej, and B. J. Cerf. 1988. Infant feeding in Bangkok, Thailand. In *Feeding infants in four societies: Causes and consequences of mother's choices*, ed. B. Winikoff, M. A. Castle, and V. H. Laukaran, 14–41. New York: Greenwood Press.

Winkelman, M. 1992. *Shamans, priests, and witches: A cross-cultural study of magico-religious practitioners.* Tempe, AZ: Anthropological Research Papers, Arizona State University.

Winkelman, M. 2000. *Shamanism: The natural ecology of consciousness and healing.* Westport, CT: Bergin and Garvey.

Wittmann, L. Schredl, M., and Kramer, M. 2007. Dreaming in posttraumatic stress disorder: A critical review of phenomenology, psychophysiology and treatment. *Psychotherapy and Psychosomatics.* 76 (1): 25–39.

Woodward, S.H., N. J. Arsenault, C. Murray, and D. L. Bliwise. 2000. Laboratory sleep correlates of nightmare complaint in PTSD inpatients. *Biological Psychiatry*. 48 (11): 1081–87.

Zadra, A. 1996. Recurrent dreams: Their relation to life events. In *Trauma and dreams*, ed. D. Barrett, 231–67. Cambridge, MA: Harvard University Press.

Zadra, A., and D. C. Donderi. 2000. Nightmares and bad dreams: Their prevalence and relationship to well-being. *Journal of Abnormal Psychology*. 109 (2): 273–81.

Zahavi, A. 1975. Mate selection: A selection for a handicap. *Journal of Theoretical Biology*. 53:205–13.

Zahavi, A., and A. Zahavi. 1997. *The handicap principle: A missing piece of Darwin's puzzle*. New York: Oxford University Press.

Index

Adaptation, 52, 60, 92–101, 148
Alien abduction, 116–17
Amygdala, 67–69, 72–73, 82, 90, 105, 109, 143
Amygdaloid complex, 16
Autonomic nervous system, 16–17, 65, 69–70, 106, 109, 114
Avian sleep, 15

Bed sharing, with REM behavior disorder, 77
Black Elk, 55

Cardiovascular system, 69–70, 72
Characters, 28–30, 43, 46, 136–41; enemies, 137–38; strangers, 136–38. *See also* supernatural agents
Children, 11–25, 65–66, 97, 107, 109; content of nightmares, 89–91; development of Self, 22–25; dreaming in childhood, 18–20; evolution of childhood, 20–21; frequent nightmares in children, 8, 19; language skills, 24–25; sleep in childhood, 13–14, 63
Compensatory rebound, 15
Conflict theory, 135–50; dream agents/characters can represent genomes within the individual, 141; dreaming and consciousness, 140–41; effects of imprinted genes on functional brain systems implicated in sleep processes, 142–43; effects of imprinted genes on psychologic systems implicated in growth, 141–42; genetic conflict and dream phenomenology, 146–48; genomic imprinting and sleep–state biology, 143–46; REM–NREM dissociations in the dreaming mind, 138–40
Content of Nightmares, 27–52, 43–47, 91; in children's nightmares, 89–90; creatures and misfortunes, 47; compared to dreams, 46–47; non-human characters, 5; in REM Behavior Disorder, 78; social interactions, 46, 89; striving, 46. *See also* supernatural agents; characters
Costly signaling theory, 75, 101–6, 149
Creativity, 75–76, 84

Dementia, 77
Demonic possession, 112–18, 135; interpretation, 119–34
Depression, 78–80

Dreams: effect on mood and behavior, 103–4; in children, 18–19; compared to nightmares, 46–47, 83–88, 91; comparison of REM and NREM dreams, 146–46; dream recall rates, 18; in premodern societies, 54–60; REM dream contents, 67

Early human groups. *See* tribal cultures
Elderly, 76–77
Environment of evolutionary adaptation, 9
The Exorcist, 112, 114–15

Fisher, C., 106
Freud, Sigmund, 106, 112
Functionality, 2, 52, 61, 87. *See also* proposed functional theory of nightmares
Fuseli, Henry, 112–13, 115–16. *See* The Nightmare

Genetics, 141–48

Hall and Van de Castle method of scoring dreams, 28–30, 139–40
Hartmann, Ernest, 107
Hippocampus, 16
Holy spirit possession, 113–15
Hormones, 16, 65
Hufford, David, 115
Hypnagogic hallucinations, 80

Identity. *See* Self
Igbo, 58
Intensity dimension, 15
Intentional agents, 14

King, Stephen, 117–18
Kramer, M., 106–7

Language, 21–22, 24–25, 98–100
Levin, R., 107–8
Linguistic Inquiry and Word Count, 39–43

Memory consolidation, 16
Mind, 135–36
Mind-reading, 86–87, 91, 136, 149. *See* Theory of Mind
Monsters. *See* supernatural agents
Motor paralysis, 71, 77

Narcolepsy, 80
Negative emotionality, 9–10
Nielsen, Tore, 107–8
The Nightmare, 112–13, 115–16
Nightmares; compared to dreams, 46–47, 83–88, 91; as compelling, 47–52, 85; content analysis, 43–47; creativity and, 75, 84; definitions, 1, 5–7; etymology, 119; frequency, 8, 73; functionality, 2, 52, 61, 87; narcolepsy and, 80; neuroanatomy and physiology of, 73; neuropharmacological agents in, 73; nightmares and REM biology, 92; pharmacology, 109; in popular culture, 111–18; and Post–Traumatic Stress Disorder, 82; precognitive nightmares, 47–52; in premodern societies, 53–61; recurrent nightmares; stage II NREM nightmares, 79; themes, 5; treatment strategies, 108–10; word count analyses, 39–43. *See also* phenomenology of nightmares; recurrent nightmares; theories of nightmares
A Nightmare on Elm Street, 115
Nightmare disorders, 6–7, 76–82; recurrent nightmare syndrome, 7; Night terrors, 14, 65
Nightmare sufferers, 4, 10, 51–54, 66, 75–82, 90; schizotypal personality trait, 92
Night terrors, 14, 65
NREM, 14–18, 63–73; in children, 16–17; comparison of REM

and NREM dreams, 146–46; REM–NREM dissociations in the dreaming mind, 138–40; REM NREM processing specializations, 138–40; Stage II NREM nightmares, 79; interactions with REM, 16–17, 64–65, 147–48. *See also* slow wave sleep

Parkinson's disease, 77
Penile erections, 71–72
Personality. *See* nightmare sufferers
PGO Waves, 68–69
Pharmacology, 109
Phenomenology of nightmares, 83–88, 90–91; automaticity, 84; basic visual features, 83; cognitive content elicits the emotion content, 84; compellingness, 85; creativity, 84; emotional atmosphere, 83–84, 91; lack of metaphor, 86; mind-reading, 86–87, 91, 136; narrative form, 85; self-identity, 85–86; self-reflectiveness, 86; supernatural agents (*see* supernatural agents)
Popular culture, 111–18
Post-Traumatic Stress Disorder, 82, 108–9, 117
Possession theme, 112–18, 119–34; caveats, 120–22; recurring patterns, 122–34. *See* demonic possession and holy spirit possession
Prazosin, 109
Precognitive nightmares, 47–52
Premodern tribal societies, 53–61, 102; child care, 21; dreams, 54–60; murderous ancestral male theory, 2; nightmare sufferers in tribal cultures, 4, 10–12, 51–54; religious behaviors, 96; Shamans, 55–61; sharing of nightmares, 8–10, 53, 60–61, 94–101

Prestige, 95–96, 99–100
Prophetic nightmares, 48
Proposed Functional theory of nightmares, 92–101; adaptive function of nightmares, 95; biological contributions to signaling "quality". 100–101; evolution of language skills, dreaming skills, and reputation, 98–99; relation of functional design to adaptation, 92–93; role of the dream/nightmare in the skill set of spiritual specialists, 96–97; role of prestige in development of self and in evolution of human societies, 95–96; signals used to identify supranormal abilities and exceptional individuals, 97; storytelling skills and prestige or reputation, 99–100; triggers of nightmares, 94–95
Psychopathology, 4, 75–82

Rebound sleep, 64–65
Recurrent nightmares, 3, 5–12, 19, 76–82, 105–6, 109; in elderly, 76–77; depression and, 76–80; recurrent nightmare syndrome, 7; treatment strategies, 108–10. *See also* nightmare disorders
REM, 10, 15, 16, 63–73, 90, 100–101, 104–6, 143–46; amygdala in, 68–69, 72–73; autonomic nervous system storms in, 70; cardiovascular system in, 70; in children, 13; comparison of REM and NREM dreams, 146–46; dream content, 67; imbalance of REM and SWS leads to nightmares, 80; interactions with NREM, 16–17, 64–65, 147–48; motor paralysis in, 71, 77, 113, 115–17; muscle twitching, 72;

REM *(Continued)*
 nightmares and REM biology,
 92; penile erections in, 71–72;
 PGO Waves, 68–69; properties,
 66; REM Behavior Disorder,
 76–78; REM latency in
 depressed patients, 79;
 REM-NREM dissociations in
 the dreaming mind, 138–40;
 REM-NREM processing
 specializations, 138–40; REM
 on REM off cellular networks,
 66–67; respiratory changes in,
 70–71; selective cerebral
 activation in, 67; suppression
 of, 79; thermoregulation in,
 71; REM Behavior Disorder,
 76–78; content of nightmares
 in, 78; in Parkinson's Disease,
 77
REM deprivation, 103

Sanders, Barb 27–52, 126–31
Schizotypal personality trait, 92
Selective cerebral activation, 67
Self, 22–25, 32, 35, 36, 85–86, 94–95
Shamans, 55–61, 96–97, 102
Sharing of nightmares, 8–12, 53,
 60–61, 94–103
The Shining, 117–18
Sleep, in childhood, 13–14, 63;
 genomic imprinting and
 sleep-state biology, 143–46;
 interaction between REM and
 NREM, 64–65, 147–48;
 rebound, 64–65; REM-NREM
 processing specializations,
 138–40; sleep architecture,
 63–64; sleep deprivation, 15,
 65, 81. *See also* REM; NREM
sleep paralysis, 80, 113, 115–17; and
 suicide, 80; two-process model
 of sleep regulation, 15, 81. *See*
 slow wave sleep
Sleep debt, 15
Sleep deprivation, 15, 65, 81
Sleep paralysis, 80, 113, 115–17

Slow wave sleep, 63; imbalance of REM
 and SWS leads to nightmares,
 80; in REM Behavior disorder,
 78. *See also* NREM
Stage II NREM nightmares, 79
Suicide, 80
Supernatural Agents, 5, 19–20, 22, 87,
 90–91, 108–10, 113, 135. *See also*
 possession

Taken, 117
Theories of nightmares, 89–110;
 arousal from SWS, 17; costly
 signaling theory, 75, 101–6; as
 evidence of extraordinary
 powers in ancestral
 populations, 53–61; Fisher's
 view of nightmares, 106;
 Freud's view of nightmares,
 106; functionality of
 nightmares, 2, 52, 61, 87;
 genetic influence, 2;
 Hartmann's view of
 nightmares, 107; imbalance of
 REM and NREM causes
 nightmares, 80; Kramer's
 view of nightmares, 106–7;
 Nielsen and Levin's view of
 nightmares, 107–8;
 murderous ancestral male
 theory, 2; standard take, 1. *See*
 also conflict theory; proposed
 functional theory of nightmares
Theory of mind, 21, 24–25, 86–87
Themes in nightmares, in children, 89;
 violence, 5, 7. *See also*
 possession theme
Thermoregulation, 71
Toraja, 59
Tribal cultures. *See* premodern tribal
 societies
Two-process model of sleep
 regulation, 15, 81

Waking state, 87–88
Women, 71, 80, 113, 115

Yansi, 58

About the Author

PATRICK MCNAMARA is Director of the Evolutionary Neurobehavior Laboratory at VA New England Health Care System and Associate Professor in the Department of Neurology at Boston University School of Medicine. He is also Series Editor for the Praeger series "Brain, Behavior, and Evolution." McNamara is trained in Neurocognitive Science. He is a member of the Sleep Research Society and the Association for the Study of Dreams. He is currently researching problems of the evolution and phylogeny of REM and NREM sleep states.